THE INNER GODDESS MAKEOVER

A Map for Empowering the Feminine Within

THE INNER GODDESS MAKEOVER

A Map for Empowering the Feminine Within

REVISED EDITION

Tanishka

First Printing: 2007

ISBN 978-0-9874263-9-0

The National Library of Australia Cataloguing-in-Publication entry:
Tanishka.
The Inner Goddess Makeover.

1. Archetype (Psychology), 2. Goddesses, Greek-Psychology,
3. Femininity - Psychological aspects, 4. Self-culture, 1. Title.

155.333

Star of Ishtar
www.starofishtar.com

Cover artwork: Elizabeth Barrera (www.redbubble.com/people/ejbwork)

Cover design: Belynda Simpson

Printed in USA by lulu.com

to the midwives of change

I would like to dedicate this book to the women who walked before me and lit the way ahead and to those who continue to take up the torch inspiring the daughters of Earth to unveil their Divine essence!

with deep gratitude...

To my Mother for the sacrifices she made to illustrate the personal cost experienced by women who are denied their birth rite of ancient women's wisdom. To her mother, my Nana for truly seeing me and sharing her love of the elemental realm.

To Lael for being a dream holder and encouraging the birth of this creative child. To Lily for being a midwife to this work experientially in women's circles and to my dearest girlfriend and emotional rock, Annie for her enduring support, nurturance and friendship. To Michelle, for her valuable editing advice. To Judith, for hounding me to get this book out in any form. To Shauna, for her unwavering confidence in my writing.

To Jen Powell for initiating me into the Mysteries and being my Spiritual Mother. To all the women who opened their souls to me in experiencing this work as initiate priestesses.

A huge thanks to JoAnne, Michael, Elinor & Richa for formatting - proof it takes not a just a village to raise a child but finish a book! Thanks :)

To my darling daughter, Ariella for possessing immeasurable strength and wisdom beyond her years. For forgiving me my human flaws in my best attempt to mother her and for everything she endured with incredible awareness as I served the greater good.

To my beloved, Michael for knowing intuitively how to really hold and support me, so I could better parent and serve the wider community with my work. For his generosity of Spirit that continually humbles me and for challenging me with sage advice as needed.

Last, but not least, to the great Goddess Lakshmi and her conduit, Radhika who introduced me to my first publisher, enabling this book to see the light of day.

author's note

In presenting the truths I uncovered in my own research into ancient women's mysteries, I realized the extent to which our modern day religions were built upon the foundations of the earlier earth based religions which were then denounced. Whilst I have felt it important to report the historical findings and social implications of these events as I perceive them, I would also like to express the view that I believe that every religion has played a part in the great wheel of evolution and all echo the one truth. This work is therefore intended as a complementary viewpoint to religions and philosophies and not as a competitive agenda.

I would also like to add that all holistic suggestions offered are the result of my personal experience and work as a Women's Mysteries facilitator. They are intended to complement rather than replace mainstream medical health modalities. All case studies have had any identifiable personal details changed to respect and protect their right to privacy.

contents

introduction

Once upon a time there lived a princess who was a spontaneous and cheeky fresh faced girl. But on the day of her 16th birthday she pricked her finger on the spindle of life's disappointments (a quaint euphemism for one's first period) and fell into a deep sleep state. With each passing year she forgot a little more about her true self as she tried to imitate the popular feminine icons of her day, hoping this charade would gift her with everlasting love, a great social life and a fabulous career. Fortunately for her, she stumbled across a magical book of ancient secrets that taught her inner heroine how to dismantle the thorny vines that had grown to hide her brilliant, unique and utterly adorable true self!

Welcome! To what was for me an exciting voyage of self-discovery; meeting each of my inner seven feminine aspects and discovering my unique feminine gifts and powers (move over Wonder Woman!) In fact, you could say I was a prime candidate for this inner makeover, as prior to embarking on my journey, I was twenty-six, in love with my gay best friend, desperately chasing 'success' to validate my self-worth and living on a smorgasbord of toxicity. (Not the picture of an empowered woman!)

One night, completely fed up with the life I had created, I got down on my knees in front of the fireplace in my groovy, overpriced apartment and bullied the Universe in the following manner, 'If you want me to be a woman, then send me some f**king role models!' In the days, weeks and years that followed that night, the old adage, 'Be careful what you wish for' has certainly proved true for me. In the space of one week I lost my flatmate, threw in my job, broke my lease, ended an eleven year project, grieved the loss of false friends and headed for the hills where I was initiated into a circle of wise women who introduced me to the Goddess archetypes: the ancient feminine heroines.

Fate then arranged for me a cottage for rent at the end of Seven Bridges Road and I began my self-imposed sabbatical, living alone in the woods where I descended into the depths of my psyche to discover my true nature and life purpose (whilst learning how to chop wood and use a water-pump). Yes, Goddesses also wear tracky-daks and gumboots!

It has now been nearly twenty years since I took that inward journey. Including ten years of research and integration that culminated in this book. And while I do believe there are a number of ways to uncover the gems of your soul, it was discovering the lessons of the seven inner Goddess archetypes that birthed within me a life changing understanding and subsequent personal empowerment. Consequently, what follows is a seven step inner makeover which is designed to introduce you to the different facets of your feminine psyche so you may express all your colorful selves in radiant harmony, creating divine balance, wholeness and personal fulfilment.

For a woman who once thought being 'feminine' meant wearing floral prints and being subservient and demure, I have now come to comprehend and experience the true power of my feminine nature. And so it is with deep gratitude to my mentor, Jen Powell who opened the door for me to the Goddess archetypes and to all of the incredible women I have since journeyed with, that I share with you the wisdom of these ancient feminine mysteries.

In Blessed Sisterhood, Tanishka

how to get the most from this book

Because this book is a step-by-step makeover, it is advisable to read the introductory chapters to give you an overall understanding of how this inner makeover process works, and what personal benefits you stand to gain from undertaking this exciting journey. What then follows are seven chapters, each one dedicated to introducing you to the seven psychological aspects which are universal to all women.

Ideally, I recommend you read one chapter at a time in sequence, taking a month to complete the exercises and observe how each Goddess archetype plays out in your life. Since we women ebb and flow with the inner tidal surges of the moon, a full lunar cycle enables us to really integrate and consciously anchor the strengths that each archetype unveils within us.

The Tantric Seven Step Stairway to Heaven!

Each Goddess archetype governs a chakra (the seven main energy centres located within our bodies), so as you consciously explore the issues raised in each chapter, you will experience internal energy shifts, clearing old blocks that have previously limited you from experiencing your fullest potential and empowerment. This seven step structure can be likened to a stairway to Heaven, with each step taking you closer to experiencing your own Divine nature.

Using universal archetypes as keys to understand and balance the seven chakras has been used to attain self-realization in numerous ancient mystic traditions, including Tantra (Sacred Sexuality) around the globe for thousands of years. I intuitively used this as a structure for empowering women long before I realized it had been around since the dawn of time. I have also used this process with countless women who continue to inspire me with the jewels they uncover and the radiance they emanate as a result.

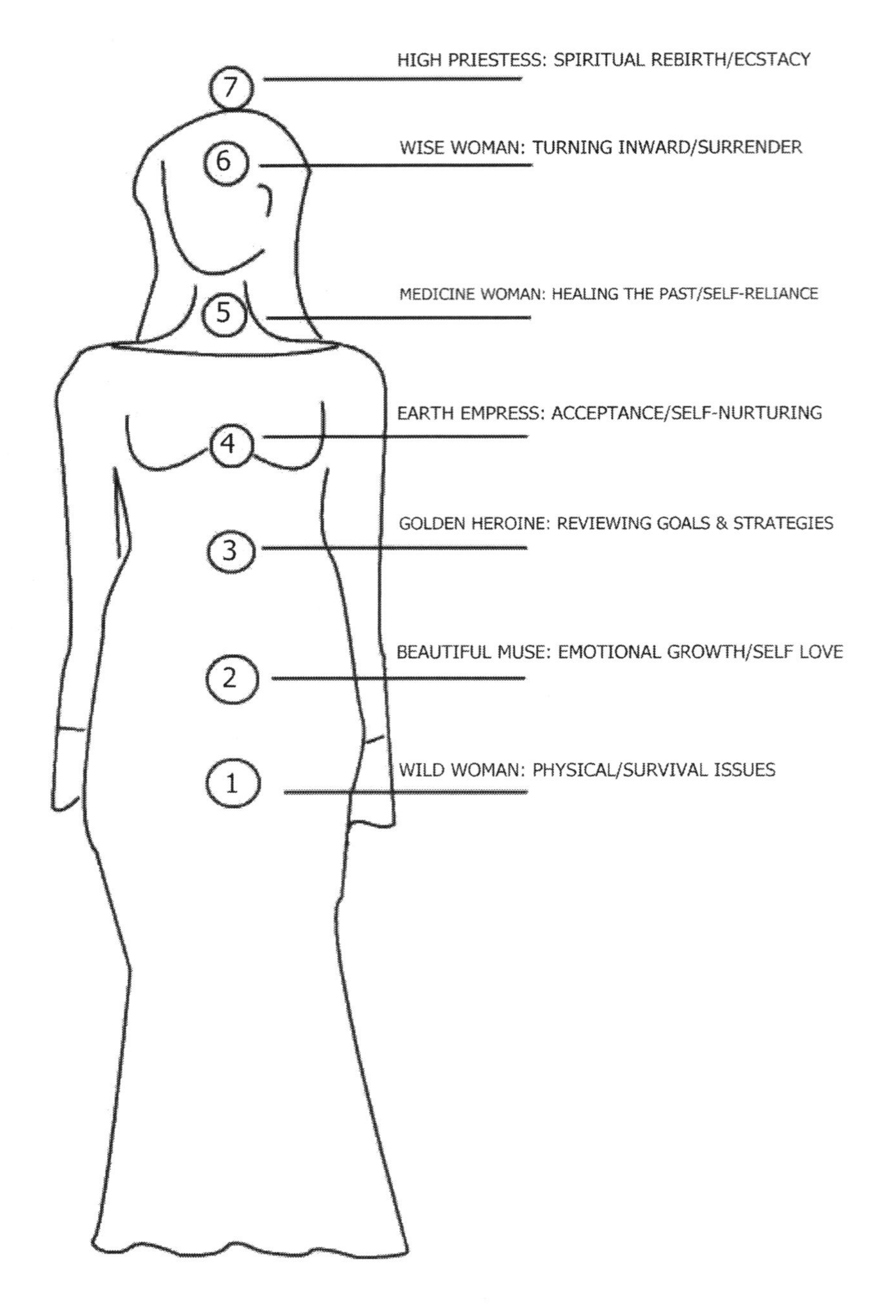

Ultimately, by focusing on a conscious journey through the feminine archetypes, we come to understand ourselves better as women so we can in turn create more harmonious relationships with those around us and manifest a more fulfilling, sustainable and balanced life.

To totally support yourself whilst undertaking this journey of self-transformation, consider gifting yourself with an energy healing each month to further assist you in integrating the psychological, emotional and energetic changes taking place. Each chapter also has many other practical suggestions to assist you along the way. I encourage you to use a journal to record your journey and as a workbook for the exercises given at the end of each chapter.

WHAT IS A MODERN DAY GODDESS?

The word 'Goddess' seems to have recently become a buzzword. In the 1950s only those immortalized on the silver screen such as Marlena Dietrich and Marilyn Monroe were referred to as 'Screen Goddesses' but now Goddesses seem to be popping out from every small screen and magazine to sell us disposable razors, gym wear and hair dyes. So what do these mortal women have that qualifies them as modern day Goddesses? And what can the rest of us do to become one?

I regard a modern day Goddess as a woman who sees and honors all aspects of herself as natural and therefore perfect and sacred. (Note: this includes spontaneous burping!) Yes, any woman can shine with liberated self-acceptance and vitality when she chooses to value herself as a unique expression of divine life force, instead of trying to become the perfect woman she thinks everyone else wants her to be.

Outgrowing the Ideal of 'The Perfect Woman'

The first step is to realize there is no such thing as the perfect woman. And of course your idea of the perfect woman is not necessarily the same as mine. Depending on which feminine archetype is ruling you, you may aspire to be a tall leggy blonde, a perfect Mother or a career superwoman... but none of these ideals will bring happiness if they are not balanced by the other archetypes.

The very idea of a perfect woman is a myth brought about primarily by marketing consultants wanting women to compulsively purchase products in the name of self-improvement. Tell-a-vision is exactly that, a vision of the world we are told to compete with, at the risk of social suicide should we fail to comply. If this sounds like a harsh appraisal, just watch daytime TV, (targeted specifically at women) and observe your self-esteem plummet like a thermometer bound for the Arctic. By 3pm you'll think your skin too white, your breasts too small, and your wardrobe inadequate, your teeth too yellow, your thighs too soft and your hair colour too drab. Which begs the question, 'So why do we buy it?'

Because we have literally been 'programmed' to want to emulate the models we see on TV. Fortunately for us, a model is only a replica of the real thing. It is not the real thing. WE are the real thing, 100% unique specimens of womanhood. After all, the word 'model' is a product description and you are not a product. You are a human being! (I, for one, strongly suspect we were never intended to have skin as smooth as the plastic on Barbie's legs or roast our stomachs golden brown like take-out chicken in the name of beauty.)

And although we may wish we had smaller thighs or tighter abs, small thighs alone do not a Goddess make. No, what does give certain women that special something (and I don't mean a yeast infection) is the self-assurance of knowing they are absolutely divine exactly as they are. That is the sole purpose of this book: to enable you to see, explore and know yourself as the utterly divine creature that you truly are. So you:

A. Never doubt it again and

B. Don't surround yourself with people who fail to acknowledge you as a fully-fledged Goddess in your own right. (That said, there's no need to convince the console operator at your local service station that you are in fact a Goddess. Just knowing this truth will suffice.)

Yes, regardless of your age or silhouette, just consciously embodying this principle from the inside out will bestow upon you a glow reserved for those proud owners of Aphrodite's best kept beauty secret.

What Is An Archetype?

Archetypes are the characters in the earliest soapies called myths. The word 'myth' comes from the term 'mythologia' coined by the Greek philosopher, Plato, which refers to the universal stories that symbolize our inner lessons.

Contrary to what a lot of us were told in high school, myths are not mere make-believe stories without a basis in fact. They are intuitive accounts of our universal human experiences. *In-tuition* being our inner guidance, *Uni-verse* referring to the one story we all live through in different ways.

Myths also demonstrate clearly the cast of universal characters (archetypes) we will meet on our life path, as well as the lessons we are guaranteed to encounter and our personal strengths and weaknesses that will aid or hinder our growth in becoming wise.

Myths (like fairy tales) with their lead actors known as Gods and Goddesses are an easy road map to understanding ourselves and our soul's mission while here on Earth. They are an interpretation of the timeless Hero/Heroine's journey that we each embark on when we arrive here in a body without a clue of what to do save for the instructions of our parents, teachers and advertising campaigns.

Myths were originally passed down via the oral tradition by ancient cultures, the same myths being common to tribes who had no means of communication, yet remarkably all featured the same Gods and Goddesses whose traits were identical, although their given names differed. This is attributed to the part of our consciousness which contains the same universal archetypes accessed by 'dreamtime' or trance states and which have been revived in our society by the work of people like Carl Jung, the Father of modern psychology and Joseph Campbell whose research of global mythology was the inspiration behind the Star Wars trilogy. (Not to mention countless wise women who passed on the wisdom of myths, folk and fairy tales to their children and their children's children!) The cast of Goddess archetypes I have chosen for this inner makeover are primarily from the Greek pantheon (with the exception of Lilith and Ishtar, the earthly and celestial feminine expressions of Spirit known as the 'Shekinah' or 'Tree of Life' amongst the ancient Hebrews.) These are the seven Goddesses that resonated strongly with my own psyche and I hope they serve as a starting point for your own journey of discovery, uncovering the hundreds of historical Goddesses from around the globe.

You may find you resonate more with the shamanistic myths of Africa, the Polynesian Islands, the Caribbean or the Norse and Celtic myths of Europe. Or you may prefer the Zen Buddhist, Hindu, Taoist or Shinto myths of the ancient Eastern cultures or even modern quest equivalents such as those from The Wizard of Oz, The Muppet Movie, and The Lord of the Rings or Star Wars. Trust your own intuition to lead the way.

Once familiar with these archetypes, you may also take great delight in watching the same universal God and Goddess archetypes enact the timeless mythical stories on the world stage. The age-old plots being continually revived by new characters in every gossip rag and newspaper ever printed and sold: *The Hopeless Love of Guinevere and Lancelot* played by Paula Yates and Michael Hutchence, *The Grief of Widowed Isis* played by Jackie Onassis or *Diana, the Huntress becomes the Hunted* played by Diana, the Princess of Wales. (Dear Gen Y readers, apologies for not offering more up to date examples.)

The Inner Makeover from Princess to Queen

This inner makeover will grant you personal insight and understanding by showing you the scripts that your seven inner feminine archetypes continually play out in your own life, enabling you to make the transition from feeling like a 'princess'; one who looks to others for approval and authority, to being a self-appointed 'queen'; a woman who trusts her own intuition and approves of herself exactly as she is. As such, this is a private and personal voyage of discovery. Unlike the quick fix exterior makeovers that fade when you hit the shower, this is a journey of enlightenment that is both life-changing and long lasting in its effect. Although I concede that I too have made life-altering shifts that began with a new hairstyle and a pair of knee high boots, at the end of the day the results of such makeovers are temporary. Changing your inner perspective creates a blossoming effect that permeates both your inner and outer experiences so you continue to glow for a lifetime.

Best of all, this is a makeover you don't need Oprah to facilitate (bless her and her work, but sometimes you just don't want a telecast viewing audience watching when you're at your messiest).

So what follows in this book are basically the seven stages of this timeless feminine metamorphosis, enabling you like the caterpillar to find your wings. Each archetype will introduce you to another colourful aspect of yourself. And with each step you will make the time honored transit across the rainbow that bridges Heaven and Earth to reclaim your true identity as a truly magical being. With each chapter you will be given the story and lessons of each feminine archetype: the angry rebel, the romantic, the career woman, the nurturer, the sex kitten, the hippy-witch and the loner. (See, there is a perfectly reasonable explanation why we can change an outfit seven times before leaving the house!) And by getting to know your seven soul sisters and their strengths and weaknesses you can avoid repeating the same painful life lessons, such as always falling for emotionally unavailable men. Which begs the question, if it really is as simple as all that...

How Come Mum Didn't Tell Me I Was A Goddess?

Women have not had the audacity (or self-love) to refer to themselves as Goddesses for approximately 2000 years. This is perfectly understandable when you consider who our major role models have been.

Our first feminine role model is our Mum. Yes, the first seven years of our life we instinctively spend studying our Earth Mother, emulating and internalizing her as our blueprint of feminine expression. This includes her strengths and weaknesses, as well as her eccentricities and mannerisms. Yes, it is our Mum who teaches us how to take care of our emotional and physical needs from potty training to bee stings.

Our major spiritual role model, however, as women growing up in a predominantly Christian culture has been Eve. Known in modern versions of the Bible as the first woman created as a partner for Adam, she was previously referred to as Pandora by the Ancient Greeks in their creation myth. What is interesting as the common theme is that both girls have since been culturally shamed for not doing 'what they were told to do', which created untold trouble for humanity, insinuating a need to punish and control women to avoid pain. The message to little girls growing up is a warning of the terrible consequences that will undoubtedly befall should we dare to think for ourselves. (Fortunately Lisa Simpson is changing the tide!)

The Myths of Pandora and Eve

Pandora is given a box by the Gods and told not to open it, but possessing a healthy curiosity, she does what any mammal with a thirst for knowledge would do and opens the box, the result being that pestilence and suffering is unleashed upon humanity. For this act she has been in grave need of a PR campaign ever since. It is however interesting to note that the name 'Pandora' means *'All Gifts – the bad as well as the good'.*

Eve has been depicted as the evil temptress for disobeying the command of God to not eat from the tree of knowledge of good and evil. In her desire to know how an apple tasted, she inadvertently inflicted untold evil upon the world by accepting the serpent's offer of an apple and enticed Adam to swap his diet of beasts for a more vegan alternative... a bite of the apple.

The Result

Consequently, with these women as our spiritual role models it's understandable that women have been viewed as demanding troublemakers who shouldn't be trusted by men. Redemption was offered to those not wanting to be an evil temptress. Yes, all your inherent sins as a female could be absolved away by simply opting for the career path of 'Virgin Mother' (easier said than done!) Life as a nun or a mother who suppressed her sexuality were as close as you could get to this ideal.

Today, one hundred years after the suffragettes first rallied for female voting rights and forty years after the feminists of the 1960s and 70s fought for our reproductive and economic rights, we still have fertile women en masse starving themselves to retain their pre-pubescent forms. This is in part our collective subconscious attempt to forever remain the innocent maiden to retain approval by our patriarchal culture, and avoid the shame and disapproval placed on older women.

We don't have to look far to see how Eve's influence has been both far-reaching and insidious. There is even a range of douching products by the name of Eve, implying that vaginas are inherently dirty and should smell like the Potpourri stuffed cane swans that graced domestic toilets in the 70s rather than their natural warm, musky scent.

The word 'Eve' is literally short for evening. Symbolically she fulfilled her destiny as suggested by her name in heralding our fall into night as a species. This 'fall' is necessary in the getting of wisdom and is a natural progression in the individuation process, as we explore the darker side of our psyche so we may learn through our experiences and evolve knowing ourselves in our own right.

BEFORE YOU BEGIN THE MAKEOVER... MEET EVE: THE INNER PRINCESS

Do not be alarmed if you recognize yourself in the following chapter. We have all made serious errors in judgment, particularly in our youth. (I have a photograph to prove it, wearing denim from head to toe in the mid-80s.) I recommend having a hearty laugh at yourself should your ego feel bruised.

It is my wish that after reading this chapter you will be happy to leave 'girl power' to the pre-teens and instead take up your rightful place as a wo-mah-n, whose power is evident in your ability to look anyone in the eye as your equal.

The Female Prototype

I prefer to think of Eve as a prototype rather than an archetype. She's like the patriarchal pin-up girl who we are programmed to 'model' ourselves on, rather than express our full range of 'archetypal selves'. (Note: Eve and Barbie are interchangeable role models.)

Eve is the part of us that doesn't like to make a fuss. She wants to be liked by everyone. Because what unconsciously drives her is the need to always be included, loved and approved of. So if our inner Eve doesn't feel approved of or loved, she'll get her fix by fantasizing about living the life of a celebrity by reading trash mags.

Eve is the aspect within us that secretly aspires to look like the reigning darlings of Hollywood in the hope of bringing some of their success to our door. This tendency to compare and clone is understood by the large cosmetic companies who headhunt a list actresses as spokeswomen.

Socially, Eve is Daddy's little girl, our inner 'good girl' who obeys the unwritten patriarchal social rules for fear if she doesn't, she will be outcast and branded as a loser/freak/weirdo/bitch or some other villainous creature when really she wants to be perceived as nice, agreeable and lovely, just like a princess in a fairy-tale. (Which is why divorce can be so devastating to a woman who has obeyed all the unwritten rules and still been dethroned!)

Whilst many post-feminist women would rather die than admit it, Eve is the hidden part within us who still wonders if there's a 2% chance an aristocrat will sweep us off our feet with a Land Rover (the modern equivalent of Barbie's pink campervan), so we can spend our days oscillating between banana lounges and pedicures, being completed provided for and protected. Hence the global success of the film, 'Pretty Woman' and reality show, 'Keeping Up With The Kardashians'.

Unconsciously, our inner Eve seeks out a Prince Charming who reminds us of our Dad. That is to say, a guy he approves of and would enjoy a fishing expedition or round of golf with. Eve respects her Dad's judgment above her own, so if her Daddy approves of her chosen prince and he jilts them both, Daddy will feel equally mortified and do what he can to rally to the aid of his little girl. The catch is that Eve dominant women expect their partners to play surrogate Daddy to their every whim and consequently use their looks and implied sexual favours to obtain credit cards, puppy dogs and new kitchens whenever they want arises.

Ultimately, our inner Eve's biggest challenge is to learn how to take full responsibility for her choices, rather than blame everyone else for what doesn't meet her ego's expectations. We can assist her with this task by understanding how and where our inner princess is calling the shots; demanding instant gratification and the fulfilment of her wants before her needs. Only when we have learnt to recognize our own inner Eve can we then enjoy a truly R rated adult version of life, (the 'R' representing those long-term gains earned by taking 'R'esponsibility for our own happiness.) For if we don't take responsibility for our personal lessons, we automatically slip into the (Eve) little girl/victim archetype whenever chaos strikes. However, when we are anchoring our inner Goddess we are less inclined to lose faith in our ability to weather each individual storm and therefore less likely to harbour resentment towards others, our self and life in general.

Eve only gives her power to others because she doesn't trust her own instincts and abilities. Eventually she must take the leap of faith in order to learn how to fly. Her journey is therefore a tale of individuation, learning to recognize and balance her polarities, achieve mastery over the four realms (material, mental, emotional and spiritual) and return home having experienced reunion with the 'source'. And it is only through each departure from her established comfort zone that she is rewarded with a greater sense of self-awareness, acceptance, confidence and deeper self-appreciation.

Each journey undertaken to reveal another archetype within our psyche creates an inner union of opposites – as we shed light upon both the light and dark polarities of each archetypal energy. In doing so we find the acceptance to express all our polarities; our rational and emotional sides, our material and spiritual pursuits, our need for independence and intimacy, as well as a lifestyle that allows for both action and reflection in equal doses.

The result is wholeness, which in mysticism is referred to as the Sacred Marriage and must first be experienced as an inner state before attracting a mate capable of enjoying an external union that is as healthy and whole for both individuals.

(You may wish to consider treating yourself to a sacred marriage ring when you complete this inner makeover, symbolizing your journey to reclaim your whole self, like a circle that has no beginning and no end but is complete in itself. Like you, it is a sacred space that contains and distils its own unique magic.)

Her Appearance

Symbolically, Eve is the girl who hasn't yet been initiated into her womanhood, (in other words she hasn't experienced puberty.) So as the pre-pubescent girl, Eve has an aversion to body hair.

To see how prevalent the Eve consciousness is within our society just watch daytime TV and you'll see daughters of Eve selling every type of torture equipment in the name of hair removal.

Typically if Eve is running us we want to look young! Whether that takes collagen, Botox or surgery, our very sense of social survival depends on it so we'll do whatever it takes to find the resources. Nowadays the quest to appear 'young' sadly means pre-pubescent with many young women banishing their pubic hair soon after they grow it to appear non-threatening to immature, porn-addicted boys of all ages. (For the relationship dynamic this 'waxxxing' sets one up for, check out my book, 'Creating Sacred Union in Partnerships'.)

An 'Eve mind-set' places increasing importance on our appearance rather than on our inner character, so whilst our complexion may appear flawless, our hair lustrous and our bottom pert, our sense of self deteriorates and we become more addicted to attending our appearance.

Our inner Eve determines her self-worth on how everybody else sees her, so she worries about what people think of her and her reputation in general. Unconsciously she can also put other women's appearance down in her own mind to bolster her own self-image.

As you may have gleaned, walking around with this mind-set would not a Garden of Eden create. Rather, an insecure and unfulfilling life that is a picture postcard but lacking in true love and joy. So, what happens to an Eve after she takes her first bite of the apple, the fruit of wisdom long held sacred in ancient Goddess cultures? She takes a good look at what she doesn't like about herself as the first step in getting real!

(Before we go any further I recommend buying yourself a journal with blank pages to record all of your Inner Goddess drawings & processes in the one place. I would also advise having on hand some crayons, pastels or color pencils to draw the visions and symbols you download from your subconscious.)

So, let's begin!

EVE'S INNER MAKEOVER ACTIVITY

On page one draw a before picture of your inner Eve.
(Stick figures are most welcome!)

Now make arrows around your Eve, with explanations about her hang-ups and insecurities. (Allow complete honesty with yourself. Remember, everyone has an inner Eve that is equally embarrassing!)

And now, without further ado let's introduce you to the star-studded cast of seven Goddesses who will be hosting your inner Goddess makeover...

Small eyes.
Striking but never been 'pretty'
paranoid
introvert
insecure
boring
socially awkward.
lumpy, arthritic hands.

THE 7 STEP

INNER GODDESS MAKEOVER

LILITH: THE INNER WILD WOMAN

The Wild Woman is the first soul sister we meet in our inner journey through the feminine psyche. Although widely unknown in our society, her presence is felt with the onset of our first period. It is her role to initiate us into our fertility and reveal to us our feminine nature, cycles and sisterhood. Unfortunately she is often subconsciously greeted with shame as a bringer of 'The Curse' (a telling colloquialism referring to how our menstruation is viewed within our culture).

How I Discovered My Wild Woman

When I was twelve years old and in my first year of high school I got my period. For months I hid it from my mother, using toilet paper instead of pads or tampons so no one would discover my secret. I found the idea of telling anyone too confronting. I felt it was a real drag having to deal with this inconvenience for the rest of my life and so I needed time to process my dilemma, as I saw it, before telling anyone else. I had never even heard of a menarche ceremony (a rite-of-passage celebration to mark the arrival of one's first period), and I dare say I would've been mortified if my mother had thought to suggest it.

But whether I liked it or not, Lilith (the Wild Woman you will soon be meeting) was making her presence known externally too; the hairs on my legs were growing darker and hair grew under my arms and on my yoni, which I then called a vagina, a word I hated but was unaware alternatives existed. Meanwhile, the other girls in my class had started shaving their legs, but when I broached the subject with my mum she forbade me to start, saying I was too young.

Yes, Lilith the Wild Woman was emerging through my pubescent form and nowhere could I see validation for her presence — not on TV, not in magazines, not at home, school, ballet or anywhere in the known universe. And so the daily taunts about my primal appearance increased until I was thrown out of the group, barred from sitting and eating lunch with the other girls, who were all devouring teen mags, applying lip gloss on the hour and getting their hair streaked blonde. To add insult to injury, each girl would produce a brush and fastidiously brush their hair prior to each class (a feat I was unable to accomplish since my hair was wild and woolly and would've tripled in volume with any attempt to imitate their preening ritual).

Then the boys caught on that I was the reigning female scapegoat and they started chanting 'Dinky Di' at me (which was a brand of dog food) whenever we lined up for class. Basically my magical thirteenth year was hell. I wasn't invited to class parties, was picked last for sports teams (probably more on account of my lack of hand eye co-ordination but which added to further social injury) and ate lunch alone or with the Christian kids (also considered outcasts). I had effectively been banished for daring to reveal my natural self, my Lilith amongst my peers.

After many tearful nights, my Mum relented and allowed me to shave my legs. I took to the bath, lathered up and laboured with a disposable razor for what seemed like hours, until at last I emerged like a plucked chicken.

And sure enough, having dismissed Lilith, I was then considered acceptable enough to rejoin the 'Eve' clones at lunchtime. However it wasn't until many years later when I allowed my natural self, both inner and outer, to be seen again that I also found my voice to speak up on my own behalf and enjoy more authentic friendships and relationships.

Please Note: I am not advocating that 'Real women have hairy legs'. I am saying that if we reject our natural self in order to win love and approval from others we are ultimately rejecting ourselves. So please, take back your power by accepting your primal erotic appearance complete, with body hair (especially in winter!). Then, when you can revel in your inner wild cat, your mind is your own again to consciously choose when you feel like preening with a pot of hot wax - not because you feel you have to, to live up to someone else's false expectations.

WILD WOMAN QUIZ

Answer the following quick quiz to find out what shape your inner Wild Woman is currently in. (Circle the answer that most describes you.)

You're at a dinner party and another guest says something that angers you, do you:

A. Take a sip of wine and respond under your breath?

B. Wait to say something in private to the host about their remark?

C. Question their viewpoint and speak your own truth at the table?

With regards to your menstruation, do you:

A. Avoid it by taking the contraceptive pill consistently?

B. Deal with it but feel it's an inconvenience?

C. Use your sensitivity at that time to reflect and nurture yourself?

You are camping with friends and realize you've left your hairbrush at home, do you:

A. Drive two hours to the nearest town to buy one?

B. Wear a hat the whole time?

C. Let yourself go feral for a couple of days?

Now add up your score. A = 1, B = 2, C = 3. *If you scored:*

1 – 3 Your inner Wild Woman is in the closet with the door locked. This next chapter may be confronting but will help liberate you in the long run.

4 – 6 You do let your inner Wild Woman out on a leash but don't feel comfortable letting people know she's with you. You'll pick up a few helpful tips in the next chapter.

7 – 9 Grrr! Your inner Wild Cat is doin' fine. Enjoy reading the following chapter.

Herstory: Wild Woman Goddesses

For thousands of years, ancient cultures around the world have honored and celebrated the wild aspect that lies within all women. Ancient Greece knew her as Medusa and in India she was known as Kali or Durga, Hindu Goddesses who both slayed demons, thereby symbolically facing their fears to gain personal power. The Polynesian people celebrated their inner Wild Woman as Pele, the volcanic Goddess, whose eruptions would wake people up. Similarly, the Egyptian wild cat Goddess, Sekhmet, was honored for her ability to recognize and destroy what was no longer healthy by raging when necessary, as did Oya, the African storm Goddess of change. The Western equivalent is Lilith, known infamously as the serpent in the Bible's creation myth. The following is her story, which has since been edited from the Bible for fear that she would set a bad example to good girls everywhere.

The Myth of Lilith

Lilith featured in the early Hebraic Creation myth as the first wife of Adam and has been portrayed ever since as the typically scorned ex-wife. So unpopular did she prove to be with reigning patriarchs overseeing the doctrines of modern religion, that she was removed from the Bible in subsequent translations, and now only appears as the nameless serpent who tempts Eve to taste the apple from the tree of knowledge of good and evil.

Early editions of the Bible stated that God made Adam and Lilith from the Earth, but he used only 'impure' sediments to create Lilith. (Ironic when you think that by modern standards, all of Mother Earth was pretty pure prior to the pollutants we've used during the Industrial Age.)

The Bible went on to say that when it came time to procreate the species, God told Lilith she was only permitted to lie beneath Adam, hence the term, 'Missionary Position' named after the early Christian missionaries who endorsed the use of this position as the norm. Understandably, Lilith objected to the constraints of a submissive position during sex and thereupon uttered the name of God (and no doubt a few other expletives), and fled to the desert to lament the fate of the feminine.

> 'According to Talmudic legend, Lilith... flew away to the desert to lament the diminishment of the moon and feminine power.' Caitlin Mathews, *Sophia, Goddess of Wisdom.*

While in the desert, the Bible reports that Lilith had sexual encounters with both incubi and succubi, referring to the masculine and feminine 'daemons' (nature spirits) with whom she interacted. (The term 'incubus' comes from the name given to the ancient temple priests who attended the womb chamber where seekers would incubate in anticipation of a spiritual rebirth or vision.) This is exactly what Lilith did during her solitude in the desert; she rediscovered her connection to all living things and as a result became a shaman who could shape shift into a serpent, a symbol of her ability to transform herself by shedding her old skin at will.

After Lilith had completed her vision quest she ventured back to see if Adam had undergone a similar inner awakening during her absence (which would qualify him to undertake the great rite of Sacred Marriage, having also achieved wholeness in his own right). However, Adam had replaced his first wife Lilith with Eve, who would lie beneath him, indicating that she would supress her own power and defer to him in all matters. (Eve was said to be created from a rib on Adam's left side, denoting the inner feminine. Judaism believed this was unnatural, as unlike Lilith, Eve was not created from the Earth Mother but from Adam's mind-set of an ideal woman, rather than his true opposite and equal.)

Discovering this, Lilith was troubled by the realization that Eve's daughters would be sure to follow her example for generations to come, so she transformed herself into the serpent and tempted Eve to taste the fruit from the Tree of Knowledge, which the Bible's patriarchal deity had forbidden. (It's interesting to note that the apple, the fruit of wisdom and the serpent, the sign of the healer, were both sacred to the earlier Goddess or matriarchal religions which preceded the God or patriarchal religions of Christianity, Judaism and Islam and their doctrines, the Bible, the Talmud and the Koran.)

> 'As in fairy-tale, a daemonic serpent prods and persuades to knowledge. One of his aspects is the female-daemon, Lilith or Melusina who lives in the philosophical tree.' Carl Jung, *Aspects of the Masculine.*

This is evident in the children's classic 'Snow White', which portrays the evil queen dressing as a witch and tempting the sweet and innocent Snow White to eat her poisoned apple. Unfortunately, the queen is not portrayed with any wisdom, perpetuating the view that mature women with a knowledge of herb lore and the natural healing arts are vindictive and shouldn't be trusted by naïve daughters of the patriarchal mind-set.

After enjoying her first taste of knowledge, Eve offered the fruit of wisdom to Adam. It was for this act that the patriarchal deity then banished the pair from the Garden of Eden and according to the Old Testament, condemned humans to live lives of toil, hardship and death. The serpent's punishment was to become the perceived enemy of humankind.

Wild Woman Profile

The Wild Woman is the part of us that will not hold our tongue to 'keep the peace' if we disagree with someone or with the status quo. Despite the fact this may result in uncomfortable consequences in the short-term, ultimately to go against our inner truth and not stand up for our principles, is to evoke her inner torment.

Our inner Wild Woman will instinctively stand up to external authority for a cause or ideal, so if a woman has acknowledged and integrated her inner Wild Woman she will risk rejection to follow her inner truth.

Ultimately, she represents the wild aspects of the feminine psyche that have been culturally shamed as 'unfeminine' and are therefore suppressed. For instance, a woman giving birth is similar to a primal animal in that she loses control over all bodily functions, grunting and screaming with abandon until the act of creation is complete. This is an image of womanhood that is largely hidden behind a medical veneer that often appropriates the credit and respect to the physician rather than the birthing woman. Therefore she is viewed more as a victim in need of assistance than a powerful shaman journeying through the realms of death and rebirth.

The wild feminine is the most powerful a woman can be, giving rise to all her natural sounds, movements and feelings without a single self-condemning thought entering her consciousness. However, many women don't allow this aspect out for fear of looking ridiculous and alienating those around them. And yet, to not have safe times and places where we can vent every shade of our inner terrain, induces isolation and neurosis.

Ultimately, the most empowering act we can do is to reclaim those parts of us that have been demonized and shamed by our society, and doing so will heal us by restoring our deep sense of wholeness. So let your inner Wild Woman have some expression every once in a while by letting your body hair grow, not wearing a daily mask of cosmetics and daring to be free, outspoken and forthright in your views and behaviour — not merely to shock but to simply be true to yourself.

Our inner Lilith is instinctual by nature, unlike Eve (our persona) whose mind-set is fashioned by Adam (society). Lilith if acknowledged will think for herself rather than blindly following rules. She would rather be alone than compromise her inner truth so her actions follow the conviction of her ideals.

On a subconscious level, many men fantasise about coupling with a Lilith woman. She, being a partner who shares the power equally by questioning him, when necessary and offering wise counsel, whilst remaining sexually liberated, spontaneous and connected with her true self. Understandably as we evolve, more men are following their inner instincts to seek out such women, as are women internally. Typically, immature males tend to seek out Lilith women for their sexual appetite, only to abandon them when they insist on equality.

An experience which can fuel the rage and disillusionment our inner Lilith may feel with men in general, until we learn to take more responsibility for our own discernment in choosing intimate partners.

> 'She is the Goddess of kundalini, the hidden fire of sexuality which lies coiled as a serpent at the base of the spine, waiting to be aroused.' Caitlyn Mathews, *Sophia, Goddess of Wisdom*.

For women, Lilith is their mysterious dark and primal shadow self that craves union with the archetype of Pan, The Horned One. Pan is simultaneously natural and wild and there is a part of her that yearns to be taken by a man and devoured sexually with no shame or remorse. Unfortunately this lustful drive often leads her to become involved with men who value her only for her sexuality and not for her natural, wise and womanly self. As such, Lilith women do well to seek out men who have consciously embraced their Pan archetype as a sacred and natural expression of their masculinity, rather than boys who lead a double life, living out their Pan archetype unconsciously by night and suppressing their wild self by day. This immature Pan is best described as Peter Pan, the boy who refuses to grow up and confront his shadow nature, despite the attempts of many 'Wendys' to reconnect him with it. (For more about the dynamic between Lilith and Pan, both internally and externally in your relationships, check out my book 'Creating Sacred Union Within')

Women who have a strong Lilith archetype value equality and will not hesitate to passionately express their concern or even outrage should they feel imbalances beginning to rise. Fortunately, Lilith also has a strong drive to understand herself and others and will therefore take time to reflect upon her part in circumstances where conflict has occurred. This gives her the ability to transform her rage into wisdom and own her shadow behaviour rather than scapegoat her partner and others for theirs. This self-awareness gives her increasing empowerment, heightening her sexual magnetism.

Often the degree to which a woman suffers during menstruation is a strong indication of how empowered her Lilith archetype really is. Prior to menstruating we tend to feel acutely sensitive (both our five worldly senses and our otherworldly senses, such as our intuitive capabilities) — this is the time when our Lilith energy is most pronounced. So what is commonly referred to as PMT, (pre-menstrual tension) is actually the time in our lunar cycle when issues that remain unresolved from the previous lunar month come to the forefront of our mind until we deal with them. Also at this time we become attuned to both our shadow traits and the shadow traits of others, as well as any areas where we find imbalances of equality. During this time in our cycle it is imperative we honor our inner truth by communicating our thoughts and feelings as much as possible. The more we can do this, the less we run the risk of hissing at others like a pressure cooker or boiling over in a fit of rage.

Many of us have stored within our physical, emotional and energetic bodies collective anger at the suppression and persecution of the feminine during the last two thousand years. This, along with the unspoken shame and lack of sacred power connected with our lunar cycles, can potentially manifest itself in our bodies in conditions ranging from pelvic inflammation, fibroids, endometriosis, irregular cycles, excessive bleeding, fainting, vomiting, diarrhoea and painful cramps. If you suffer from any of the above complaints, in addition to seeking medical/naturopathic treatment, take some tips from the Wild Woman Get Wise and Inner Makeover sections, and take some time out for yourself as much as possible on the first day or evening of each period.

Questioning the attitudes towards menstruation is another healthy place to start. For example, using cloth pads and returning the rich nutrients in your blood to Mother Earth (or your pot plants) is a great way of honoring the magical life-giving blood that cycles within our bodies, the alternative being expensive non-biodegradable pads that resemble nappies or medical dressings that are thrown out with the garbage and anchor the belief that our lunar blood is dirty and worthless. (It is interesting to note that the word 'sanitary' means hygienic or clean, insinuating that menstruation is in fact dirty.) Or worse still, tampons that don't allow your uterus its monthly rinse cycle but instead plug you up so you can pretend you aren't even bleeding — the ultimate denial of your womanhood and feminine power. As if to prove this point, on my last trip to the supermarket I saw a brand of pads called 'Barely There'!

It has been said that when a woman is bleeding she is at the point where she is most likely to rebel and question those in a position of authority. It is for this reason that menstruation has become such a taboo within our society because simply, where there is fear, there is power. And women who are connected with their lunar cycle, with their inner Lilith, will not lie down and allow others to dictate to them how to behave.

Just before our moontime (menses), we often feel dark and destructive (especially if our period coincides with the phase of dark moon, which is the most common). This is followed by a sense of drawing inward when our lunar blood begins to flow.

We consequently need to still our sensitivities and attune ourselves to our inner needs. If we steer away from artificial lighting (which plays havoc with our endocrine system which governs our natural cycle) and rest with warming herbal teas, such as ginger and chamomile, instead of frolicking in the surf like the white bikini-clad girls in sanitary pad ads, we probably wouldn't feel half as irritable. (Ironically, swimming in cold water is one of the fastest ways to bring on menstrual cramps!)

Further facts

Lilith, the archetypal Wild Woman was said to have resided in the philosophical Tree of Life, the branches of which are often depicted as coming out of Lilith's head. The Tree of Life, (known also the Shekinah to the Hebrews) represented the two poles of the divine feminine principle. At the top resided the Queen of Heaven, God's Consort, Ishtar. At the bottom of the tree, Lilith, the Earthly aspect whose role as Ishtar's handmaiden was to use her primal powers of seduction to lure men away from their business concerns and into Ishtar's spiritual temple to focus on their soul needs.

The following three case studies illustrate scenarios where women have suppressed their Lilith energy and suffered as a result:

Elizabeth

Elizabeth came from a family where women got things done. As a result, she was an ambitious woman who had her own business. Her husband, on the other hand, was an artist and a sensitive man who cared for her and their children deeply but was absorbed in his creative projects and was unable to contribute a consistent financial wage to the family budget. Elizabeth provided the family income, a decision that displeased her. Over time, this imbalance was made known within Elizabeth's womb in the form of fibroids and ovarian cysts, alerting her that she needed to nurture herself and address her feminine needs. At first, she tried to soldier on with painkillers and prescription drugs. Then she had a number of medical procedures in order to rectify her troubled womb, until finally, fed up with recurring problems, she had a hysterectomy and became very depressed. During this time she identified her true feelings of anger and resentment toward her husband for not sharing the provider role in the relationship and realized she shouldered the burden for so long for fear of confrontation.

Joan

Joan was one of twelve children brought up in a strict Catholic household. When she came to a workshop of mine she was in her sixties and the very mention of a snake had her recoiling in disgust and horror as her conditioning equated serpents with the devil. For the first day she had trouble even hearing what I had to say for the fear of betraying her parent's beliefs but slowly she recognized herself in the information she was being offered. It was not until the following afternoon when the class participated in a kundalini awakening trance dance that she felt the power of her own inner serpent (Lilith) rising and was able to express the emotional pain which had kept her defenses up.

Nicki

Nicki's father was a successful businessman who was well respected within their local community. Nicki's mum also had a public profile as she organized various social events and charity fundraisers. Nicki, on the other hand, had no desire to follow in her parent's footsteps and left her home town after high school to pursue an Arts degree. Whilst at university she became involved in a number of feminist groups, became a vegan and eventually dropped out to live with a community in a native forest. Nicki smoked a lot of cannabis to suppress her fury at her parents and mainstream society in general. Fuelling her anger was her mother's criticism of Nicki's decision to grow her body hair and not conform to family expectations of being a 'good girl'. Unfortunately, whilst Nicki had embraced her own Wild Woman, she was similarly scapegoating those who had not done the same and unconsciously used her righteous indignation to intimidate others who didn't share her views.

This last example illustrates that unleashing one's wild self is only half of the journey. For without the humility to reflect upon one's own flaws and wrongdoings, the archetype of Wild Woman judges others harshly, using rage to dominate the opinions of others.

Wild Woman Strengths

The following is a description of how we behave when our Wild Woman archetype is appreciated and expressed:

- I feel confident knowing my natural self is sacred.
- I revel in my ability to be spontaneous, original, free and unconventional.
- I will not compromise my values, my appearance or my feelings just to please others. I go with my instincts, even if that means being outcast by the 'in crowd'.

- I have the inner strength to sacrifice situations that don't serve me, shedding my 'snake skin' in order to grow.
- I stand my ground and risk objections to be true to myself.
- When speaking my truth I exercise diplomacy and compassion for others.
- I value my anger as an indication that something needs to be understood and transformed within myself, as well as externally.
- I allow my primal erotic nature free orgasmic expression.
- I use shamanic practices to ground and energize me.
- I honor my lunar cycle by turning inwards to connect with my inner self and the elemental cycles of the Cosmos.

Wild Woman Shadow Traits

The following is a list of how we behave when we suppress the Wild Woman within our psyche:

- I tend to view men as incompetent and inferior.
- I sometimes suppress my anger for fear of what others would think. I hold back from being honest for fear of hurting myself or others. I don't express my authentic self for fear I'll be rejected.
- I don't take full responsibility for my choices, instead I am quick to blame others. I tend to judge others harshly, without compassion for their naiveté and fears.
- I second-guess the urge to assert myself and act on my instincts.
- I often rebel and only hurt myself, rather than look at what pain my anger is masking. I can focus on the 'enemy' outside rather than on my own inner patriarch.
- I will silence and dominate others with my righteous anger and indignation rather than really listen to their point of view.
- I am afraid, deep down, of becoming disempowered within a committed relationship, fearing I will compromise my values to avoid being rejected.

Wild Woman Lessons

To balance your Wild Woman's strengths and weaknesses, try the following suggestions:

- Educate your partner to accept and value your inner Wild Woman.
- Say 'No' to situations that do not honor your highest truth.
- Confront issues of inequality in all your relationships.
- Be humble enough to face your own shadow, enabling you to be emotionally honest with yourself and others.
- Honor and value each person's individual process.

- Delight in your and other people's primal erotic nature without judgment.
- Don't stay in a relationship where you're appreciated more for your wild sexuality than your soul's unique expression and wisdom.
- Seek wisdom to understand your own inner conflict so you don't project it externally on to others.
- Learn to recognize where and how you attempt to exert power over others to get your personal needs met.
- Do not conform or 'keep the peace' at a cost to your sanity.

Wild Woman Relationship Patterns

Personal

The Wild Woman is the part of us that announces in a relationship, 'Honey, we need to talk.' She is often responsible for the end of the initial 'honeymoon phase' and represents our need to 'get real' and consciously acknowledge our shadow traits and resolve differences. She is the stormy element of change who challenges her mate to understand themselves more fully and to grow emotionally. Without her willingness to get to the heart of each matter, relationships remain psychologically immature and unable to last the test of time. Partnerships that suppress Lilith's need to question their dynamics often result in marriages that over time offer only companionship without passion, as any sign of opposition is dulled in the name of peace, so is the spark that ignites the sexual union.

The other extreme is the volatile relationship that is either emotionally or physically combative. The result is sex ends up being used to resolve disputes instead of true intimacy and understanding, the intense opposition creating a desperate need for reunion after each storm passes. This pattern keeps many women in abusive relationships, repeatedly being hooked in emotionally by the passionate reunions, at the cost of their psychological and psychic well-being. Often 'good girl' Eves who appear shy of expressing their inner Lilith side are unwittingly attracted to bad boys who play out their dark, destructive side for them.

Famous Wild Women

In the 1960s with the dawning of the Age of Aquarius, Lilith literally came back from her exile in the desert with women like Germaine Greer and Janis Joplin voicing the primal rage of the Wild Woman who had been relegated to waxing floors for fear of upsetting the apple cart. The acceleration in women's empowerment has since snowballed.

However, after the mass roar of disgruntled women worldwide in the 1960s and 1970s, there was a backlash that saw feminists portrayed as dark, angry she-devils, particularly in Hollywood.

Glenn Close in the 1980s thriller *Fatal Attraction* is an example of how the wild and passionate side of a woman can be portrayed as demonic. As a result, the philandering behaviour of the husband (played by Michael Douglas) is downplayed. His character is sympathetically depicted as he is stalked by the psychotic wrath of a woman scorned.

Also in the 1980's hit comedy, *Cheers*, Lilith was the aptly named first wife of Frasier, played by Kelsey Grammer. Intellectually his equal match as a psychiatrist, she was dark-haired, forthright with her views and generally feared by the show's male characters. However, by the 1990s her attributes were found more deserving of recognition from Frasier (in his own self-titled sitcom). He turned to her for insight into his personal issues in times of crisis, even acknowledging his sexual attraction to her, despite their ongoing personal confrontations.

Fortunately the lead up to the new millennium saw the global serpent of kundalini awaken the primal power of Lilith in both men and women en masse. So now we have an increasing number of both men and women speaking out against inequality to change the corrupt status quo. So too, more outspoken women are being celebrated (instead of shunned) as agents of change, with many men offering their services to actively support them. This includes the Dalai Lama, who in 2009 was quoted as saying at the Vancouver Peace Summit: 'The world will be saved by the western woman.'

Wild Woman Makeover Kit

Below is a list of practical tips to further hone the instincts and personal power of your inner Wild Woman.

Suggested Styles

Although clothes do not 'maketh the man' (or woman), they certainly do influence our code of behaviour. That said, when choosing to evoke your primal Lilith energy, being totally 'naturale' is not always a viable option. So here are some other suggestions you may find useful:

- *Wear leopard, tiger or snakeskin prints.*
- *Wear or adorn your house with faux furs.*
- *Let your body hair grow (even if just under your winter woollies).*
- *Use less or no make-up.*
- *Let your claws (fingernails) grow.*
- *Wear your hair out or tease it for a wild look.*
- *Consider tattoos and body piercing (permanent or semi-permanent).*
- *Wear neck to ankle bodysuits (to feel serpentine).*
- *Try body painting with ochres or henna.*

Alternatively, going feral is a great way to experience Lilith first-hand. You may wish to not shower for a day or go camping and let your natural self-hang out. Perhaps consider walking barefoot around the house, leaving your underwear and bra in the drawer and trying some kundalini yoga, shamanic drumming, chanting or trance-dancing.

Wild Woman Colours

If you feel drawn to wearing the following colours, know that change is imminent as Lilith is in the driver's seat. Similarly, if you see someone wearing these colours or decorating their car or apartment in this colour scheme, tread carefully so as not to incur their wrath.

Black and Red

Black and red are colours symbolising death and rebirth. Black represents all that is unconscious; the void or abyss of pure potential which is not yet made manifest and the chaos of that which is not yet seen and therefore consciously understood. Red is the surge of new life, of the passion and enthusiasm needed to instigate new possibilities, as well as our blood engorged genitalia that creates physical life through the joining of opposites. Red is also associated with the planet Mars, which is sub-ruler of Scorpio and the God of action and war. It's the energy of frustration that surfaces when we know we need to make changes in our life.

Wild Woman Associated Chakra

Base Root

The base root chakra or energy centre is located at the base of the spine and represents our survival issues and fears. It is the power centre that grounds and connects us with the Earth, so when we lose our connection to our wild, primal woman, we in turn feel ungrounded and disempowered. The colour of this energy centre is red, reflecting our blood, which boils in rage if our passions are not afforded positive expression. When this energy centre is weak, our physical health can suffer or it may manifest as a tendency to become a victim to our own fears. To help clear energy blockages in this chakra, consider active meditation CDs such as *Dynamic Meditation* and *Kundalini Mediation* by Osho or *5 Rhythms* by Gabrielle Roth. To help energetically free your base chakra from limiting survival fears consider either the book, *Cutting the Ties* by Phyllis Krystal or *E.F.T, the emotional freedom technique.*

Wild Woman Essential Oils

Sandalwood

Helps to dissipate fear.

Sage

Promotes wisdom and clears negative energies.

Clary Sage

Both uplifting and grounding and handy for adding to a base oil, such as sweet almond to rub into your abdomen and lower back for menstrual cramps.

Wild Woman Flower Essences

The following are vibrational essences which distil the healing properties of various plants. When taken orally they promote emotional balance and wellbeing.

Hornbeam

Activates inner strength needed to face life's challenges.

Rockrose

Gives you the courage to overcome fears.

Wild Woman Minerals, Crystals and Stones

Garnet

Strengthens and purifies the blood. Also harmonises the base root chakra's kundalini energy. It's red in colour and helps strengthen our Earth connection and immune system.

Bloodstone

It's also red in colour, and has the potential to ground our energy. Bloodstone oxygenates the blood while balancing iron deficiencies. It also stimulates the base root chakra, activating kundalini whilst strengthening the heart and reducing emotional stress.

Serpentine

Activates the kundalini energy up through the chakras. It is green with ochre red, yellow and white markings. It's great for the relief of menstrual cramps and muscular aches and pains if you hold it on the area. It also assists the absorption of magnesium, a mineral available as a supplement which assists the nervous system integrate the rising kundalini energy when it awakens.

Wild Woman Food

Apples

Apples symbolize immortality – the acceptance of the death and rebirth cycle that is eternal life. They were common to most Indo-European mythologies as a magical fruit dispensed by the Goddess.

Avalon, an ancient mystery school made famous by the legend of Kind Arthur, was said to be the 'Apple Isle' sacred to the Triple Goddess (the maiden, mother and crone). The use of an apple in the Judeo-Christian creationist myth may have been influenced by the Gypsy wedding custom of the bride and groom cutting an apple horizontally in half to reveal the pentacle (representing wisdom), which they fed to their beloved. This indicated they would willingly eat from the Tree of Life, acknowledging their partner as the paradox of divine perfection and human flaws, a mirror upon which they could reflect to become wise.

Blood Plums, Red Wine, Red Meat and Tomatoes

Celebrate Lilith with red foods that are guaranteed to ignite your life force. Being a primal Goddess, Lilith enjoys chewing bones, so if you're a carnivore, bless the soul that has sacrificed its physical form so that you may enjoy a barbeque or suck the marrow out of an osso bucco stew or marinate some spare ribs. If you're vegetarian, try some chilli con carne with red kidney beans, a curry with red lentils and root veggies slow cooked and shard around an open fire!

Wild Woman Flower

Lily

With its pronounced stamen and powerful scent, the lily is a symbol for our inner Wild Woman's sexuality and fertility. (The oriental equivalent is the lotus, which was sacred to Ishtar, Lilith's polar opposite, who resided at the top of the Tree of Life.) The lily or lotus represents genital magic and the transformation that sexual initiation heralds. The lily was also a symbol of the miraculous impregnation of the virgin (maiden) Goddess. The 'Blessed Virgin Juno' was depicted holding a lily and was later replaced by the 'Blessed Virgin Mary', whose lily appeared in the male Archangel Gabriel's hand. (Some Christian authorities claim the lily in Archangel Gabriel's hand filtered God's semen, which entered Mary's body through her ear! Sounds like a biblical version of the game, Twister.)

Biologically the blue lotus that was sacred to Egyptian priestesses is considered to have the same healing properties as Viagra. This is significant to Lilith, as her female lust and primal urges are the initial forces that introduce us to transformative powers of the feminine temple through the sexual gateway of psychological death and rebirth, the yoni.

Wild Woman Hangouts

Below is a list of places where Lilith feels right at home. Allow yourself a Lilith pilgrimage and commune with her in your own creative way and time.

The Desert

In the arid landscape of no distractions we are forced to contemplate our true nature and transcend our lower instincts. The feminine or yin aspect in nature is considered to be moist, fertile and lush so this landscape provides an experience with the opposite polarity for women to become whole.

Moon Lodges / Red Tents

Traditionally women would gather together during their moon time (period) to meditate and channel wisdom for the greater community. Consider creating your own Red Tent in your boudoir with red fabrics, plush cushions and candles you can retreat to during that time of the month. Better still, check out what Red Tent women's events are happening in your local area or consider starting a Red Tent women's circle once a month.

To find out more about my online course that teaches you everything you need to know to create a Red Tent, visit http://www.starofishtar.com/portfolio/red-tent-facilitator-training-course/. To find the nearest Red Tent women's circle to you, visit http://www.starofishtar.com/community-2/womens-circles-mens-circles/

Earth Festivals

Celebrated around the world to commemorate the holy days of the seasonal cycle, earth festivals such as the Glastonbury Festival in England, Burning Man in America and Confest in Australia are great opportunities to let your shamanic self out to play in a natural environment.

Wild Woman Astrological Sign

One does not need have a Scorpio sun, moon or rising sign or have a lot of planets in the eighth house to exude Lilith traits – but it helps! Alternatively, keep an eye on the moon when it is in Scorpio during each monthly cycle by consulting a moon calendar or during the month when the Sun transits through Scorpio, October 23 to November 23.

Scorpio

This is the sign of transformation as the lower nature of the scorpion seeks out its higher nature in the form of a phoenix, a regenerative bird, reborn form the ashes in the Tree of Life. Scorpios are renowned for their charismatic sexual magnetism, as well as their struggle to find a balance between external and inner power. Scorpio is also renowned for their intense duality, with a tendency to swing between its hedonistic lower self and its mystical higher self. Scorpio colors are red and black.

N.B. The 13th sign, Ophichus known to the ancients as 'The winged serpent' is considered the second half of Scorpio. So when the sun transits through Ophichus November 30 - December 17 each year this is a particularly potent time to raise one's kundalini. Observing this sign does throw out the traditional dates of the astrological signs. Below are the dates of the signs when we acknowledge the 13th sign.

Capricorn: Jan. 20 - Feb. 16.
Aquarius: Feb. 16 - March 11.
Pisces: March 11 - April 18.
Aries: April 18 - May 13.
Taurus: May 13 - June 21.
Gemini: June 21 - July 20.

Cancer:	July 20 - Aug. 10.
Leo:	Aug. 10 - Sept. 16.
Virgo:	Sept. 16 - Oct. 30.
Libra:	Oct. 30 - Nov. 23.
Scorpio:	Nov. 23-29.
Ophichus:	Nov. 29 - Dec. 17.
Sagittarius:	Dec. 17 - Jan. 20.

Wild Woman Symbols

If you want to know when Lilith wants to have her needs addressed, simply pay attention to the signs. Should you encounter any of the following symbols in your day-to-day travels, take it as a personal invitation from your subconscious to tend to her needs.

The Pentacle

A symbol for hermetic wisdom (the intuitive insights we receive in solitude) which has been demonized as a sign of devil worship by Christian theologians. It represents the five elements: air, fire, water, earth and spirit as well as the physical human form of the body.

The Tree of Life

The Tree of Life Goddess (Ishtar) is best known for handing her fruit to the first man while her serpent of wisdom (Lilith) lay entwined in the branches. She was worshipped as early as 2000 BC in the East and in Avalon, Hesperides and Eden, and was said to possess life-giving apples.

Wild Woman Totem Animals

Serpent

Snakes are feminine creatures that are subtle and fluid in their approach and are susceptible to being charmed. They signify a metaphor for the awakening kundalini or passionate life force that lies dormant till aroused in the base of the spine. It is interesting to note that the Ouroboros, the glyph of the snake eating its own tail, is a symbol for wholeness in The World Tarot card, and the entwined snakes have long been used as a symbol for healing, representing shamanic transformation.

Spider

Another symbol of potent feminine power is the spider, again largely feared in the West. The medicine of Great Grandmother Spider was said to weave the fate of the world and possessed the dual powers of creation and destruction using ingenuity and skill. She also represented the interconnectedness of all things.

Owl

The owl is said to be sacred to Lilith, as a symbol of wisdom.

Wild Woman Relative Parts of the Body

Menstrual Blood

Worshipped by the ancients for its magical healing and life-giving properties, menstrual blood has long been used to bless crops with fertility, assist manifestation in ritual, and to charge talisman with healing power, especially the first drop of 'moondew' or menstrual blood.

Christ's communion ritual where followers are instructed to worship his blood when they drink of the wine is an assimilation of earlier rites that used menstrual blood and bread baked by women, which were commonly referred to as moon cakes. Nuns have continued this tradition baking the wafers for the Christian sacrament.

The Buddhist Dakinis, the Hindu Tantrikas, Native American communities, Celtic and European Pagans and Gnostic worshippers celebrated this earlier rite. Blood is symbolic of passion, heat and anger – all are traits that Lilith possessed. So if your menstrual flow is problematic, take the time to sight the moon each evening to reconnect your cycle with Luna's.

Spine

Our spine or backbone signifies our ability to stand up for ourselves. It is also the channel through which our life force or kundalini ascends when we use our energy consciously. A good remedial therapist, osteopath or chiropractor is a great help if working through Lilith issues.

Rectum

Sometimes we just need to ask 'What's giving me the shits?' to understand why we may have an irritable bowel. If you're not expressing your anger on a regular basis, it may make itself known in your rectum or a little higher up if you're 'holding it in' symbolically. Scorpio rules the elimination organs so it may help to clean out all the garbage in your life and diet to assist your bowel.

WILD WOMAN INNER MAKEOVER ACTIVITES

So, you've let your armpit hair grow down to the floor, you've skinned a goat, made your own drum and legged after an antelope to reconnect with your primal self. Now it's time to do some inner work and put out the welcome mat for Lilith, Lily to her friends.

Speaking the Truth

Get real with yourself and everyone else and be honest about the changes your inner self wants to make.

Write a list of ten things you wish to say NO to in your life.

Consider what fears stop you from speaking your truth.
Make a commitment to begin honoring yourself by not going against your instincts.

Owning Your Own Shadow to Become Wise

Think of someone you dislike and write down all of their traits that annoy you. Be totally honest; no one need see this but you.

Now substitute their name with your name for each shadow trait. Changing pronouns such as they, she or he with I, my, me, and read through the list again. Take your time with each one, allowing the truth of each statement to drop in and take effect. Contemplate how you also possess that same trait, or perhaps treat yourself in the way that they treat others, i.e. being judgmental.

Now close your eyes and visualize that person with white-feathered wings holding a mirror up to you. Thank them for showing you what you've been blind to in yourself.

Now visualize any anger or judgment you have felt towards them as a red light which spirals up your spine into a purple flame, transmuting old karma between you into white light, which showers down upon you as resolved energy returning to its original state.

Addressing the Balance of Power

Write down in your journal relationships that come to mind as not being equal.

Consider what strengths you fail to appreciate in the other person or why you may be undervaluing your own or the contribution you each make to the relationship.

Once you've clarified your thoughts on the written page, make a time to discuss your feelings and possible solutions with the other person involved. If they are not agreeable to a discussion, call upon Lilith to help you face your aloneness rather than compromise your inner needs and personal power by accepting an unbalanced status quo.

Reclaiming Anger, Reclaiming Passion!

Anger has been by and large considered very inappropriate for 'ladies' during the last two thousand years, and as a result many women regularly suppress their anger. If anger does surface but is feared, it usually dissolves into tears, making it difficult for women to express their dissatisfaction. To get what they want, girls are conditioned to cry like victims instead of screaming like enraged banshees. Anger is, however, a valuable warning sign that a boundary has been crossed and that something needs urgent attention to be resolved.

Write all the things that irritate you and then note what you can do about each of these situations. It is good to connect with what you are passionate about, but don't just get angry; use that energy for change.

Try meditating daily, visualizing a planet of peaceful people and living a more peaceful existence by uncovering what you are angry about and resolving it.

Try going to the op-shop (or second-hand shop) and purchasing some old plates and playfully smashing them in turns with a friend, child or partner, yelling to the heavens about what makes you mad.

Alternatively, let your family or housemates know when you are feeling fed up and angry so they know to keep a wide berth and make allowances. This lets everybody know that you acknowledge your anger, which is safer than projecting it onto anyone in your path.

Deriving Power from the Source

This following meditation is akin to filling up your energy from the cosmic petrol station. A quick and simple technique, you can do in your own time, sitting on a train or in the shower every morning or whenever you're feeling low on energy, because when we feel energized, we feel empowered.

Tree of Life Meditation

N.B. I have recorded an MP3 version of this meditation which you can listen to as a daily guided meditation to start your day. Available at: http://www.starofishtar.com/meditation/

Sit with your weight evenly distributed either cross-legged on the floor or upright in a chair. Take your awareness to the base of your spine and visualize roots extending out from your coccyx, down through the floor and deep within the Earth. Visualize your roots extending all the way down to the core of Gaia, Mother Earth (an orb of glowing red energy) and wrapping themselves around like large tentacles.

Feel the rush of red energy surging up from her center through your root system and into your physical body, energizing and grounding you with Earth energy. See your body fill and glow with red energy.

Now take your awareness to the top of your head and visualize branches growing out through your crown, up into the sky, through the clouds and beyond the stratosphere, all the way out to Sol, Father Sun. Feel your branches wrap around this bright, solar orb of masculine energy, filling you with optimism, hope and a celestial lightness of being.

Feel the rush of golden yellow energy surging down through your branches, in through your crown, filling your body with this golden light, a sense of purpose that merges with the red already present in your body. Allow the two colours to co-exist, creating a sense of wholeness and harmony.

Finally, seal yourself off in a large egg shaped bubble that contains both of these energies. You are now ready to start the day!

What's in a Name?

Below is a list of titles that were used in the ancient world to describe Lilith:

She of the Night, Storm Goddess, She-Devil, Mother of Demons, Lilutu, Lil, Child Killing Witch, Lamashtu, Tree of Life Goddess, The Serpent, Snake Woman, The Dark Goddess, Wife of the Devil, Queen of Sheba, Screeching Owl, Dame Donkey Legs, Vixen Bogey, Blood Sucker, Woman of Harlotry and Impure Female.

Consider some of the nicknames your Lilith has received over the years, both from people you know and in literature, music and the media.
Some examples that sprang to my mind include: *Dragon Woman, Monster, Alien Woman, Bitch, Witch, Hag, Dyke, Snatch, Festy, Dirty, Filthy Whore, Enchantress, Donkey features, ET with Plaits, Evil Woman, Scary Lady, Hairy Legs, Feral Bitch and Man Eater.*

Words are powerful.

Circle any of the names that jump out at you and question why they carry a charge for you. Who was it that used the word in a derogatory way? Do you still want the approval of that person?

Consider how you can now reclaim that label in a positive and fun way. Write a poem, get it screen-printed on a t-shirt or make a cake and write it with icing on the top and decorate with candles, marking your Lilith rebirth day.

Art Therapy: You as Lilith

In your journal or on a sheet of paper draw yourself as Lilith. Draw yourself as you would look at your most feral. You might be screaming with rage, hair standing on end, sporting hairs on your legs long enough to weave a blanket.

Know this energy is accessible whether you feel your survival is at stake or you need to stand up for yourself. You may wish to hang this picture up in your room or place it on your altar while you are working with your Lilith energy so you can face your fear of expressing her.

Food for thought

Could it be that the lump known as Adam's apple is metaphorically Lilith's apple of wisdom that he just couldn't swallow?

Embracing your Wild Woman: Further Suggestions

- The key to anchoring the shamanic power of Lilith is to reconnect with nature. Here are a few pointers you may wish to try to tune into the natural cycles. Purchase a moon diary or moon planting astrological calendar and observe how you feel with the lunar changes as the moon moves into a different astrological sign every two and a half days. Also attune your activities to the phases of the moon so you are working with the natural energies and not against them. In other words, rest at dark moon and socialise at full moon.
- Study the beauty of the artist, Frieda Kahlo in herself portraits, complete with moustache and mono-brow. Eat with your hands, get some dirt under your nails and do picnic wees in the bush or backyard.
- Go to the reptile enclosure at your nearest zoo or animal sanctuary and make eye contact with a snake. Admire its beauty, breathe deeply into any fears it may arouse in your body and acknowledge its great wisdom and sacredness in a telepathic conversation of thought.
- Be eccentric. Take delight in being your own woman and not conforming to society's cta-tions of a well-behaved lady. Enjoy!

Get Wise

The adage 'Knowledge is Power' is an oldie but a goodie. Below is a list of other books you may find helpful in understanding and addressing some of your Wild Woman issues.

Wild Woman Non-Fiction

Shakti Woman by Vicki Noble

Sister Moon Lodge by Kisma Stepanich

The Wild Genie by Alexandra Pope

Buffalo Woman Comes Singing by Brooke Medicine Woman

Blood, Bread and Roses by Judy Grahn

When God Was A Woman by Merlin Stone

Moving Into Ecstacy by Amoda

Moon Diary by Shekinah Morgan (an annual publication)

The Wise Wound by Penelope Shuttle and Peter Redgrove

Women who Run with the Wolves by Clarissa Pinkola Estes

Estes Sophia, Goddess of Wisdom by Caitlin Mathews

The Woman's Encyclopedia of Symbols and Sacred Objects by Barbara Walker

Wild Woman Fiction

The Red Tent by Anita Diamant

Eva Luna by Isabelle Allende

Topics for Discussion

Next time you get together with your female friends for a cup of tea, consider throwing a few of these conversation starters in the mix for general discussion. Alternatively, you may like to start An Inner Goddess Makeover Group or book club that meets on a regular basis to share your collective wisdom or experiences as you complete your personal journey, using this book as a guide.

- How has your or other women's wisdom been devalued in your experience?
- How have you or women you know been scapegoated socially for allowing your/their inner Lilith to be seen?
- How did you receive your first period and was it celebrated?
- Did you banish Lilith in your own life in order to be accepted by society?
- What is the most primitive experience you have had and how did it change you?
- How can you honor Lilith more in your own life?

Questions for Personal Reflection

- If I am strong, will people still like me?
- If I show my true strength of power, will it threaten my existing relationships?

Secret Woman's Business: Best Times to Celebrate Lilith

PMT – Pre Menstrual Tension is when we feel the presence of Lilith and we become sensitive psychically and emotionally. It is in this state of heightened awareness that we realize what has rendered us powerless in the last lunar cycle. If we fail to take responsibility for our choices and address it at this time we may lash out on those around us as if our very survival is being threatened.

So pay particular homage to Lilith in the two weeks after ovulation every month, a good time for consciously letting go of what isn't serving you. Act on the intuition you receive at these times to honor her needs, including her heightened sexual appetite just prior to menstruation if this feels appropriate.

Wild Woman Rite of Passage Ceremony

This is a great way of anchoring Lilith's energy within you so you can draw upon it when you need to access her power.

You will need:

Modelling clay that doesn't require firing

Leather strapping

Rhythmic music

Ochre/berry juice/personal moonflow

Step One

Put on some tribal, enigmatic earthy music – I like *Earth Heart* by Vicki Hansen or alternatively *Dynamic Meditation* by Osho. Close your eyes and take three red breaths into the base of your spine then begin to dance in whatever way your body instinctively expresses the music, peeling off layers of clothes as you fire up. Allow your mind to travel and journey to places beyond the room you're in, invoke Lilith as you dance, visualizing yourself as the Wild Woman.

Step Two

Ask to be shown a symbol. Sit down and begin forming your symbol out of the clay. (If you don't receive one consider making a serpent, coiled around as a spiral, signifying the feminine descent inwards or an Ouroboros – the serpent who eats its own tail, representing self-fulfilment or whatever feels right for you.) If bleeding, you may wish to mix a drop of your magical moon flow with the clay. Let this amulet dry and place it on a red altar or buy a piece of leather strapping to tie it with and wear it around your neck. You may wish to varnish it when dry.

Step Three

Take either the ochre, berry juice or your own menstrual blood and draw your symbol on your womb reclaiming your power as a woman. Ask Lilith to anchor her strengths within you.

Wild Woman Act of Beauty

Consider making yourself a red mandala. This is simply a circle, which you then intuitively fill with colours, images, shapes, patterns and textures that symbolize your inner Lilith. You may wish to consider making this small enough to place on your own representation of the Tree of Life – along with mandalas for each of the other chakras at the end of the Inner Goddess Makeover. This Tree of Life may take the form of a tapestry, cross stitch, painting, quilt or canvas wall hanging. In Tantra this practise is known as a Yantra and helps assimilate the lessons of the major chakras. Do take a pic of your Act of Beauty each month and share it on our Inner Goddess Makeover Facebook page, along with your experiences with each of your inner Goddesses throughout the journey. I look forward to seeing you there! Visit me and others around the globe awakening their Goddess mojo at https://www.facebook.com/pages/The-Inner-Goddess-Makeover-by-Tanishka

Consider also making a red altar for the next month by covering a small table with a red cloth and placing on it a red candle and any objects or images that feel appropriate to empower your inner Wild Woman.

APHRODITE: THE INNER BEAUTIFUL MUSE

The Beautiful Muse is the second soul sister we meet on our feminine journey. She is the glamour puss who often arrives as we banish Lilith's new pubescent changes from public view with an assortment of cosmetics, hair products and coquettish new clothes. She is often apparent long before puberty but firmly takes the reins around the age of fourteen. It is usually around this time that we develop a 'crush' on that special someone and test out our attractiveness on our dad or any other passing male. However girls who experience sexual abuse often suppress their playful Venusian expression for fear of unwanted sexual advances or they become extremely flirtatious, basing their identity on how others have seen them in the past.

How I Discovered My Beautiful Muse

When I was a kid, my inner Aphrodite (the archetypal Beautiful Muse), strode out of her closet early. Like many young girls I was enrolled in dance classes, which meant an unofficial apprenticeship in sequins, show tunes and sickly smiles. Precocious as this was, I thoroughly enjoyed being able to dress up and apply make-up. I even learnt to apply my own false eyelashes with the dexterity of a drag queen from the age of eleven.

But despite being born in 1970 with a very hip afro, my natural beauty wasn't celebrated in the regimented world of ballet which required a strict code of hair styling; a hair bun. So the ingenious solution amongst the 'Ballet Mothers' was to individually lacquer down each of my rebellious curls with 200 bobby pins and attach a round pot scourer (covered in a hairnet) to the back of my head, much to my Venusian horror.

This, along with always being cast as a 'boy', caused me to feel like an impostor who needed an extreme makeover to appear pretty like the other girls, rather than being appreciated for my unique features. And so as I entered my teenage years, I sought refuge in make-up – regularly rushing home from school, tying a t-shirt around my hair and painting my face with enough Max Factor to please Joan Collins in an effort to convince myself that I really was beautiful.

Unfortunately, because I felt my appearance too freakish without the aid of Dulux, so too did all the boys in my grade, including the boy whose timetable I learnt off by heart for three years – a secret infatuation I kept well hidden for fear of ridicule and rejection.

This behaviour continued throughout my twenties, with a number of serial infatuations and short-lived romances that ended in tears. Then, just like the mythical protagonist Psyche, who served an apprenticeship to the Greek Goddess of Love, Aphrodite, I swooned and fell in love with a beautiful and unattainable Eros, a gay boy who broke my heart like Greek crockery and caused me to rethink my approach to love as I drowned in a sea of self-pity and love songs. Following my fall I met and lived with a man, an industrial designer who like Aphrodite's husband, Hephaestus was crippled (emotionally and psychologically), and for two and a half years I tried to be the beautiful object he would choose to marry. But when he chose someone else I moved on, having two short-lived romances with unsuitable suitors. The first was like the God Mercury, quick-witted and charming but unable to fathom the depths of his own soul, let alone that of another. The second was a philandering Zeus who was still emotionally bonded to his ex-wife (and mother of his child) despite his sexual flings with nubile Aphrodites, which ended when they questioned his emotional commitment.

And so, thoroughly disillusioned with love, I gave up my search for Mr Right. At the time I was living with a dear old friend of mine, Annie, and finding ourselves in need of a third housemate. On Christmas Eve we agreed to a young man moving in (on a temporary understanding), as he was considerably younger and recovering from an intense affair with the underworld rave culture.

As it turned out, he demonstrated an intuitive wisdom well beyond his years and took to our holistic lifestyle with all the appreciation of a native shaman. In due course we invited him to stay and we went on to enjoy a warm and honest friendship. During this time I continued to burp, fart and speak gibberish about the house as I didn't consider him 'relationship material' so it came as quite a shock during an energy healing when I realized how deeply this unlikely candidate had touched my heart. Without any of my usual seduction I confessed my realization to him immediately afterwards and we agreed to tentatively begin a loving partnership. This was my first experience of being loved for who I was rather than the glamour I projected. We married and had a beautiful daughter. The marriage lasted three years until we realized we did not have enough in common to continue growing together so self-love instructed me to end the marriage. For eight years I focused on balancing my own inner feminine and masculine strengths and after writing my book, 'Creating Sacred Union Within' I met my life partner, a soulful, wise man, whose ability to honor and revere all aspects of the feminine won my heart.

BEAUTIFUL MUSE QUIZ

Answer the following quick quiz to find out what shape your inner Beautiful Muse is currently in. (Circle the answer that most describes you.)

You meet someone you feel attracted to at a friend's place, do you:

A. Feel self-conscious and freeze up, unable to communicate freely?

B. Start flirting with them and fantasizing about the future?

C. Engage with them and speak openly about yourself and your life?

You need to buy a dress for a formal occasion, do you:

A. Rebel against the idea and wear dress pants and a top?

B. Try on dresses, feeling secretly horrified by what you see in the fitting room mirror?

C. Enjoy the opportunity to try on dresses with your best friend?

It's time for the work Christmas party, do you:

A. Make an excuse and not turn up?

B. Get drunk and flirt with your boss?

C. Offer to host some party games or office awards?

Now add up your score. A = 1, B = 2, C = 3. *If you scored:*

1 – 3 Your inner Beautiful Muse is currently on ice. The following chapter should help to melt her inaccessibility.

4 – 6 Your inner Beautiful Muse needs a little TLC to avoid potentially sticky situations. You'll pick up a few helpful tips in the next chapter.

7 – 9 You have the grace and charm of Audrey Hepburn. Enjoy the following chapter!

Herstory: Beautiful Muse Goddesses

Throughout history, the Beautiful Muse was worshipped by the ocean, in honor of the emotional depth she beckons us to experience. She is the essence of romance, the inspiration behind great works of art, poetry and music. In the case of Freya, the Norse version of this archetype, she even inspired the naming of the day, Friday (which is short for Freya's Day) as it is ruled by the planet Venus – also the Roman name for the Goddess of Love. Throughout the Caribbean she was invoked as the mermaid Goddess, Yemaya and in Brazil as Oshun, who adorned herself with beautiful things. In the West, we have revered her as Aphrodite, the classical Greek Goddess of Love and Beauty. She was often portrayed naked and revered for her luminous beauty, which yielded a power so great, it was said she could enchant both Gods and mortals alike. What follows is her story.

The Myth of Aphrodite

Aphrodite was born while her parents were having a domestic argument. In fact, their disagreement became so heated that her Titan mother, Rhea told her son Cronus to sever his father Ouranos' genitals with a sharp sickle and cast them out to sea — a task that Cronus dutifully carried out. While floating on the water Ouranos' genitals produced a white foam, out of which rose Aphrodite, fully grown as a young beautiful woman.

She then rose from the waves on a seashell and stepped ashore at Paphos on Cyprus. (As depicted in the famous painting by Botticelli where Zephyrus, the wind and Flora, the spirit of spring blew her gently ashore amidst a shower of rose petals.)

Once arrived, she met the astonished townsfolk of the small seaside village who soon married her off to one of their local Gods, Hephaestus. Hephaestus was a humble blacksmith who, despite a crippling disability, was a talented craftsman whose creations displayed both ingenuity and beauty and won him favour amongst the other Gods and Goddesses on Mount Olympus. This, however, was not enough to satisfy the appetites of Aphrodite, who indulged in passionate affairs with both Dionysus, the God of Food and Wine and Ares, the God of War.

Tired of Aphrodite's indiscretions, Hephaestus set about constructing a net of durable, fine gold thread to cast over the lovers when next they met. He stealthily laid his trap and ensnared the couple, bringing them before the other Gods in search of retribution. Unfortunately for poor old Hephaestus, the other Gods fell about laughing at his tireless and obsessive effort to capture a woman's heart who was not his for the taking and as they wiped the tears from their eyes, Poseidon, the God of the Sea persuaded Hephaestus to release Aphrodite and Ares from the net.

Aphrodite never again married but had two children to Ares, a daughter and a son whom they named Harmonia and Eros. Later she had another child, with Hermes, the God of Wisdom. It was called Hermaphrodite.

The Moral

Aphrodite represents the nubile maiden, who having been born out of family conflict, is driven by a strong inner drive to heal her childhood issues through the coupling with her opposite. She does in time learn through her choices in love, preferring not to be kept by a man who sees her as yet another beautiful object to possess, nor a man who places war before love but who values wisdom above all else. And so she has a child who is a hermaphrodite, signifying her healed and whole emotional state.

Historical Appearance

Aphrodite loves being nude and carries no shame or self-consciousness about her body or state of undress. It is her innocence and self-acceptance that makes her utterly adorable to onlookers. As a result, she has long been a muse for sculptors who have replicated her sensual curves; the *Venus de Milo* and the *Aphrodite of Chidos* are amongst the most renowned works of art she inspired, and many modern day artists are reviving her popularity in various mediums and forms such as the film, *The Muse* with Sharon Stone playing a modern day Aphrodite (complete with spangly fish woman wardrobe). Aphrodite is often seen wearing scallop shells as the famous painting, *Venus Rising* by Botticelli portrayed or, alternatively, as a mermaid, dripping in pearls and frolicking with dolphins in the ocean. In less fantastical depictions she is captured as a beautiful maiden holding flowers or a dove. She sometimes pops up as an advertising icon as can be seen in my home town where she's used to sell fish and chips!

The Greeks commonly used the word *golden* to describe her, as celestial love energy radiated from her being (this is distinct from the charismatic force field of ego which can be projected by those attempting to prove their attractiveness to the world). This golden glow was attributed to her personal alchemy, her ability to transform the mundane into transcendent experiences by perceiving life through a creatively inspired lens.

As the Goddess of artistic inspiration, many poets and composers through the ages have waxed lyrical about her flashing eyes, beautiful breasts and soft skin. And to more high-brow suitors such as the Greek playwright, Homer, it was her wit that gave her an irresistible charm, as she laughed freely and engaged skilfully in social repartee.

Beautiful Muse Profile

Aphrodite is a force of nature, her energy urging us toward relationships. She is both the bringer of joy and the feared harbinger of passion. She is the Goddess of Love and the essence of feminine beauty and grace. She is also easily spotted for her social charm, being well versed in the art of conversation. She is considered unconventional and often has artistic or bohemian friends who mirror her flamboyance and aesthetic flair. In fact, so impressive is she in social situations that her social network can become almost unmanageable. (So many invitations, so little time!) She is also considered a 'man magnet', not necessarily for her bombshell looks but for her genuine interest in and love of men. Being feminine and watery (emotional) by nature she is an enigma who intrigues all she meets, but none more so than her polar opposite, a fiery man.

The Goddess Aphrodite showed that the human experience could be blissful. She demonstrated this by being completely unself-conscious in the celebration of her own beauty and the beauty of others. As a result of her ability to see the beauty in all, she enjoyed lovers of both genders, illustrated by her passionately kissing cowry shells, a pseudonym for female genitalia. It is interesting to note that Aphrodite was born a fully-grown woman, indicating that there is a certain maturity needed to be completely uninhibited and self-fulfilling. If, however, our inner Aphrodite is immature her immediate concern is to find 'the perfect lover', an aim that can override her common sense, resulting in other areas of her life being neglected as she pursues her latest fancy. Stopping at nothing in her quest for love, she will use all her enchanting powers in order to possess her chosen love object, with glamour being her tell-tale preferred weapon of choice.

The archetype of Aphrodite is by no means virginal; often dismissing contraception in the heat of passion, despite the personal risk. This impetuousness is also exacerbated by her deep psychological need to know and merge with another which can lead to co-dependent relationships as her personal boundaries tend to be as watery as her emotions.

This Beautiful Muse aspect within us also has a great capacity to be empathetic towards others who are in emotional pain. If this aspect is dominant, we tend to be sensitive and compassionate as a result of our own experiences. However, if our empathetic tendency goes unchecked, we can be easily drawn into other people's dramas rather than stay detached and able to be of true benefit, both to ourselves and to others.

Aphrodite, like the sirens whose enigmatic singing drew boats off course in the myth of Odysseus, can be seen today on pop music charts wailing out tortured lyrics while dressed to kill (or privately in lounge rooms belting out emotionally unbalanced lyrics like *I Can't Live, If Living Is Without You* demonstrated beautifully by Renee Zellweger in the film, *Bridget Jones' Diary*). A scenario which illustrates how our inner drama queen if indulged completely can reduce us to a state of complete hopelessness. (Pre-Goddess makeover I often warbled along with melancholic songbird, Sade, while imbibing red wine. Post-Goddess makeover I warble along with Aretha, singing uplifting Gospel tracks while washing the dishes!)

Aphrodite was also renowned for her poetic and persuasive speech and her ability to emotionally move us, which is why drama schools are a beacon for Aphrodites in search of a stage on which to shine and emote.

Venus, the ruling planet of Aphrodite and the astrological sign of Taurus, gifts us with the quality of appreciation. There is no one who will make you feel more appreciated than a woman in full

Aphrodite mode. Just observe a recipient basking in her unwavering gaze that is until she turns her attention elsewhere to pursue the next passing interest. This ability of hers to live thoroughly in each moment can be both a boon and a drawback, depending on how deliberate her intentions are. It may lead her to be impulsive financially, purchasing exquisite pampering items that appeal to her sensual nature or fashion accessories that thrill her vanity but max her credit card.

Above all, Aphrodite represents the transformative power of love. For it is when we are 'in love' that we see the world through Aphrodite's rose-coloured glasses and everyone and everything in it appears ideal. Unfortunately, if this state of love is not achieved through spiritual awareness and reconnection, this temporary ecstatic bliss can leave us hankering for more, whatever the cost, leading to an emotional rollercoaster created by the false belief that it is only this one person who can evoke such feelings within us. So the challenge that Aphrodite ultimately presents us with is to experience this state of transcendent love without needing 'the other' to act as a catalyst. Otherwise, we feel anxious and blue whenever they are not around. It is for this reason that many Aphrodite women become addicted to 'being in love' and fall in love often, breaking more than the heel on their designer shoes every time they fall.

If Aphrodite is a dominant archetype within you, you may find it hard to maintain a balance between work and play. With a large network of friends and acquaintances, you are easily distracted from completing the task at hand. It is important that your work stimulates your creativity so you will find the commitment needed to complete each project.

In our culture many Aphrodites struggle with the outward signs of ageing, particularly if they have depended on their looks rather than fully develop their inner character and talents, (a trend illustrated by the growing cosmetic surgery industry). Fortunately, there are some Aphrodites who age gracefully, retaining their youthful vitality through their creative and spiritual passions and as a result, attract friends of all ages and from all walks of life.

The following case study illustrates a woman who feared and therefore repressed Aphrodite's power:

Beth

Was a woman whose feelings ran very deep, despite having been raised by a mother who prized her intellect above all her other gifts and shamed any sign of emotional vulnerability. As Beth grew older she learned to hide all her intense romantic desires and vulnerabilities for fear of ridicule and, as a result, outwardly criticized other women who did express their Aphrodite aspect. For fear of judgment from her mother, Beth renounced all outward signs of self-beautification, viewing it as a pre-occupation that confirmed she needed to be validated by men. Unfortunately for Beth, this mind-set prevented her from loving herself unconditionally and suppressed her ability to experience moments of spontaneous joy. This in turn inhibited her socially, isolating her from making friends and meeting potential partners, which gave rise to further feelings of resentment and envy towards those who were socially affable and popular.

Beautiful Muse Strengths

The following is a description of how we behave when our Beautiful Muse archetype is appreciated and positively expressed:

- My natural charm wins people over and I consciously use my gift for persuasive speech, storytelling and inspired penmanship to spread love, joy and laughter.
- I possess an empathic understanding and am good at giving emotional counsel to help others.
- I only surround myself with people who are able to express love for me, even if that means distancing myself from those I most want love from.
- I exercise self-love in all of my decisions, rather than be manipulated by other people's emotional needs.
- I enjoy beautifying my environment, using beauty to heal and uplift.
- I value harmony above potential dramas, making me a peacemaker committed to resolving disputes by exercising compassion for all concerned.
- Having reflected on my own emotional lessons, I have a great understanding of myself and therefore, of the human psyche in general.
- My active imagination, sense of play and fantasy enhances mundane experiences, making them special and unforgettable.
- When speaking to people, I give them my full attention, appreciating their uniqueness, which in turn brings out the best in them.
- I let others see my vulnerability. I have compassion for myself and value my emotional responses as great teachings.
- My ability to dazzle others is ageless, as I know the elixir of life is love.
- I love and appreciate my unique body and features so I don't feel the need to constantly try and attain 'perfect' looks.

Beautiful Muse Shadow Traits

Below are some of the ways in which we can behave when our Beautiful Muse archetype is not understood:

- I am constantly looking for the perfect partner or trying to change my current partner into one.
- I choose partners who aren't emotionally available and so become tormented by uncertainty as I hopelessly try to convince myself that they really do love me.
- Obsessive infatuation can prevent me from being available to other more loving potential partners.
- I'm addicted to the honeymoon phase of 'being in love'.
- Emotional dramas can take my focus away from my practical responsibilities.

- I'll spend my pay packet on an outfit in an effort to enchant someone into liking me rather than see if they like my true self and choose me for my heart.
- I constantly compare my looks with others.
- I try to be the perfect girlfriend so I won't be rejected.
- I can be a drama queen, gossiping and bitching about other people's problems.
- I sometimes fantasize about being worshipped as a celebrity and being the centre of attention.
- I often throw my plans and friendships to the wind to be available to my partner.
- I can be inconsistent and stand people up if I become engrossed in what I'm doing.
- I enjoy surrounding myself with 'attendants' who live through my amorous adventures.
- I derive my self-worth from how lovable or attractive others find me.
- I tend to take all the responsibility for my relationships working and am reluctant to leave if my partner is not equally committed.
- I can be emotionally self-absorbed, using friends as sounding boards for each unfolding chapter of my continuing drama.

Beautiful Muse Lessons

To balance your inner Beautiful Muse's strengths and weaknesses, try the following suggestions:

- Appreciate your unique curves, features and silhouette as divinely beautiful in their own right.
- Clarify your intentions if someone mistakes your appreciation of them as genuine romantic interest.
- Admit your flirtatiousness to others so their emotions aren't hurt.
- Free yourself from destructive attachments by loving yourself until you outgrow the desire for someone who is incapable of loving you.
- Acknowledge we can only love others as much as we've learnt to love ourselves.
- Devote yourself to 'The One' (Spirit) not wait for 'the one' (Prince/ Princess Charming) to save you from your unhappiness.
- Take steps to heal your emotional wounds from childhood.
- Derive your 'natural glow' from the light of spirit not a tonne of cosmetic products.
- Practise compassion and acceptance for yourself and others, despite perceived imperfections.
- Own your inner victim and take steps to strengthen your ability to take care of your own needs so your femme fatale doesn't seek men to rescue you and create unwanted karma drama.
- See and consecrate yourself as a Goddess so you don't need a man validating you to feel divine.

- Value your soul as irresistibly lovable, regardless of your external appearance or relationship status.
- Be happy for others to be the centre of attention, as well as yourself.
- Be fully present to the gift in each moment.
- Learn to be receptive but not passive.

Goddess tip

Art therapy is a good tonic for Beautiful Muses recovering from the emotional bruises of 'love gone wrong', enabling them to channel their pain and frustration creatively, thus transmuting it. This is because Aphrodite is also the Goddess of Artistic Inspiration and so provides an outlet for those unexpressed desires that have been romantically evoked, enabling them to find a natural resolution. The 'process not the artistic end result' is what's important.

Beautiful Muse Relationship Patterns

Personal

Our inner Aphrodite's main concern is with her love life. She is a shameless romantic but needs to 'come back down to earth' when shopping for a mate. Otherwise she'll fall for someone's charm and overlook their inability to emotionally connect with and commit to her, thereby creating endless dramas. At her worst she will try to seek out evidence that he really does love her even if his actions indicate he wants nothing further to do with her. Unfortunately, such a fixated obsession often prevents her from being available to a loving relationship with anyone else. (Friends of Aphrodite-dominant women please note, it is virtually impossible to get through to your lovesick friend – so be blunt if you're tired of hearing her delusional ravings.)

In fact, Aphrodite's love radar often seems to hone in on guys who are creative with no aspirations of marriage, such as emotionally withdrawn musicians or artists, whose allure may be their mysterious, complex, and unresolved psychological problems. Other variations include men who don't respect them or treat them badly.

Sadly, many Beautiful Muses spend months or even years relegating the rest of their lives to be 'on call' should their man get the urge to 'catch up for a drink'. Also common amongst Aphrodite women is a penchant for sensitive, well-dressed men who are the 'ultimate challenge' – homosexual men. Aphrodites beware! Although you may have so much in common, for instance fashion, gossip and interior design – walk away if you can't accept that they may totally adore you but are unable to take things further. (This Aphrodite had one gay man literally run several kilometres on foot to escape her romantic proposal... my wish is for all women to be spared such humiliation and heartbreak.) Fortunately, when most Beautiful Muses hit thirty (the traditional age when the Mother phase kicks in), they 'get serious' in their desperation to evaluate and learn from past mistakes in their relationships.

Ultimately, everyone's inner Aphrodite would do well to realize how she can need others to constantly validate her lovability, which can then drive her subconsciously to dress and behave seductively towards everyone she meets. This unconscious drive for everyone to love her can create needless dramas in her life. For example, should she be unconsciously flirting with a married man and incur the subsequent wrath of his wife, she will be hurt that his wife doesn't like her and will be oblivious to her own flirtatious behaviour.

The more your Beautiful Muse within can love herself in her practical choices, the more quickly you'll see her personal life improve (rather than constantly trying to manipulate her life to match the fantasy she has been dreaming about and obsessively trying to replicate romantic comedies). Ultimately her challenge is to relinquish the notion of the 'perfect partner', that being the shopping list of traits she projects onto all possible partners in her bid to create the idyllic life. Just as the sculptor Pygmalion became besotted with his statue of Galatea and based this creation as the yardstick against which all other mortal women were compared, culturally we have adopted the same diseased way of thinking.

Like the ingénue in George Bernard Shaw's play, 'Pygmalion' we try to conceal our true identity in a bid to appear as 'perfect partnership material' to others with our carefully constructed feminine persona.

Famous Beautiful Muses

Aphrodite icons abound, as she is one of the few archetypes who has been celebrated throughout our patriarchal culture as an acceptable role model for women. However, a conscious understanding of the archetype has been sadly lacking, with taboos placed on women extolling Aphrodite's free love approach to life. For example the term nymph referring to a woodland nature sprite has since been twisted into a dark psychological disorder known as nymphomania, when a woman is addicted to sex.

Cleopatra, Marilyn Monroe, Madonna, Meg Ryan, Jennifer Aniston, Katy Perry, Nicole Kidman and Kylie Minogue all qualify as Aphrodites. All have been revered for their beauty but their vulnerability has also been aired as they have suffered publicly in affairs of the heart.

Audrey Hepburn is another example of a public Aphrodite, particularly in her older years, as she exuded the grace and transpersonal love of an emotionally wise Aphrodite in her dedication to serve the world's children as an ambassador for UNICEF, rather than spend her days in a Los Angeles doctor's surgery to compete with the maidens on the red carpet at the Golden Globes. Similarly, the shadow side of Aphrodite's insecure vanity and fear of ageing was depicted in the film 'Death Becomes Her' starring Goldie Hawn and Meryl Streep.

Beautiful Muse Makeover Kit

Below is a list of practical tips to positively anchor your inner Beautiful Muse.

Suggested Styles

We enter the realm of Aphrodite when we adorn ourselves with garments that highlight our best assets and make us feel feminine and romantic.

Here are a few ideas:

- *Watery hues such as blue, green or turquoise. Soft rose or shell pink fabrics.*
- *Cowry shells such as those woven into chokers or belts.*
- *Pearls, opals and jewels that have an oceanic quality.*
- *Shimmering gold body dust and copper-toned hair or make-up. Girly, strappy sandals.*
- *Anything glamorous, such as evening wear with matching accessories.*
- *Sarongs. (Clothes that expose our collar bone or cleavage, revealing an open heart.)*
- *Soft lines, such as necklines that fall off the shoulder, skirts with elegant long side splits or plunging back lines.*
- *Fresh flowers in your hair.*
- *Any type of 'pretty' ornamentation such as hats, ribbons, beading, lace or feathers, especially accessories that enhance mystique such as fascinators on hats and hand-held fans.*
- *Fabrics that are ultra-feminine such as chiffon or jersey and will drape around the curves of the feminine form. (Nothing tailored that cuts your energy and appearance into segments.)*

Remember, Aphrodite is renowned for her artistic flair so design your own outfits and either sew them yourself or have them made up by a seamstress or tailor.

Alternatively, don't be afraid to experiment with more bohemian, avant-garde combinations of pieces found in bargain bins and op shops. You may wish to create a social event just to give your Aphrodite an outing such as a medieval masquerade ball, fantastical moonlit fairy picnic for Midsummer's Eve or a Goddess Debutante

Ball to unveil your inner Aphrodite. (Chances are, your Aphrodite may not have had such an opportunity to impress since your school prom – which for many of us self-confessed Aphrodites was more about the dress than the event.)

Beautiful Muse Colours

If you don't have any garments in these colours, chances are your Aphrodite's been too weighed down with commitments and responsibilities to let loose and enjoy the more frivolous side of life. Take the next available opportunity to treat yourself to a piece in one of the following colours and notice how it makes you feel.

Pink

Pink represents the heart chakra. The combined energy of both the red of desire and the white of spirit. The centre that Aphrodite must strive to find within herself if she is to break her patterns of love addiction.

Turquoise

Turquoise denotes her affinity with the ocean and is alluring in its intensity. It is also the colour of the higher heart chakra that sits over the thymus gland.

Beautiful Muse Associated Chakra

The Sacral Chakra is the second energy centre that is both our lower emotional centre and the point from which we connect with the astral plane, the plane of low psychic phenomena, which we engage with when we fantasize (connect telepathically) with the energy of another person. Such flights of fantasy only fuel feelings of addiction and dependence when the reality isn't there to support such emotional attachment. Located in the abdomen, this energy centre connects us to others through feelings of dependence and the arousal of desire. It also represents obsession with self-gratification. Its colour is orange, which is also linked to joy through creative expression, one of the best therapies Aphrodite can undertake to transmute her emotional disillusionment into a sense of self-fulfilment.

To assist with clearing blockages in this chakra, consider having a Reiki Healing or the Emotional Freedom Technique to ease emotional pain. Archetypal Chart Readings, Psychotherapy or Soul Centered Psychology are also helpful to assist subsequent understanding of your personal relationship patterns. Art Therapy, Beauty Therapy and any sort of Water Therapy are also extremely beneficial when healing and empowering your inner Aphrodite.

Beautiful Muse Essential Oil

Rose Oil

Rose oil opens the heart to the vibration of love and is also an antidepressant, favoured by Cleopatra as her signature scent. She would have her ship's sails drenched in it so her people would smell her coming up the Nile! (Could be a tad expensive to emulate.)

Beautiful Muse Flower Essences

The following are vibrational essences which distil the healing properties of various plants. When taken orally, they promote emotional balance and wellbeing.

Honeysuckle

Honeysuckle is helpful in releasing past events and emotions.

Chestnut Bulb

This essence assists in identifying and integrating past lessons so they don't need to be repeated.

Beautiful Muse Minerals, Crystals and Stones

Pearls

Pearls were sacred to Aphrodite and the 'pearly gates' used in Christian symbolism originally referred to Aphrodite's yoni (the Tantric term for vulva) leading to Heaven. In Tantric practice, 'polishing the pearl' was the term used for female self-pleasuring. The 'pearls of wisdom' also referred to knowing the wisdom of the Goddess.

Scallops and Cowry Shells

Both were said to be shaped like Aphrodite's yoni. Among the Ancient Greeks, the word *kteis* meant a vulva, a cowry shell, a scallop or a comb. Gypsy women have long valued cowries as an amulet for feminine energy.

Rutilated Quartz

Venus Hair is the name given to clear quartz crystals that contain slivers of titanium dioxide, giving them the appearance of fine golden threads. These stones were widely regarded as a love charm for their association with Aphrodite.

Rose Quartz

Pink in colour, this is a great crystal for healing the heart. Handy to wear a piece near your heart or sleep with a piece beside your bed.

Copper

Said to resemble Aphrodite's hair colour, copper offers healing benefits when worn. It aids the joints, nervous system and flow of blood. It also aligns the physical and emotional bodies.

Gold

Gold balances and develops the heart chakra, aligning it with the sacral and crown chakras. As Aphrodite was commonly referred to as 'golden', both golden goblets (signifying her emotional vessel, the heart) and golden jewelry (her penchant for adornment) are symbolic of her energy.

Beautiful Muse Food

Fish and Shellfish

Both have long been accredited as an aphrodisiac (which is itself a derivative of the word Aphrodite) because of their association with the love Goddess and their aroma and taste being synonymous with the alchemy of sexual fluids. (Bouillabaisse soup is a personal favourite. Fry up plenty of onion and garlic in oil, add whatever combination of seafood and fresh fish you desire along with some passata, fresh oregano, thyme, sage and rosemary. When it's ready to serve add some fresh basil, cream, pepper and salt. To thicken, remove the fish, add some bread and puree then return the fish & serve. Quick to make and delicious.)

Confectionary

Mimicking the sweetness felt emotionally when we are in a state of love, sweets such as chocolate release 'feel good' endorphins into our bloodstream. Unfortunately many 'L plate' Aphrodites eat sweet foods to surrogate what they aren't getting emotionally and spiritually. However, if chocolate is abused as a comfort food, the long-term effects can contribute to diabetes.

Golden Apples

Sweet fruits in general but especially golden apples, which are the totem fruit of the Goddess, as they possess a golden quality such as that attributed to her appearance.

Beautiful Muse Flowers

Rose

Roses have long been sacred to the Goddess. Romans knew it as the flower of Venus. Roses were worn as a badge by her priestesses who served her temple by performing acts of love. Roses were also symbolic of female genitalia, the ancient Gnostics believing that the first rose sprouted from the first menarcheal blood of Psyche, the Virgin Soul – which is where the rosary or rose wreath originated as a Christian honoring of the Virgin Mary.

Narcissus

Narcissus are white-petalled flowers with gold centers. Their name is a derivative of the Greek word *narke* meaning 'a drugged stupor' which is an apt description for many Aphrodites who become obsessed with winning the affections of a suitor who is as good for them as heroin. Narcissus was also an alternative name for the Greek God Adonis with whom Aphrodite became infatuated. It has also been suggested that as the flower has six petals, it's symbolic of the sacred hexagram that is used to signify the sexual union of Goddess and God.

Pansy

The pansy was said to grow on the mounts of Venus. Venus being the Roman appropriation of the earlier Greek Goddess, Aphrodite.

Waterlily

As a lotus symbol of an open heart on the water of emotional stillness, the water lily is a beautiful adornment for any water feature adorning a shrine to Aphrodite.

Beautiful Muse Hangouts

Ocean

The ancients used to believe that the ocean itself was the watery body of the female serpent, Oceanus, undulating her tidal rhythms in tune with the moon. As the home of Aphrodite, the ocean offers restorative benefits for our emotional well-being as a reminder of the need to go with the flow and not fight the current, lest we drown in it.

Waterfalls, Fountains, Streams and Ponds

All are locations where bodies of water converge and where the energy of Aphrodite will flourish. These areas are usually surrounded with lush and damp vegetation such as ferns and moss. As with the ocean, the negative irons in the atmosphere absorb and transmute our own negative emotional energy.

Beauty Spas and Hair Salons

Self-pampering is key to Aphrodite's enjoyment of life, so if you've left it too long or never made it a priority to treat yourself to some TLC in the form of beauty therapy, make a date to let the world float away whilst you relax in good hands.

Clothes and Accessories Outlets

It is no surprise that most Beautiful Muses are titillated by ornamental trinkets and handbags that are utterly useless but are 'must have' items because of their exquisite beadwork. That said, know that most specialty retail outlets trade on our inner Aphrodite's impulsiveness (and vanity) so do your best to only purchase that which you 'fall in love with' to ensure you get good use out of it. (Don't go shopping when you're pre-menstrual and don't spend beyond your means.)

Florists

Fresh blooms are appealing for Aphrodites the world over. So if it's been a while since someone crossed your path with flowers, treat yourself to a bunch to put a smile on your face.

Beautiful Muse Astrological Sign

Taurus

Ruled by Venus, the lesson of Taurus is to overcome desire. Taureans or those with Taurus prominent in their natal charts tend to be led by their five senses. (I have Taurus rising, so my persona is ruled by Venus and hence I have a hard time leaving a buffet table.) Similarly in the *Tarot*, the lesson the maiden must learn in '*The Lovers*' card is to transcend the transient pleasures afforded by her five senses: taste, touch, sight, smell and sound to pursue a more subtle but ultimately fulfilling pleasure – the reconnection with her spiritual nature.

Beautiful Muse Symbols

Below is a list of all the symbols pertaining to Aphrodite, so should you have regular sightings of any of them, make a mental note to reconnect with your inner Aphrodite.

Flower of Aphrodite

Comprising of six points joined by six arcs at 60 degrees, it was considered the flower of Aphrodite as six was the number of feminine sexuality – which is why later religious authorities decreed it as the evil number of the beast.

Cups

As a symbol of the receptacle of heart energy that is poetically said to 'runneth over', cups are synonymous with Aphrodite. In the *Tarot*, the suit of cups represents the Fool's journey through his (or her) emotional lessons.

Beautiful Muse Totem Animals

Should you encounter or have a special affinity with any of the winged, feathered or finned friends listed below, take it as a sign that Aphrodite's blessing is close at hand.

Doves

Doves have long represented Aphrodite and were carved on her temples, jewelry and coins. The Holy Seven Sisters or Pleiades star system also referred to as the Seven Doves were said to have been born out of the mouth of Aphrodite, Queen of the Sea, who was then depicted as a dolphin. Christian imagery assimilated this symbol, changing it to one holy dove with seven rays of light emanating from it.

Swan

As a water bird possessing grace through the water and wings to fly heavenward, the swan was sacred to Aphrodite. White feathers are also considered a calling card of Aphrodite's. Swans are also loyal in love so their symbolism is not merely for their beauty, but for their pairing.

Dolphins

Dolphins are symbolic of bliss, playfulness and sexual ecstasy and have long been associated with the Mistress of the Sea. In Syria, Aphrodite was worshipped as *Derceto*, a mermaid whose name meant both womb and dolphin.

Fish

Before early Christians claimed the fish as a symbol, based on the notion that the Greek word for fish, *ichthys* was an acronym for Jesus Christ, Ichthys was the name of the son of Atargatis – an earlier version of the Sea Goddess, Aphrodite.

Beautiful Muse Relative Parts of the Body

Sinuses, Lungs and Bronchial Tubes

These represent the element of emotion as well as the salty fluids of our bodies, such as tears. This is why many Beautiful Muses are prone to suffer chronic sinus, bronchitis or asthma – all of which are representative of unexpressed tears.

The Digestive Tract

If our stomach is upset, chances are so are our emotions. Bowel complaints such as irritable bowel syndrome are also synonymous with Aphrodite issues. For example: diarrhoea can represent a fear of rejection and constipation, a tendency to hold on emotionally to what isn't serving you.

Skin

Aphrodite was said to have luminous skin, and consequently there's been a large number of body glitter products released since the re-emergence of Goddess consciousness.

Mound of Venus

This is the curve of the female pubis bone. Similarly in palmistry, the mound of Venus relates to the raised fleshy area that extends down from your thumb.

BEAUTIFUL MUSE INNER MAKEOVER ACTIVITES

Now it's time to have a look at the shape of your inner Aphrodite. The following processes are designed to illuminate some of her universal lessons. I recommend doing all of the processes even if you are in a committed relationship, as there are always deeper levels of self-love and acceptance to be learnt and enjoyed. Try not to just skim through them, but rather take the time to do each segment. This is where alchemy will occur – through self-love in action.

Narcissistic Love

In the *Tarot*, the first lesson in love is encountered by the Page, the youth who needs to grow emotionally. It is the lesson of Narcissistic love.

Here is a brief retelling of the story of Narcissus.

Narcissus was the son of Leriope, a nymph and the river, Cephissus. When he was born, Leriope consulted a prophet to ask if he would have a long life. The prophet replied that he would on the condition that he did not come to know himself. And so Narcissus grew to become a very good-looking youth and was admired by both boys and girls, although he never returned their affection.

One young nymph, Echo, became hopelessly enchanted with him and monitored his every move. Unfortunately for Echo, her girlfriends asked her to keep Zeus's wife, Hera, entertained with endless chatter while they provided Zeus with sexual favours. When Hera discovered Echo's deceit, she cursed her with only being able to utter the ends of other people's sentences.

Unable to express her true feelings for Narcissus, the lovesick Echo faded away until she was nothing but her namesake... an echo.

Meanwhile, angered by the vanity of Narcissus' arrogance, another local youth prayed to Nemesis, the Goddess of Retribution, to assert a just punishment for his actions. And in the coming days, his wish was answered when Narcissus, hunting on the slopes of Mount Helicon came upon a clear pool where he paused momentarily to drink. No sooner had he stooped to quench his thirst that he caught sight of his own reflection and became instantly entranced. Desperate to connect with his ideal mate, Narcissus tried all of his charms in an attempt to get the boy to respond. Unable to accept that his newfound love would not embrace him, he faded away.

Later when his friends came looking for him, the only remaining trace they could find by the pool was his namesake, the flower called Narcissus.

Ask yourself the following questions:

Am I looking for someone to prove to me I really am lovable?

Do I have a pattern of falling for people who are in some way unattainable or 'a challenge' and then proceed to try and make them fall in love with me?

Do I have a pattern of falling for people who are similar to me? For example, in the same profession?

Do I have a tendency to become infatuated with someone, even if I know that person is unable to really embrace me?

If you answered, YES to any of these questions, chances are you could use some time becoming enamoured with your own reflection instead of hoping someone else will.

Try these suggestions:

Stare into a mirror and admire your features. Look deep into the eyes of your own soul and notice any negative thoughts that arise and replace with thoughts of acceptance and appreciation.

Develop your wholeness so you don't rely on others to complete you. Make a list of all the traits you fell for in your current or ex-partner. Now reflect upon those same traits that are within you and how you can embrace and nurture them in yourself.

Establishing Conscious Union

Your next step is to learn to resist 'happily ever after' fantasies until you've really spent time getting to know a good deal about a potential partner. Consider their inner character traits and ask yourself the following questions:

How emotionally mature are they?

Are they interested and able to commit to a monogamous relationship with you?

Are they responsible?

Are they able to speak their feelings openly and honestly to you and respond to yours?

Have they resolved their past emotional hurts? Do they flirt with other people?

Are they aware of and sensitive to your needs?

Do you feel comfortable being with them when you're at your messiest?

Am I more loving or unloving towards myself?

Write down in your journal ten things that you did for yourself this week that were loving and ten things that were unloving. Compare which actions dominated and resolve to do more of the loving actions.

If I loved myself 100%

Write down what you would do if you loved yourself 100%. Start incorporating some of these actions practically into your life.

A Love Letter

Find a time and a space when you won't be disturbed and put on some tranquil music. Take one of your favourite pens and a nice piece of parchment and write a love letter to yourself. Allow your soul to express all the love you feel for yourself, the beauty your soul sees in you and even what your inner self would like to do physically to express that love. It might be poetic, complimentary, appreciative, supportive, sensual or erotic... it's up to you.

What I love about my inner self/outer self

Get together with a girlfriend and take it in turns to stand up and say what you love about your outer self (body/appearance) for two minutes.

Now repeat this process, taking it in turns to say what it is you love about your inner self (character traits/soul gifts).

Alternatively, you can do this speaking into a mirror. It may feel silly but there is more power in speaking and witnessing your truth than just thinking about it.

Mirror, mirror on the wall

Write down a list of things that you are dissatisfied with in your current or ex-partner. Don't hold back, be explicit and leave nothing out. Now read the list back to yourself exchanging their name for your name, i.e. 'I hate that Jeremy couldn't commit to me' becomes 'I hate that I couldn't commit to me'. Now reflect on how your partner mirrors the way you treat yourself.

What's in a Name?

Below is a list of some of the titles by which Aphrodite was known throughout the ancient world:

Amaterasu, Atargis, Tirgata, Derceto, Salacia, Pelagia, Delphine, Mari, Maria, Marina, Marian, Mariamne, Myrrhine, Myrrha, Mari-Yamm. Mari-El, Oshun, Titania, Queen of the Fairies (who was renowned for her vanity), Yemaya, Venus, Freya and Stella Maris (meaning 'The Star of the Sea').

What nicknames has your Beautiful Muse been given over the years?

Peruse the following list and circle any that carry an emotional charge for you.

Consider when it was that you first heard that term and who used it.

Reflect on whether their discrimination is one that you wish to continue to carry within yourself.

Vamp, vixen, drama queen, show-off, legend in her own lunchtime, glamour puss, femme fatale, siren, lipstick lesbian, valley girl, dumb blonde, ditzy broad, airhead, flaky chick, fag hag, dolly bird, fake, exhibitionist, starlet, ham, over the top, too much, model, blondie, beautiful person and bimbo.

Art Therapy: Let your Siren Shine

In your journal or on a large sheet of paper draw yourself as Aphrodite. Allow your imagination to soar, depict yourself in your most divine gown or set of scallop shells. To get your creative juices flowing, put on some truly transcendent music. (I recommend '*Yanni Live at the Acropolis*')

Know that Aphrodite's energy is within you to access, whenever you feel frumpy or notice negative thoughts undermining your self-love and acceptance. I recommend hanging your Aphrodite picture up in your room or alternatively, placing it on your altar while you are consciously cultivating the positive traits of Aphrodite so your ego is constantly reminded of the treasures and beauty within your heart.

Embracing your Beautiful Muse: Further Suggestions

- Admire the beauty in every moment. Look out for those 'special' moments in time, people and places.
- Swap a pedicure, head massage or facial with a friend regularly. This also helps take pressure off your partner to fulfil all your sensual needs.
- Rent films like 'Himalaya' or 'The Green Mile' that celebrate the transcendence of spirit rather than romantic comedies, which reinforce the fairy-tale ending. Also try to play ecstatic celestial music rather than romantic pop ballads such as *I'm nothing without you* and other disastrous lyrics.
- Throw out or give away clothes that don't do your body justice and affirm that you are open to receive clothes that do.
- Pamper yourself regularly with inexpensive natural beauty products such as lemon for your face which cleanses, tones and is great for pimples. Try an egg white face mask or a lavender foot oil.
- Splurge on some natural beauty products made with essential oils.
- Take yourself to a meditation or Reiki circle once a week to reconnect with the soul love offered to you by your celestial guides and ancestors.
- When something upsets you, try as a first response putting on some music, closing your eyes and gently allow yourself to feel and express any emotions that surface. Ask for angelic support to gather around you and grant you grace and acceptance (before reaching for biscuits, cigarettes and other emotional suppressants).
- Remember, there is room for every Aphrodite to shine. Avoid comparisons and focus on your own unique appeal. Don't allow trends of the day to dictate your personal Aphrodite style — fashion is fickle. In Elizabethan times a woman was revered for having beautiful hands and if she had lovely hair, it was thought that this was a karmic payback for having cut it all off in a previous life as a nun!

The power of love

The most famous statue ever built to commemorate Aphrodite was made on the island of Kos by an artist called Praxiteles. When at last she was unveiled, the local council members were so shocked by her nudity that they rejected her and she was instead purchased by the people of Knidos, whose temple to Aphrodite was recently rediscovered by the aptly named Professor Love. All that remains of the statue is its base and an inscription telling of a man who was so enamoured of the artwork that he attempted to copulate with the statue!

Get Wise

Below is a list of books you may find helpful in understanding and addressing some of your Aphrodite issues.

Beautiful Muse Non-Fiction

Return to Love by Marianne Williamson

The Mythic Tarot Book by Juliet Sharman-Burke and Liz Greene

Goddesses in Every Woman by Jean Shinoda Bolen

The Goddess Within by Jennifer Barker Woolger and Roger J Woolger

Beautiful Muse Fiction

Feminist Fairy Tales by Barbara G. Walker

Topics for Discussion

Below are a few conversation starters you may like to raise with your female friends over a cup of freshly brewed Brazilian on a sunny Sunday morning:

- What are my inner thoughts when I see a woman who is not my idea of 'beautiful'?
- What are my inner thoughts when I see a woman who is my idea of drop-dead gorgeous?
- What negative and positive comments from others have I held onto about my appearance? (And why?)

- What is the most loving thing I have done for someone else?
- What changes can I make in my life to actively appreciate both myself and others on a daily or weekly basis?

Questions for Personal Reflection

- How do I invalidate my natural beauty?
- What could I do to honor the Aphrodite in my own life?
- Am I judgmental of other Aphrodites and if so, how am I suppressing this energy within myself?
- Does my life reflect that I really do love myself?
- How do I emotionally invest in dramas, be they my own or other peoples?
- Do I ever mistake the intensity of emotional pain for true love?
- Do I consider both romance and beauty frivolous pursuits rather than sacred expressions of my inner Aphrodite?

Secret Woman's Business: Best Times to Celebrate Aphrodite

Valentine's Day

Although a modern celebration of romantic love, it was originally an ancient Roman festival to celebrate the Goddess Hera (wife of Zeus).

April Fool's Day

Which is when the Romans celebrated her to commemorate Spring. (Northern Hemisphere.)

The Equinoxes

When there is a perfect balance of yin and yang energy, as both the length of day and night are equal in the yearly cycle. This happens twice a year, in autumn: around March 21st in the Southern Hemisphere (September 21st in the North) and spring: September 23rd in the Southern Hemisphere (March 23rd in the North).

Dusk and Dawn

As they are romantic, magical times dappled in rose gold light.

Spring

In general, particularly on a full moon.

Beltane

Traditionally celebrated in the Northern hemisphere as the 31st of April. (31st of October in the Southern hemisphere.) I personally like to celebrate it when the full moon is in Taurus (ruled by Venus, accentuating our sensuality) and the sun is in Scorpio (ruled by Pluto, accentuating sexual magic), which occurs in early Spring.

Friday, the 13th

Each Friday is ruled by Venus, i.e. Freya's Day (Freya was the Norse version of Aphrodite or Venus). Friday the 13th was particularly sacred to Aphrodite as the number thirteen honored the old calendar based on the thirteen lunar months. The Romans contrived our calendar of twelve months based on the transits of the sun. The ancients used to celebrate Friday, the 13th by taking the day off work and making love. This did not sit well with the work ethic of our industrialized modern culture and was hence branded a day of evil by puritanical cults.

Beautiful Muse Rite of Passage Ceremony

You Will Need:

Mirror with a wide wooden frame

PVA craft glue

Golden glitter (optional)

Additional seashells (optional)

Six rose quartz crystals

Six tea light candles

Rose essential oil and moisturizer

Relaxation music

Step One

Take yourself to the beach. Sit and meditate on the vastness of the ocean that makes your dramas seem so small and then close your eyes and take three breaths into your belly (sacral chakra) invoking the Goddess of Love, Aphrodite. Next, swim in the ocean or walk along the shallows. Swimming in saltwater always leaves us feeling reborn, as salt and water are two of the elemental processes used in the ancient practice of alchemy. The combination cleanses your aura (energy field) and the salt binds damaged hair treated by chemicals!

Step Two

Collect some shells, driftwood, coloured glass worn smooth by sand and wind and any other treasures you find.

Step Three

Arrange and glue the seashells and assorted treasures on to your mirror frame.

Step Four

Make a sign that says 'The Face of the Goddess' and place it on the frame of your mirror. Put on the relaxation music. Place the six tea lights in a circle, invoking the angels as you light them. Then add the six rose quartz crystals and invoke the healing properties of the stones, visualizing pink light connecting the circle. Now remove your clothes and invoke the energy of Aphrodite, asking her to anchor her strengths within you. Look into the mirror, deep into your eyes and say the following: *I Love You, You Are Beautiful.*

Step Five

Scent the moisturizing lotion with rose oil and lovingly apply tender care to each part of your body. (If pregnant use only Rose Bulgar or Rose Maroc.)

Beautiful Muse Act of Beauty

Consider making an orange mandala for the sacral chakra using orange art supplies and fabrics. You may also wish to create an Aphrodite altar in your home for the next month and place on it any objects or pictures that feel relevant.

ATHENA: THE INNER GOLDEN HEROINE

The Golden Heroine is the third soul sister we meet along the path. She is often activated as we reach the end of our secondary schooling and consider our career options. She usually rears her head as an overachiever, studying hard and taking on positions of authority, such as being a school prefect or president of a committee. She may have a tug-of-war with your Aphrodite energy as you set out in the world and encounter the lessons of love and war simultaneously. She presides over your ability to face challenges in the world of business and academia.

How I Discovered My Golden Heroine

The middle name my parents gave me, *Louise*, means 'Warrior Maid' which indicates why my Athena archetype has always jostled to be amongst the top three archetypes within my psyche at any given time. This was evident early at the age of five when I threw off my childish dreams of becoming an air hostess and stated that my precocious new ambition was to be a famous star of the stage and screen.

A few years passed with no talent scouts spotting me at the local supermarket, followed by the realization that they only cast 'city kids' in the *Smarties* commercials. Frustrated with my parent's apathy, I began staging regular 'Mommie Dearest' episodes, cajoling and bullying my parents to relocate from the country so I could audition for the TV show 'Young Talent Time' and get my lagging career underway.

When this failed I turned my attention toward excelling academically. Being born in the Chinese horoscope Year of the Dog, I needed regular pats on the head and rewards for being 'good'. Of course what I was really seeking was constant love and approval from my parents, who seemed most pleased with me when I behaved well and achieved. As a parent I appreciate how easily this message is given.

At school I became a house captain, prefect, member of many committees and organizer of bun fights small and large. I then left home to study performing arts at University and graduated, moving to Melbourne so I could at long last audition for my big break on TV. Again, years passed waiting tables with only token acting jobs in training films and as a featured extra in commercials. I decided to take matters into my own hands and carve out a profile as a stand-up comedienne. Not one of my brighter ideas.

For one year I terrorized myself with crippling stage fright as my unconscious Athena kept sending me back out in front of tough pub audiences to try and win their approval. This all came hurtling to an end one Sunday when one of the promoters took me aside and told me that no one wanted to hear what I had to say. In tears I left the building, unable to return for six years.

Meanwhile, still desperate to create opportunities to showcase my talent I also tried to create and produce a television pilot called, 'Good Morning Unemployed'. This venture took me on a journey that lasted eleven years and taught me many valuable entrepreneurial and life lessons, despite feeling grief stricken that my creative child would never live to see the light of ratings season.

This career failure left me feeling totally disillusioned with life in general and severely doubting my own abilities. It was then that I discovered the Goddess and began reading Tarot and doing fairy parties on weekends to pay the bills. I found this healing for my deep-seated fear that nothing I did was ever good enough.

I then began a short-lived business hosting Goddess theme parties for hen's nights and birthdays. Although I enjoyed creating and hosting these events, I undervalued my efforts and subsequently undercharged, which left me feeling drained and defeated and I closed up shop, convinced the market wouldn't bear a price increase for such a largely untried and novel experience. It was then my inner Shirley Temple resurfaced and conspired with my shadow Athena, who together plotted an ambitious plan, and sent me to do their bidding, despite resistance from most of my other archetypes. And so it was I returned to stand-up, quivering in my knee-high boots as I feared the mob would throw more than insults and put a permanent dent in my jester hat.

I justified this decision with the belief I couldn't fail since I was armed with golden insights about my realization that I was an omnipresent deity – a modern day Goddess. So imagine my surprise when I shared my holy grail only to be met with perplexed male faces that stared back at me, with beers suspended in mid-air!

It was then I decided to start a business, this time with the support of a girlfriend, running inner Goddess makeover workshops for women. This venture titled, 'Woven Women' saw me repeat many of my old patterns, namely undervaluing my services, which again left me burnt out and poor by the end of the first year. Fortunately, I also completed a small business course during this time, which helped to refine and ground my ideas. Then I fell pregnant and my best-laid plans were laid to rest.

When I wrote this book, (which took seven years research and three years writing), I began to realize all seeds require their own germination time and consistent, humble effort is required to produce any worthwhile tangible result. As I write the revised edition seven years later I have finished my first national tour and am about to embark on my first international tour. Thanks to social media and technology I have been able to expand my work so it's accessible to more people around the world. I am now able to support myself financially doing my soul's calling. Something my dear Dad did not think was possible. Ultimately working toward that goal has taught me some of my greatest personal lessons. This was summed up beautifully by a bumper sticker I read recently, 'Every successful person has failed many times!'

GOLDEN HEROINE QUIZ

Answer the following quick quiz to find out what shape your inner Beautiful Muse is currently in. (Circle the answer that most describes you.)

Which of the following best describes your work situation:

A I am unemployed or working a job that I don't enjoy.

B I am in a respectable line of work that I'm good at and enjoy the challenge.

C I am either studying or making my income doing what makes my heart sing!

You receive your weekly pay cheque, do you:

A Blow it having the best weekend ever?

B Spend it on bills, groceries and still not have enough to cover rent or mortgage?

C Invest 10% of your earnings via direct debit in a savings plan?

In an average week, which of the following best describes you:

A I work all week then try to forget about work on the weekend.

B I find it hard to have a day that is totally work-free.

C I love my work but have a rich home and social life.

Now add up your score. A = 1, B = 2, C = 3. *If you scored:*

1 – 3 Your inner Golden Heroine is in need of some courage to pursue her dreams. The next chapter will help you to identify that you're a diamond in the rough.

4 – 6 You tend to bolster your self-worth by attracting dragons to slay but are exhausted from fighting constant battles. You'll pick up a few helpful tips in the next chapter.

7 – 9 Look out Xena Warrior Princess! You have learnt the true value of your inner gifts and share them with the world. Enjoy reading the following chapter.

Herstory: Golden Heroine Goddesses

There have been many heroic Goddesses celebrated around the globe who used their wits to uphold justice and serve the common good. Among the most notable are Maeve the Irish Warrioress; Minerva the Roman Goddess of Intelligence and Handicrafts; Sophia the Greek Matriarch Goddess of Wisdom; and Maat the Egyptian Goddess of Law, Order, Truth and Justice. All were renowned for their integrity, strategic planning and cultural contributions to city life, but none more so than our host and tour guide, ancient Grecian Goddess, Athena.

The Myth of Athena

Athena's Father, Zeus, had been warned by the God Uranus that if he had a child to Sophia, the Goddess of Wisdom, the child's intellect would surpass his own. Alarmed by this eventuality, Zeus swallowed the pregnant Sophia in the hope he would avoid being shown up intellectually by his unborn daughter.

The day arrived when Athena was ready to be born and unable to find a suitable exit point, she began pounding away on the inside of her father's head, determined to live and fulfil her destiny. As a result Zeus experienced an excruciating headache until finally, she cracked his head open and stepped out a grown woman, wearing golden armour and holding a spear.

It was said that so momentous an occasion was this that the whole of Mount Olympus shook and a large shout of exaltation arose from deep within Mother Earth.

In Ancient Greece Athena was known as Pallas Athena. (Pallas was her childhood friend whom she inadvertently killed when the pair tested their skill at fencing.) The name Pallas means storm or battle, which is indicative of her ultimate battle with her own ego. Killing her childhood friend is symbolic that her own ego was pierced by the sword of truth, a necessary preparation for her destined role of stateswoman, enabling her to selflessly serve and lead her people.

So successful was her reign the Greek city of Athens was named in her honor. According to legend, the Ancient Greeks built an affluent city and were in need of a patron God/Goddess to protect their inhabitants and wealth. Athena and the God Poseidon both responded proposing they should fight for the honor. The townsfolk suggested a competition would be a more peaceful way of deciding who should bear the title and asked both Olympiads to bring forth a gift, on which they would be judged.

Poseidon produced a horse, which created great excitement from all the judges who warned Athena she would be hard pressed to better Poseidon's offering. Athena then revealed her gift of an olive tree, explaining that its fruit would provide oil for cooking, lighting, perfume and food. She went on to explain the plant's leaves could produce medicinal tonics, shade from the sun and the bark could produce wood for building materials and paper – all goods for export to add to the city's wealth. Most importantly she made the distinction that the horse would prove in hindsight to be used more as an implement of war, whereas the olive branch would be recognized as a symbol for peace. (This is where we derive our modern euphemism for an act of peace-making, 'to extend the olive branch'.)

Further facts

Despite her image as the stately virgin warrior Queen, Athena was a civilizing Goddess, presiding over battle strategy in wartime, and domestic arts in peacetime. She was a warrior by nature, although she only fought to defend truth or uphold justice, deploying strategy to resolve disputes and avoid war.

Athena was a patron to all craftspeople, indicating her respect for artistic creations that were purposeful in their use, such as pottery. Festivals to celebrate Athena were particularly popular amongst classical artisans. She was also accredited with inventing the Greek alphabet, flute, plough, chariot, horse bridle and various ships, including the Argo for Jason of the Argonauts.

Athena was particularly fond of heroes and heroines who undertook difficult quests, whom she assisted through her patronage, protecting and mentoring them to achieve their goals.

The Moral

As there are three short myths, so there are three morals. Firstly, to individuate from her father's influence and find her own sense of self, Athena needs to question the thoughts that keep her confined to her father's view of the world, which is not necessarily that of her own. The myth is reminiscent of the archetypal father who fears being surpassed by his sons, so Athena being the daughter most gifted with masculine traits, also piques his fear of competition. I have also seen women with dominant Athena energy 'swallowed' by their fathers as a result of sexual abuse. The father's lack of feminine energy being something he selfishly devours in his offspring rather than consciously develop within himself.

Secondly, Athena's downfall is her killer instinct that can have her falling on her own sword should the need to win become more important than her respect for those who are playing the game. Finally, her ultimate challenge is to use her wits to outsmart her opponent, whilst still upholding her ideals.

Historical Appearance

Athena is the only Olympian Goddess portrayed wearing armour (although the visor of her helmet is often pushed back to reveal her striking features), sporting a shield over her arm, a spear in her hand and sometimes a bowl or spindle in the other. If there was a doll created in her image it would be an action figure!

Her breastplate was made of goatskin and she bore the head of Medusa on her aegis (belt) over a long white tunic. Intertwined snakes were shown on her shield or on the hem of her robe, which again demonstrated her affinity with feminine wisdom as her main mode of defense. She is often depicted with an owl, the bird most associated with wisdom, as well as with prominent eyes, two of her notable traits. The Greek playwright, Homer referred to her as 'shining grey eyes'.

Golden Heroine Profile

Athena loves a challenge. She enjoys the endorphin hit from achieving against the odds but also needs to explore and own her vulnerabilities or she risks sabotaging her efforts and blaming others for her misfortune. It is imperative for her to remember that a good leader owns their mistakes, whereas a tyrant scapegoats their wrongdoings onto others.

In the *Tarot*, Athena is represented by the suit of swords, the mental element of air. She uses a sword of truth, representing 'the double edged mind' to analyse and cut away what is no longer needed for her own mental clarity. Alternatively, if she is out of balance her mercurial sword of truth can be used against herself and others in the form of self-criticism and judgment. This is why it is healthy for her to filter new ideas against her intuitive feelings, rather than hide behind an attitude of cynicism, closing her mind to new possibilities. Cynicism is often a defense mechanism we develop when we feel the need to hide our true feelings in an environment that feels emotionally unsafe.

Women with strong Athena personas often closely emulate or vehemently rebel against their fathers. For example, the daughter who becomes a lawyer just like her dad or one who drops out of conventional society and becomes an environmental activist to unconsciously spite him.

Often we look to our father to gauge our sense of self-worth. For example, you may doubt yourself and your capabilities if your dad wasn't able to see and nurture your individual strengths. As a result, you may get caught up in trying to prove your father wrong or right in an attempt to prove your own self-worth. This is of course a complete waste of energy, for we are the only ones who can heal and restore our self-worth by accepting and appreciating ourselves exactly as we are, thereby freeing us from behaviour that's geared towards winning approval. Many inner Athenas would also do well to remember that often the underlying reason their father seems uninterested in their achievements is because it highlights his own feelings of inadequacy or he just 'doesn't get' what it is that they do.

Another repercussion of low self-esteem is that we consequently experience issues in relation to money, as well as conflicting inner beliefs about the accumulation of material assets. This is because when our self-worth is low, we tend to crave money, recognition and outward signs of 'successes as proof of our self-worth. However, if on the other hand we value ourselves for who we are, rather than what we achieve we are then free to pursue what we really enjoy doing regardless of whether it's acceptable to others.

For many women with a strong Athena archetype it is a challenge to summon the courage to pursue their chosen field of endeavour and not undermine their efforts by undercharging for their skills and level of expertise. This can also translate into a work ethic that keeps one 'working like a Trojan' for little in return as we come to identify with struggle as part of our self-pride and have an inability to perceive our true worth.

Alternatively, many unconscious Athenas are prone toward control and may work in a job that gives them financial security but little enjoyment. This appeases their inner patriarch (the stern inner father) who rewards them for being 'sensible' and not indulging in a more unconventional path, despite the fact that this would lead to a greater sense of fulfilment.

Many of us who grew up with an absent father, be it physically or emotionally often struggle with expressing our Athena energy. For instance, if your dad failed to mentor you in life skills such as changing tyres, mowing lawns, changing light bulbs and offering financial advice, chances are your inner masculine is a little immature and insecure.

This used to be the acceptable societal norm as the traditional form of partnership encouraged women to find a father surrogate to fulfil their masculine roles rather than become healed and whole in their own right. But as we move beyond this form of co-dependency and into holistic relationships, we need to address these inner gender imbalances or forever remain a victim damsel in distress at the first sign of trouble. Just as women have been demanding that men get in touch with expressing their emotions and doing their share of child rearing and housework, we also need to allow our 'balls to drop' and take responsibility for our physical and intellectual needs.

That said, I believe one must first work to strengthen, understand and heal the gender they have physically incarnated into before addressing the needs of their opposite gender polarity, as summed up beautifully by Robert A. Johnson in the following excellent use of her masculine characteristics; but if masculine characteristics dominate her basic personality, she will at best be only an imitation male.

For our inner Athena to become truly wise we must also encounter the lessons of success and failure, which are crucial if we are going to make any valuable contribution to public life. In fact, it is often the catalyst of perceived career failure that reconnects many Athenas with the feminine, as a sense of failure often brings our vulnerability to the surface, provoking subsequent reflection and life changes.

Goddess tip

All Athenas would do well to remember the lesson of King Midas; namely, all that glitters is not gold. If we chase that which seems the largest victory we can often miss out on all the small gems along the way such as friendships, creativity, quiet reflection and communion with nature. As it is the sum of all of our experiences that makes us truly rich.

Athena also ensures success in her career ventures by spending adequate time and resources planning, researching and implementing practical strategies to achieve the targeted goal. This must include time and resource management if her plans are to prove realistic. These practical skills are particularly important for women whose inner Aphrodites are dominant to avoid feeling repeatedly disillusioned with their efforts to construct their ideas.

Athena loves to feel like a winner. The ancients often described her as 'promachos' meaning champion. Unfortunately, she can want to win so badly that she'll deceive her friends to possess the perceived coveted prize. Shadow examples of this attitude caricatured in action include Nicole Kidman in the film, 'To die for' and Reese Witherspoon in the film 'Election' where both characters play out dark sides of their psyches in an effort to outsmart all competitors. In her shadow aspect, sisterhood is a completely foreign concept to her, as she sees herself in direct competition with everyone in her bid to become 'Top Dog'– again illustrating a masculine hierarchical pecking order.

Growing up she may also show an aptitude for computers, economics, chemistry, physics and other male-dominated subjects, often thriving on the opportunity to compete with the boys. For this reason she will often opt for a co-ed secondary school, technical school or defense academy rather than choose an all-girl community in which to learn.

Many young Athenas seek positions of external power from a young age and power plays often arise in the marital home over the allocation and use of money. Many Athenas have grown up watching their traditional 'stay at home mothers' feel powerless as their fathers controlled the purse strings, giving rise to an inner commitment to be a financial success and to aim for autonomy. This can also manifest as a judgmental attitude towards their mothers and women who assume a more traditional role, as 'subservient breeders', rather than fully appreciating the intangible benefits of remaining within the home to rear children.

The fear of becoming like their mothers can lead many of our inner Athenas to try and 'do it all', resulting in chronic exhaustion as we juggle partnerships, children and long working hours in an attempt to maintain our income and professional status. All we can do to preserve our own equilibrium is question our values and priorities and make balanced life choices.

Goddess tip

Are you being driven relentlessly by an inner slave driver? Chances are if you have 'To Do Lists' longer than your shopping docket you are attempting to wear your underwear on the outside and be Super-Athena! Try affirming at the end of each day that you are satisfied with what you have accomplished instead of mentally whipping yourself for all the things you were unable to do.

Above all, our inner Golden Heroine is a tactician, using alliances and networks to achieve her ultimate aim. She knows that intellect and skill are not enough to achieve her ambitions and knows that mentors, allies and sponsors are crucial for her career development. She is direct in her negotiations, unless her shadow need to prove herself is still subconsciously driving her to be deceptive both to herself and others.

Athena was a virgin Goddess, in line with the original meaning of the word 'virgin' which meant, 'a woman unto herself'. She was also referred to as, 'chaste' in that her intellect could not be swayed by sentimental emotions. This gave her the ability to interact with men without any accompanying sexual or emotional tension distracting her from the task at hand. Although handy to employ at work, this same trait can prove an obstacle at home as she can be so cool and logical that passion and intimacy are not high on her list of priorities.

Below is a case study illustrating how the archetype of Athena, if not understood, can wreak havoc and threaten all that you hold dear:

Bronwyn

Bronwyn had been a genetic scientist and was amongst the top in her field. She worked long hours and hectic travel schedules meant she was often away from her family. This resulted in a communication and intimacy breakdown between her and her husband, leaving her as a divorced single mother of two. The strain of trying to care for three people and a demanding career took its toll on her health when her body rebelled, insisting that she slow down and nurture herself. It was at the age of 43 that she was diagnosed with breast cancer. Having left motherhood till later in life, her children were still very young. Fortunately, she ceased all her work commitments to focus on healing and reprioritizing her time — in case she didn't have much time. Subsequently, as a result of the collapse of her career, she discovered new talents and hobbies and now is a creative writer, a career she can pursue from the comfort of her own home.

Golden Heroine Strengths

The following is a description of how we behave when our Golden Heroine archetype is appreciated and expressed:

- I am prepared to endure short-term pain or loss to achieve my career goals. I keep my head in a crisis and apply lateral thinking to create a win-win solution. I am an excellent negotiator who can see both sides of an issue.
- I am confident enough to ask for what I need and want.
- I am happy for others to succeed, knowing that every dog has its day. I do not define myself by my job description.
- I can assert my difference of opinion to my father without getting angry.
- I appreciate the process of learning through failed attempts, so I don't expect myself (or others) to be perfect.
- I believe in my own unique gifts enough to invest time and money into nurturing their growth.
- I don't compare my talents with others, knowing that everyone's distinct gifts are needed for the whole plan to work.
- I can financially provide for myself and those dependent on me.
- I enjoy honing my skills so I can turn what I love doing into a marketable commodity. I stand up publicly for what I believe in.
- I dedicate my career efforts to making a difference, rather than just achieving external status, power and wealth.
- I value my intuitive wisdom as much as my intellectual knowledge.
- I make sure I grasp a concept with its inherent strengths and weaknesses before embarking on its construction.
- I am physically fit and active.
- I am flexible enough to change course if my current one is proving counterproductive.

Golden Heroine Shadow Traits

The following is a description of how we behave when our Golden Heroine archetype is disempowered:

- I bring work home routinely.
- I never feel as if I'm good enough.
- I don't stop to enjoy a job well done and celebrate my own achievements. I lack the courage to pursue what it is I'd really like to do.
- I blame my failures on others rather than humbly examine my own wrong-doing. I am not consistent in applying a patient step-by-step process to achieve my goals.
- I study or work in a profession I think will eventually meet with my father's approval rather than follow my own instincts.
- I may not be supportive of other women in my attempt to be accepted as 'one of the boys'.
- I do not see and value the intangible strengths of the feminine, both in myself and in others.
- I may be so competitive that true trust and friendship with women is impossible. I am so fixated on the goal at hand I can only 'talk shop' in social situations.
- I can be very cutting and lack empathy for other's vulnerability. I sometimes value results above ethics.
- I judge myself and others on income, qualifications and achievements rather than on their strength of character.
- I am unmoved by spiritual or artistic experiences.
- I can drain the life force out of others with my obsessive need for rational proof and 'the facts'.
- I can squash other people's dreams with my fear-based, conservative thinking. I may dismiss my mother as weak and incompetent at 'things that matter'.
- I may be subconsciously trying to fulfil the role of the first born prodigal son. I may project my need for achievement on to my children.

Golden Heroine Lessons

To balance your inner Golden Heroine's strengths and weaknesses, consider the following points:

- Realize your self-worth is not dependent on what you do, how much you earn, your IQ or your achievements but rather on your inner being, which is priceless.
- Accept you need a balance of productivity and reflection to 'succeed' both personally and professionally.
- Mentor those younger or less skilled rather than fear they will outshine you.
- Access your own intuition so you can be your own authority figure and not try to please those you perceive as externally powerful.

- Identify what inner gifts fulfil you the most and commit to them.
- Appreciate the inherent divine blessings present when things don't work out the way your ego planned.
- Fully appreciate both your father's gifts and flaws and own them in yourself.
- Validate your emotions by expressing them rather than just rationalizing to avoid feeling.
- Use money wisely to cover your needs before your wants.
- Acknowledge the infinite wellspring of Spirit behind your ideas.
- Exercise the chastity of pure reflection – not influenced by personal desire.
- Don't resent others who have acquired more power materially, but see it as a mirror of what's possible if you apply yourself.
- Open yourself to physical touch and close interaction with others, e.g. being hugged.
- Discover your playful inner child so you don't take everything so seriously.
- Appreciate that everyone on your path has something to share and teach you to help counteract any feelings of intellectual superiority.
- Approach new situations and concepts with an open mind.

Golden Heroine Relationship Patterns

Personal

Athena is often married to the job, so likely unions often stem from her professional alliances. She has a tendency to date those who are upwardly mobile as she respects ambition as a character trait. She is also likely to seek out men who are older 'father figures' both for their perceived power and subconsciously to win the approval of a father surrogate. She is attracted to power and therefore does not feel enticed by men who openly reveal their sensitivity. If she doesn't date her boss, she may still seek out a suitable mate within the corporate ranks, using subtle negotiations to become his 'right hand woman'. Once his loyalty is assured, she will staunchly defend him and guard his privacy as aligning with his power gives her a sense of self-importance.

She can be very choosy and matter of fact when sifting through potential partners, preferring to analyse their credentials with her head instead of her heart. These were the women of old who were praised in Victorian culture for making a 'good match' by marrying for profit and status in preference to love.

When it comes to expressing herself sexually, Athena dominant women tend to be totally practical, viewing sex as a recreational activity rather than as a means to connect emotionally and sensually. They tend to want to be 'good' in bed, as their perfectionist streak extends into every avenue of their life. In fact, they prefer brain sex above all else, spending time with their closest ally and confidante reading the weekend papers in bed instead of 'dirtying' the sheets with bodily fluids.

This lack of unbridled passion can result in our inner Athena aspect being blind to our partner's need for sexual and romantic stimuli which may lead you to respond to news of an adulterous affair with an equal lack of passion, logically convincing yourself that steadfast loyalty and joint leadership could never be threatened by a transient fling's affections. There are also many lesbian Athenas who enjoy the companionship of another high achieving, professional woman without having to access their inner Aphrodites. (An archetype which can feel downright uncomfortable if they grew up emulating the masculine, sensing that the feminine enjoyed little, if no external power in our patriarchal society.)

Although one could be forgiven for thinking that Athena is not the marrying type, many Athenas like the stability of a legal partnership and run their household like a tight ship, providing heirs and managing the family budget like a CEO. As parents they really come into their own once their children hit puberty, giving them the autonomy and responsibility they are so keen to acquire. If divorce becomes a necessary course of action, Athena women are very matter of fact in dividing assets, with little of the spiteful behaviour that can be displayed by shadow Aphrodites who are frightened they won't have what it takes to support themselves without their partner.

In marriage an Athena-dominant woman may be seen behind the throne, such as a political wife, rather than pursue her own career. She may guide her partner in his decision-making, as in the myth where Athena advised the warrior Achilles to hold back rather than strike his leader Agamemnon in anger as a tactical manoeuvre. Or she may excel as his 'hostess', preparing beef stroganoff at a moment's notice should he bring home his associates.

Famous Golden Heroines

As children, young girls have had Athena figures such as Wonder Woman and Xena, Warrior Princess to aspire to, although the media does not abound with public recognition of positive real-life Athena role models.

Anita Roddick who created The Body Shop chain of cruelty-free cosmetics springs to mind as someone who embodies the positive traits of Athena, making a difference through her business practice of trading with those third-world communities who have been previously exploited by commerce and industry. Although many more shadow Athenas abound in public life, such as countless female politicians who are completely disconnected from their feminine wisdom, prioritizing short-term economic gain over long-term environmental and social policies.

Golden Heroine Makeover Kit

Below is a list of practical tips to strengthen the self-worth of your inner Golden Heroine.

Suggested Styles

Modern day Golden Heroines tend to prefer classic, 'no nonsense' clothes that don't date with passing fashion trends. So if you need to organize your life, get your career back on track, assert yourself more often and keep a cool head when those around you are losing it, try wearing a few of the following suggestions from Athena's wardrobe to help you anchor the positive traits of this archetype.

- *Keep hair short, pulled back or pinned up in a roll or bun.*
- *Wear tailored shirts, skirts and suits, commonly referred to as 'power dressing' clothes items to ensure you will be taken seriously in a man's world.*
- *Wear navy, white, black and beige – colours that don't scream for attention.*
- *Use simple modern pieces of jewelry.*
- *Buy clothes which are easy to care for and maintain.*
- *Wear pin stripes, braces, lapels, ties and dress pants, emulating the English fashions befitting true gentlemen.*
- *Wear comfortable shoes!*
- *Wear sensible and comfortable undergarments in neutral shades.*
- *Wear simple lines and block colours rather than prints.*
- *Wear glasses with elegant but unobtrusive frames.*
- *Wear men's pyjamas to sleep in.*
- *Wear athletic gear (preferably used to exercise in, not just a trip to the video store in the car!)*
- *Wear the obligatory black dress and pearls for evening wear.*
- *Wear pants rather than skirts.*

Goddess tip

Traditionally Athena was depicted as wearing a helmet. This was her proverbial 'thinking cap'. Symbolically this represents Athena's ability to intellectualize attacks made upon her, allowing her to assess the best course of action and not take insults personally. Coincidentally, many Athenas prefer to wear boyish caps rather than more feminine hats. You may wish to embroider one with the title, 'Thinking Cap' to assist you whenever you need to assess a situation by exercising detachment. Alternatively, you may wish to block out external distractions by pulling the visor down on your invisible helmet.

Golden Heroine Colours

Whenever you step into an environment where the following colour scheme dominates, the Golden Heroine is the most respected archetype. Similarly, if needing to study or complete your annual accounting, try dressing the part in these colours for mental clarity and decisiveness.

Black and White

These tones represent the polarities of light and dark which need to be balanced internally. Athena was considered beyond corruption in her decision-making because of her conscious integration of her darker aspect, Medusa. Without this she would not be truly wise and therefore unable to rule from a point of personal balance. These colours are shown on the Tarot card of Justice as the pillars of wisdom between which she stands.

Beige

Often Athena dominant women will stick to safe, sensible, neutral tones that won't draw needless attention to their appearance so it doesn't distract from what they are trying to communicate.

Golden Heroine Associated Chakra

Solar Plexus

This energy centre is located above the stomach and governs the pancreas. It rules our personal power, will and sense of autonomy. When it is functioning effectively we feel confident, optimistic and able to achieve our goals... life feels sweet. When this power centre is blocked or too open we swing between arrogance and inferiority and tend towards bitterness. Its emanating colour is yellow. When our inner Athena is operating in her shadow aspect we are prone to experience nausea and stress pains in this area. As well as considering any sort of energy healing to repair and balance this chakra, do consider having an Archetypal Chart Reading to identify and clarify what negative beliefs are unconsciously sabotaging you since Athena governs the intellect.

Golden Heroine Essential Oils

Sandalwood

This is ideal for dissipating fear and is good to use before a high-pressure meeting or presentation.

Peppermint, Pine and Eucalyptus

All of these oils clear the head, making it easier to think. These are great to burn at work or if studying for an exam. They are also invigorating after a workout or to help you breathe easier.

Golden Heroine Flower Essences

The following are vibrational essences which distil the healing properties of various plants. When taken orally they promote emotional balance and wellbeing.

Beech

Beech eases perfectionism and criticism of self and others.

Rock water

This is good for releasing the need to control everything.

Impatiens

This essence helps one in adopting a more relaxed and diplomatic approach to situations.

Larch

Larch builds inner confidence.

Golden Heroine Minerals, Crystals and Stones

Citrine

Citrine is considered the stone of abundance.

Clear Quartz

Comes in various forms and is great for mental clarity.

Silver

Wearing silver will help to anchor the positive aspects of the feminine polarity. It strengthens the pituitary gland that rules the third eye (balancing Athena with wisdom and insight) and assists clear speech and thought processes.

Amber

This is actually fossilized resin from prehistoric pine trees and is soothing and harmonizing.

Tiger Eye

Tiger Eye enhances connection with personal power and will, aids clear perception and assists the solar plexus chakra.

Yellow Jade

Known for helping to achieve clarity, modesty, courage, justice and wisdom. It also helps dispel negativity.

Golden Heroine Food

Olives

As a fruit of the branch of peace, olives are ideal to include in any feast that honors Athena. You may also want to include other traditional Greek foods such as dolmades (stuffed vine leaves), fetta cheese, spanakopita (spinach and fetta pie) or tzatziki (yoghurt and cucumber dip).

Nutritional Foods

Often Athena dominant women will eat foods that are perhaps a little on the bland side but offer practical fuel for the body. Foods such as salads and stir fries rather than foods rich in fat, starch or sugar.

Golden Heroine Flowers

Sunflower

Though not considered a traditional symbol of Athena, I have chosen to include them as they radiate the positive qualities of the masculine – optimism, hope, boldness and courage and their colour is that of Athena's associated chakra.

White Flowers

Elegant but simple flowers such as Trumpet Lilies which incorporate Athena's colours, white and gold would be ideal for an altar or congratulatory bouquet.

Golden Heroine Hangouts

Law Courts

As an arena for the defense of justice, you will find the legal system teeming with Athenas. (She is still portrayed in judicial emblems above the bench balancing the scales of justice.)

The City

Athena is at home in the 'civilized world' as her values intellect over instinct and nature. In any major city you will see the streets teeming with Athena women as they climb the rungs of the corporate ladder.

Schools, Universities and Technical Institutions

Many Golden Heroines are perpetual students or teachers who have an on-going thirst for academic knowledge or self-improvement courses.

Research Laboratories and Hospitals

Science is a field that attracts many Athena women who one day aspire to be someone who helps save the world whilst wearing the symbolic gown of the patriarchal authority figure, the white coat.

Publishing Houses, Libraries and Bookstores

As she is renowned for her thirst for knowledge, books are synonymous with Athena. Many Athenas are literary buffs who are not content to read books but want to be a part of the great literary tradition and either write, publish or sell great works.

Military Barracks

These are your die-hard Athenas who really want to be heroic in a masculine sense and work within a highly structured environment.

Parliament

Another gladiatorial ring for aspiring Athenas who want to provoke change and do so amongst the established power brokers.

Sporting Clubs, Facilities and Gymnasiums

Whether spectating or competing, Athenas love to pump iron, push themselves hard and test their limits.

Print and Broadcasting Media Networks

Although this industry also attracts Aphrodites hell-bent on soaking up the limelight, Athenas who want to know what's going on (and preferably before anyone else) do well as journalists, columnists or critics in all aspects of the media.

Craft Exhibitions, Supply Shops and Classes

As a patron to craftspeople, all crafts and their tools are sacred to Athena.

Golden Heroine Astrological Sign

Although all the air signs pertain to the faculty of the mind, I have attributed Libra as her ruling sign, as the Libran symbol, the scales of balance and justice are also sacred to Athena. That said, if you are an air sign, chances are Athena will be a dominant archetype. Do take note, when the moon is in Libra it is an excellent time to settle outstanding disputes and let go of old, limiting beliefs.

Libra

Despite being ruled by the planet, Venus, Libra is not an impulsive sign, weighing up all possibilities and seeing a situation from every angle prior to making a final decision. Libra is the sign of the peacemaker and those with Libra heavily expected in their charts will avoid confrontation at all costs. Balance and partnerships are also key areas of growth, including business and psychological partnerships of yin and yang energies.

Golden Heroine Symbols

The Scales of Justice

Which indicate the need for balance in all decisions.

The Sword of Truth

An emblem which is symbolic of the ability to cut through illusion.

The Olive Branch

This was sacred to Athena as a symbol of peace. The Romans also used olive branches to make crowns for their returned soldiers after victory in battle.

The Shield of Protection

Used as an emblem under which a warrior fought. Originally these sigils were magical totemic themes, later becoming family heraldry banners and today we see them as commercial logos.

The Yin/Yang Symbol

A well-known Chinese symbol for the balanced union of opposites. Usually associated with masculine and feminine or sun and moon polarities, they were originally both symbolic of the light and shadow aspects of the feminine.

Golden Heroine Totem Animals

Take note, if you see the recurring symbolism of any of the following animals or if any should visit you in your dream state. It's a sign that Athena is looking over your shoulder, offering insight to clear your mind.

The Owl

Athena was usually portrayed with an owl sitting on her right shoulder, in honor of her mother, Sophia, the Goddess of Wisdom. The Athenian people valued her wisdom as her strongest asset, featuring the owl on the obverse side of their currency and Athena's head on the other.

The Spider

This creature is synonymous with Athena's patronage over the art of weaving. Although her urge to compete with other women is highlighted in the story of her encounter with the spider woman, Arachne, who is reported to have piqued the envy of Athena when she produced weavings that displayed talents surpassing that of Athena's.

The Dragon or Snake

These figures symbolize Athena's dark Goddess aspect Medusa with her protruding tongue and snake-like hair which was said to represent the menstrual secrets of the feminine mysteries. The eldest of the Gorgons and the destroyer aspect of the divine feminine, Medusa's head appeared on Athena's aegis (belt) as her source of true power.

The Dove

Doves appeared on many of Athena's temples as a symbol of peace.

Golden Heroine Relative Parts of the Body

Below are the areas of the body that tend to be affected when Athena is out of balance.

The Head

Athena tends to be ruled by her intellect, so she can be prone to tension headaches if she doesn't get enough relaxation to reflect and unwind. Our inner Athenas can fall into the same trap as many workaholic men and come to rely on alcohol or other recreational substances to relax instead of natural remedies such as chamomile tea, warm baths, yoga and massage. And should you come down with a head cold, take it as a sign that your head is too full of problems to solve!

The Hands

Women with strong Athena archetypes are often typically gifted at handicrafts even if they have no prior experience and they benefit enormously by using their hands which stills their overly active minds. Whether its renovating furniture, making tapestries, knitting or attending pottery classes, using the hands will alleviate mental pressures, and decrease sleepless nights spent listening to incessant head chatter.

GOLDEN HEROINE INNER MAKEOVER ACTIVITES

Below are a number of activities to contemplate and complete that will get your inner Golden Heroine into shape by shedding light upon any dark and limiting inner beliefs that may hinder your efforts to outwardly achieve.

Individuation from Zeus

For Athena to stand on her own two feet, neither rebelling against nor seeking approval from her dad, she must first understand his good and bad qualities.

You may wish to consider any actions or decisions you would like to take in your life but are concerned about what your father might think or feel. In other words, how does your mind belong to your father and not to you?

1. Make a list in your journal of ten of your dad's shadow traits, weaknesses and fears.
2. Examine the list and consider whether you acknowledge these shadow traits in yourself. Do you value, scapegoat or deny each or any of these traits? Write down how these traits affect you in your life.

Write down ten of your Dad's strengths, gifts or skills.

Now consider how you share the same gifts, where you may have denied the origins of those gifts and how they enrich your life.

Note. Even if your father was not physically present throughout your childhood, complete the list with the traits of those men who have influenced you. Those who have impacted upon you the most will have helped to shape the blueprint of your inner male.

The Middle Path

The Athenians tried to uphold the principle known as 'The Middle Path' – which simply meant to follow the middle path of moderation in all matters. The following is an activity to ascertain what imbalances need to be addressed for you to experience 'The Middle Path' in your life.

Draw on a page in your journal a large circle and divide it into halves, then quarters, then eighths. Creating what looks like spokes on a bicycle. This is your Wheel of Life.

Now label your sections:

- *Career*
- *Health and Exercise*
- *Rest and Relaxation*
- *Relationships*
- *Self-Growth*
- *Intellectual Stimulation*
- *Spiritual Union and Creative Expression*
- *Attending Chores and Material Concerns*

Write down approximately how many hours you spend on each aspect in an average week.

Note one thing in each section that you can do to redress any imbalance.

What's in a Name?

As with all the Goddesses, Athena's traits were worshipped in feminine deities by other names. The Roman version of Athena was known as Minerva. In Egypt she was worshipped as Maat who would weigh a soul's heart against that of a feather and in the Celtic tradition she was known as Maeve, the warrioress who could outrun horses.

Other titles she was known as include:

Athene-Gorgo, Pallas-Athene, Blodeuwedd, Anath, Thought Woman, Thinking Woman, Arachne, Kokyangwuti, Tsitsicinako, Aunt Nancy, Anansi, Spider Woman, Metis, Sophia, Medusa and *Amazonian Woman.*

Other names that carry Athena's energy include *Louise* meaning *Warrior Maid, Bridget* meaning resolute strength, *Marcella* meaning warlike, *Laura* meaning a crown of laurel leaves (indicating victory) and *Briana* meaning strong.

Reflect on what nicknames your inner Athena has heard or received over the years, knowing that this has shaped how you also see her. Below are a few examples. Should any of these spark a reaction within you, note it and the situation when you first heard it used and consider the mind-set of those who spoke it.

Workhorse, four-eyes, betty-bunhead, bookworm, dragon lady, vinegar tits, Sherman tank, yuppie, up yourself bitch, hard-headed woman, workaholic, woman in army boots, Thatcher, know-it-all, iron lady, iron-willed, lady of steel, muscle monkey, controlling, matriarch, matronly and *ball-breaker.*

Art Therapy: Express Your Inner Heroine

In your journal draw yourself as a Golden Heroine. Your inner Athena may choose to express herself like a caped crusader such as the TV character, Wonder Woman or as a Grecian stateswoman draped in white robes or even as an Olympic athlete. Try not to pre-plan how she will manifest on the page. Instead, try closing your eyes and putting on some heroic music such as the soundtrack from the film, *Chariots of Fire* and let your hand lead the way.

Embracing your Golden Heroine: Further Suggestions

- Be assertive. Dare to ask for what you want, from both friends and those in public life. If you don't ask it isn't likely to happen.
- Feed your mind to avoid your double-edge sword turning in on itself with negative thinking.
- Go to the self-improvement section of your library or bookstore and get yourself a motivational book or tape to inspire you to reach your potential instead of diminishing your mind with tell-a-vision. I recommend entrepreneurial books by women such as Anita Roddick of The Body Shop. Alternatively, go and see someone you admire speak.
- Write down all of the things your inner male feels inept at from changing light bulbs, mowing lawns, knowing about financial investment or even getting your motorcycle license. Now consider which of those things you would like to learn and tee up with a friend who can teach you or enrol in some lessons. If your dad didn't mentor you to do something, find someone who can.
- Take up a handicraft such as pottery, tapestry, jewelry making or a spiritual body practise such as yoga, tai chi or jiu jitsu to align your body and soul. Martial arts are great as they also encourage your spiritual warrior energy that is necessary for your inner Golden Heroine to mature.
- Have a think-tank session with a friend to brainstorm how you could find greater career satisfaction by channelling your inner gifts and collective skills into a marketable commodity.
- Check out available short business courses such as the New Enterprise Incentive Scheme run in Australia through TAFE, which also offers financial funding to start your own business through Centre link. Alternatively, create your own crowd funding campaign to raise the start-up capital for your creative vision, study course or career move. (This is how I raised the shortfall in funds I needed to do my first national speaking tour as a single Mum.)
- Write down what you see as your father's life lesson. For example: did he dream about doing many different projects but not have the self-esteem to commit to any of them? Talk to your dad about what he wanted in his life and how his early experiences shaped him. Now consider how you have also internalized this lesson and how as his offspring you have been trying to complete this for him.

- Have a fun game of totem tennis, pool or darts with a friend to test your skill and give your sense of competition a safe place to express itself or maybe chess or backgammon to improve your sense of strategy.
- Review your investments such as your superannuation fund and where possible reinvest with a fund that is ethical both environmentally and socially. Most super funds have a sustainable resource fund, although the onus is on the customer to ask. Consider enrolling in a one day feminine finance workshop to learn simple strategies to save and invest and feel more empowered about the world of money.
- Stop saying or thinking, 'I can't afford it!' as a mantra and allow everything to be a possibility even if you can't see how at the time. Don't allow your mind to limit your reality. Accept and relax into the tidal cycle of abundance. When the tide is out don't focus on monies going out but rather focus on what you have to be grateful for.
- Stand up for something you believe in, whether at a dinner party, by joining an organization such as Amnesty International or by volunteering to help a cause.
- Put your life in order. Clean out and discard clothes, books, jars, and computer files etc. that are cluttering up your life.

Get Wise

The following books are great for doing further work with your inner Golden Heroine.

Golden Heroine Non-Fiction

Femininity Lost and Regained by Robert A. Johnson

The Secrets of the Rainmaker by Chin-Ning Chu

Sacred Contracts, Awakening Your Divine Potential by Caroline Myss

A Woman's Worth by Marianne Williamson

The Seven Laws of Success by Deepak Chopra

The Seat of the Soul by Gary Zukov

Unlimited Power by Anthony Robbins

The Life You Were Born to Live by Dan Millman

The Twelve Trials of Hercules by Alice Bailey

Vein of Gold by Julia Cameron

Business as Unusual by Anita Roddick

Topics for Discussion

Below are a few ideas you may wish to throw around with your friends as a forum to identify and strengthen Athena's influence in your life:

- Pass a $100 note around the circle and say the first three things you feel. This quick word association will show you what powers you endow money with and the emotional charge it triggers.
- Discuss to what extent your dad has mentored you and appreciated your unique gifts and personality traits.
- Discuss your greatest fear of failure. For example, walking on stage to address a conference with your dress caught in your pantyhose or being a bag lady, destitute on the street.
- Discuss and laugh at all the ways you still seek approval from others, including your pets!

Questions for Personal Reflection

The following is a list of suggestions and questions to enable you to clear any negative money issues:

- See money spending as an addiction. Instead of spending to 'feel better' commit to 'feel better' by beating your addiction. Affirm your inner spirit is stronger than this substance.
- Get 'good hits' from comforting/nurturing treats that don't cost anything.
- Make a list and keep it in your wallet and replace 'energy losing' habits with 'energy giving' habits. For example: a fresh juice, DIY pedicure or simply lie in a hammock with a great book! Ask, 'Why am I really buying this?' For example, to look more lovable, to comfort myself or to reward myself? Ask, 'Can I really afford this now?' and consider lay-by or the peace of mind you will feel by honoring your survival needs and investing in your long-term goals.
- Try and be resourceful with what you have. For example, sell old books, clothes and CDs and cook at home more often (embodying the Earth Empress, our next archetype as a counter-balance). Try to be resourceful by considering half-price movie nights, buying cheap vegies from the market before they close or organizing clothes swaps.
- Limit your intake of TV, magazines and window shopping that feed the ego with a sense of want. You can't miss what you don't see.

Secret Woman's Business: Best Times to Celebrate Athena

Midsummer (also known as Summer Solstice)

Celebrated on December 22 in the Southern Hemisphere and June 22 in the Northern Hemisphere. This is when the sun is at its zenith point, which was the traditional day the Ancient Greeks celebrated Athena by taking her statue to the sea and washing it, renewing and purifying her, after which she would be robed in a new tunic made by local craftswomen. This was followed by the festival, **Panathenea** – games followed by feasting.

You may wish to organize your friends into teams wearing togas and play a game in her honor followed by a barbeque. The feast traditionally occurred on August 15 (in the Northern Hemisphere or January 15 if you're in the South), which may be a better time for a social event with the solstice right on the doorstep of Christmas.

The dark moon in November (Northern Hemisphere) or May (Southern Hemisphere) is when the women began work on Athena's new robe. This rite was called **Chalkeia** and would be an auspicious time to dedicate a new project and ask for Athena's blessing and patronage to launch a business or open an exhibition of fine art and craftwork. Alternatively, you may wish to do a ritual or simply light a white or yellow candle asking for Athena's assistance with your career.

In Rome the **'Day of The Craftspeople'** was the Quinquatrus on March 19 (Northern Hemisphere), September 19 (Southern Hemisphere), when artists, teachers and craftsmen and women would feast in honor of Minerva, the Roman equivalent of Athena.

Golden Heroine Rite of Passage Ceremony

You Will Need:

Hay, string or fabric, stuffing, pins, scissors, needle and

Thread Paint, paintbrush or pen

Peppermint oil

Acorns, bay leaves, coins, white/golden fabric and flowers

Yellow candle and toothpick

Clear quartz crystal

Step One

Make a poppet (a small doll) using hay from a pet supply shop and string to tie the arms, legs and head. Alternatively, you may wish to make a small doll using fabric, stuffing and needle and thread. Next, make a simple tunic for her out of remnant fabric, which you can hand paint with her symbols.

Step Two

Prepare an altar where she will spend the coming year using acorns, coins, bay leaves and a list of your goals for the coming year. Consider using yellow fabric and a vase of yellow or white flowers with perhaps an oil burner that you can burn pine or peppermint oil to assist your mental processes. Dress a yellow candle with peppermint oil and inscribe the word SUCCESS in the candle with a toothpick.

Step Three

Light the candle and holding a clear quartz crystal, close your eyes and take three deep breaths, breathing yellow into your solar plexus chakra (the upper tummy region). Invoke Athena and ask her to anchor her strengths within you. Ask her to guide you in your decisions to achieve your goals if they are for your highest good, anoint yourself and her statue with peppermint oil.

Golden Heroine Act of Beauty

You may wish to create a yellow mandala representing the solar plexus chakra using art or craft supplies and fabrics to help heal and balance this energy centre which can be attached to your Tree of Knowledge. Consider also decorating a golden altar dedicated to your inner Athena.

DEMETER: THE INNER EARTH EMPRESS

The Earth Empress is the archetype of the mother. Her role in our life is to nurture our bodies and physical needs so that we may sustain ourselves and give birth to healthy children, both physical beings and creative ideas. Without a healthy expression of Demeter (the Greek Goddess of Motherhood), we rebel against doing what is good for us and remain scattered and ungrounded. Integrating Demeter allows us to enjoy natural abundance in all its forms and therefore a better quality of life.

How I Discovered My Earth Empress

When I was twenty-six I attended a ritual, wearing a mermaid costume, so sure was I that Aphrodite would call me as her initiate. You can imagine my shock when the High Priestess called me forward and asked who it was that called me and the name 'Demeter' unmistakably popped into my head, the archetype I associated with daggy terry towelling slacks, financial powerlessness and subservience — I was mortified! Beneath my veil I sobbed so loudly for over an hour that I thought I might never stop.

Later that day I found a quote in Cailtin Mathew's book, *Sophia, Goddess of Wisdom*, it read 'only A Goddess Could Mourn So Extravagantly', which adequately summed up how I felt and inspired me to draw a picture of myself in true Scarlet O'Hara style; alone and silhouetted by the burnt destruction of all I'd lost, my hands held skyward in surrendered anguish.

What I'd lost was my creative child, a television show I tried in vain to produce for a number of years, which was rejected by ABC TV after the completion of our pilot episode. It was then I realized that grief was perfectly normal after a creative miscarriage and this marked the beginning of my conscious relationship with the archetype of Demeter.

For three months I grieved, not just for my immediate losses, but for all the wounds of my childhood and what fell away with the tears was my constructed facade of glamour and capability. Having moved to the country, I started gardening, baking, baby-sitting and teaching drama at the local primary school and for the first time since childhood I stopped wearing make-up and started wearing hand-me down clothes. Months passed and I found myself relaxed and happy, having reconnected with the cycles of the Great Mother. In Spring I marvelled at the wattle in full bloom and paddocks spotted with lambs and calves, in Summer I swam in waterholes and picked fresh berries, apples and vegetables from my friend's garden. In Autumn I walked through the fallen leaves on forest walks and in Winter I chopped wood and cooked stews. Life returned to the same good-natured simplicity that I experienced as a child, growing up in the 'Bay of Plenty' in New Zealand. This change marked the first stage of my Demeter training, 'learning to nurture myself, as I decreased my levels of toxicity, ate natural yogurt by the bucket and intuitively did psychic surgery to clean and reclaim my womb.

I then returned to the city to resume my second stage of Demeter training, 'giving birth to my creative projects'. This proved a more difficult task as again I failed to appreciate the timing, patience and consistency needed to nurture my various projects to full-term. Eventually, I started Woven Women and began running regular Goddess workshops and completed a short business course so my efforts would be more grounded in reality.

Seven years after being called by Demeter, I fell pregnant. I was delighted, having recently become engaged and my 'clucky' urge was stronger than lust after having spent two and a half years playing with five-year-olds as a fairy at birthday parties. The first trimester was hell, as I grappled with the sheer terror of becoming my mother, which manifested as 'morning sickness' 24 hours a day and hormonal mood swings that rivalled Liz Taylor in *Who's Afraid of Virginia Woolf*? Not the picture of the serene, glowing mother-to-be with quaint cravings for pickles and ice cream that I had been fed by the media and society at large.

Mid-term I felt a growing urge to birth our baby at home rather than in the sterile environment of a hospital, so we hired a lovely midwife and a birthing pool, affirming that on the big day I would, 'Open like a lotus!'.

The day came (at the crack of dawn) and I had the all-important 'show' – which turned out to be a blob of pink jelly (very impressive!). This was followed by a strong urge to evacuate my bowels, which unfortunately was shared by my husband who intercepted my ablutions to use the toilet so I sat on the nappy bucket opposite him to continue, painting a memorable moment as I looked at him and said, 'Do you think we're shitting ourselves about becoming parents?'

(Diarrhea pouring out the back of us in unison.)

He then readied himself washing dishes compulsively, lighting candles and arranging lotuses and Kwan Yin statues, ready for the quintessential new age birth... I took my crystal wand in hand and began opening the four directions to consecrate the birth space. The following is an excerpt of what I experienced and subsequently wrote in my birth journal.

I felt the need to use the wand above my head and felt a Divine spiral enter through the wand and into me as I asked for assistance to journey with our baby through the gateway of time and space for our experience through death and birth.

Feeling decidedly inward, I began calling in the directions telepathically instead of verbally.

EAST

I stood to call in the East. Being the direction of birth, I welcomed in angel spirits (singling out Archangel Michael) and I was overwhelmed as the room filled with their energies and tears of euphoria and gratitude poured down my cheeks.

The water undines called to me from deep within the pool and I was transported back to the cave at Mount Gambia and greeted by the Earth and water spirits I met there who were with me now for this experience. I saw the lotus open underneath the floorboards of our house (which had been created during our belly blessing ceremony), which quickly multiplied into a lush garden of lotuses, water features and streams which seemed suspended in the cosmos. Meanwhile, the salamanders (fire spirits) were creating rainbow streaks of energy consecrating the birth tub in a sphere of luminescent light.

NORTH

I then called in the North's elemental fire spirits and the room filled with Tinkerbell-like fireflies that danced about the candles and cleared the Shakti (energy) about the birth pool by showering golden streams of light from a central point. They then began clearing my energy and more tears of joy flowed as I described the scene surrounding me to Adrian.

WEST

I then joked to Adrian that I had inadvertently sat in the West, my element of water (with tears of joy streaming down my face). As I opened the portal, in came the priestesses of Avalon to scry into the pool. Walking down steps on either side of me, they led me into an ocean cave with a mouth similar to the yoni image in the blue agate crystal slice (gifted to me by my friends Vanessa and Shannon who had given birth the previous month).

The ocean waters lapped at our feet, like the salty fluids that resided within the feminine yoni. Inside the entrance, the walls were lit by candles and as the Mother Mary candle crackled with excitement behind me, the priestesses sat me on a scallop throne and began initiating me in to their temple of Isis, the Great Mother. They washed my hair using jugs of rose scented water and bathed my feet. They then placed a pale blue scarf over my head and placed a crimson lotus on my crown, commenting 'as above, so below' I would open and allow the universal energies to flow through me. Isis then placed me in a pale blue lozenge-shaped energy field, affording me her welcome and protection. I was also increasingly aware of the mid-wife crone Goddess, Hecate standing in the South-Eastern corner, holding her staff and watching over all the proceedings. (I had also felt the energy of my mum around me just prior to starting the ritual.)

SOUTH

The portal opened to the South and I saw a tunnel of exquisite gems and jewels (notably gold, rubies and emeralds) and was told by the Earth entities that Adrian had the ability to amass great wealth as he had discovered for himself what was truly precious in life. They said I provided the watery inspiration from the Netherworld and he, the practical know-how to build my visions in this realm. I then felt the need to disrobe and dance (the 'dance' consisting of me turning to face each of the four cross-quarters and breathing in the energies of our Native American Indian ancestors by drawing their breath through my arms which were now clasped in prayer position above my head). I did this three times in each direction. I called in the spirits of my relatives who had passed over such as my nana and my aunt Cerridwen and the energies of our friends.

Throughout this ritual I felt a man standing behind me with dark features and a divine presence that emanated Christ-consciousness, which looked remarkably like a drawing I had done before conceiving, that depicted me holding a baby with such a man standing behind me. This gentle and supportive masculine energy was also communicated to me by Adrian who was doing everything to support my inner journey, whilst connecting with me regularly with his eyes, heart, body and soul.

Three days later we left for hospital on the recommendation of my midwife (as I had an infection that would need hourly penicillin shots if I stayed at home) and I was so exhausted it was deemed time to get induced. Despite my earnest visualizations to 'open like a lotus' my cervix had only dilated one centimetre!

Having consented, I had no idea that being induced meant seizures so severe I looked like a deranged animal, my back arching and eyes bulging with each drug-induced contraction whilst my husband, midwife, dear friend Lael and hospital staff held me like a contestant riding a mechanical bull whilst strapped to an electric chair. Finally we consented to abandon the 'drug free' birth plan and summoned the anaesthetist. The clock ticked on and no one appeared, whilst I, noticing it was lunchtime began cynically assuming the anaesthetist was in the cafeteria eating egg sandwiches while I was in the jaws of hell.

Finally (an hour later), the anaesthetist arrived and I went from giving him the evil eye to looking upon him like the saint that he was, as my legs, pelvis and back filled with the sensation of fairy floss.

I went to sleep while my cervix was dilated and I woke as the drugs wore off and began pushing (and vomiting), and felt my vagina stretch wider than I thought possible and was gifted with a divine little girl, a gift from the Goddess, who we called Ariella Willow. I have since watched her blossom into a remarkable Goddess in her own right. Mothering has been the most humbling process imaginable! I am continually awed by her strength of character, clarity of selfhood, sense of humour and love of life. She is my greatest blessing!

EARTH EMPRESS QUIZ

Answer the following quick quiz to find out what shape your inner Earth Empress is currently in. (Circle the answer that most describes you.)

A friend calls who is feeling down and wants to talk. You are in the middle of something that requires your full attention, do you:

A. Feel uncomfortable that she's rung you asking for help and suggest she call someone else?

B. Stop what you're doing and listen to her whilst quietly feeling anxious about how long she's talking?

C. Explain your circumstance briefly and commit to return her call when you're finished?

Most nights of the week your dinner would consist of:

A. Take out or frozen dinners.

B. Meat and vegetables from the supermarket, followed by after dinner treats.

C. Wholefoods such as brown rice, lentils, organic vegetables and free range meat.

Your home environment is best described as:

A. A place where you sleep and not much else.

B. A show home that feels ordered but not warm and inviting.

C. A sanctuary that feels warm, happy and nurturing.

Now add up your score. A = 1, B = 2, C = 3. *If you scored:*

1 – 3 Your inner Earth Empress is petrified of becoming a doormat should she ever put on an apron. The next chapter may help you to see how you can nurture yourself and others without becoming subservient.

4 – 6 Your inner Earth Empress is putting other's needs before your own. You'll `pick up a few helpful tips in the next chapter.

7 – 9 Yo Mama! Your inner Earth Empress is in fine form. Enjoy reading the following chapter.

Herstory: Earth Empress Goddesses

There are various other names by which we have come to know and honor the mother aspect. They include Mother Mary as a figurehead of compassion and mother of the saviour child in Christian theology; Kwan Yin, the female Bodhisattva, who is also renowned for her compassion, as well as her patronage to mothers and children as a midwife Goddess; Hathor, the Egyptian cow Goddess who gave birth to Ra, the sun God and Europa, mother of the continent, Europe. Early agricultural societies honored the aspect of the Earth Empress in regular festivals where they asked for her assistance in blessing and sustaining their crops and way of life. She was known as Ceres in ancient Rome, Pacha Mama in South America and in ancient Greece first as Gaia, then as Demeter who shall guide us personally through the mysteries of the Mother.

The Myth of Demeter

Long ago in ancient Greece, Demeter lived with her daughter Persephone, sheltered from the quarrels of the world. Each year Persephone learnt more from her wise and loving mother who showed her where to find the fruits and natural wonders of each changing season, as well as how to lovingly care for and tend to the needs of those around her. Together, they enjoyed a close and warm connection until the day came when Persephone turned fifteen years of age. So keen was Persephone to venture out without her mother as her guide to see the wonders that lay beyond their land that she gathered her friends and set out in the sunshine for a day of games and flower picking. They walked through pastures and fields, past farm animals and a bubbling brook until they came upon the most picturesque valley they had ever seen.

The valley was filled with flowers as far as the eye could see and the girls scattered like dandelion seeds, discovering new intoxicating scents and colours that defied the natural palette of Divine creation.

It was then as a cry of delight pierced the air, that Persephone sighted what had to be the most exquisite creation ever handcrafted by the Goddess and she stooped to admire the petals of the exotic narcissus that beckoned her to take a closer look. No sooner had she plucked the delicate specimen from its grass-knitted bed that the ground shook and tore apart before her startled eyes.

Then she heard a deep throaty laugh echoing from within the canyon, followed by a gust of wind as six horses thundered out from within the Earth, their flanks glistening as they snorted steam and pounded the soil with their hooves. Behind them loomed a chariot steered by a swarthy man who bellowed to the frightened girl, 'I am Hades, God of the Underworld and you are to be my bride!'

And with that, his coarse hand grabbed her roughly about the waist and threw her down onto the cold seat beside him and they plunged deep within the almighty crevice of the Earth which returned, as if by magic to its former sleepy state, disclosing nothing as though not even a grass seed had ever been disturbed.

When Persephone's friends arrived back at Demeter's cottage unable to speak clearly for lack of breath and tears, Demeter calmed them enough to unravel the tragic news. As the shock set in, a metallic nausea spread throughout her body, so she draped herself in a woollen shawl and set off to visit Persephone's father to see what might be done.

Wet and cold, her breath shallow with fright, she arrived on the doorstep of the God, Zeus to share with him the terrible fate that had befallen their daughter. He then deadened her nerves to the very core by disclosing that he had himself granted permission to his brother Hades to abduct Persephone, explaining that she was no longer a child and would have a distinguished title as Queen of the Underworld, where she would continue to reside.

He then dismissed his secrecy as necessary for the girl's individuation, as they both knew full well that Demeter would never have consented to such a match. He went on to say that Demeter would always see her daughter as a child rather than the nubile maiden that she had in fact blossomed into and so ultimately she would do well to accept the fact she now had a new son-in-law.

Demeter, wild with rage screamed at Zeus for his betrayal and then left, blinded by tears and began wandering roads and countryside crying out for a word or a sign from her missing daughter.

The months wore on, as she walked from town to town, her stooped frame caging a form whose flesh had been eaten away by overwhelming sorrow. Many people sighting her tried in vain to rouse her from her grief but the only one to enjoy any measure of success was the clown Goddess, Baubo who simply lifted her skirts and began telling the filthiest jokes she could muster by using the lips of her vulva as a mouth through which to deliver her crude material!

Finally, she reached the town of Eleusis, near Athens and whilst bathing in the town square, made the acquaintance of local noble women who were so impressed with her ability to braid hair that before the afternoon sun had set she was offered work by the local Queen as a nanny to her son,

Demophoon. Glad to have the tender love of a child to nurture, Demeter decided she would raise the mortal boy as a God, feeding him ambrosia and holding him nightly in the fire of transformation to grant him the gift of immortality. This however was unfortunately interrupted when the boy's mother walked in on Demeter holding her son over the fire and grabbed him, preventing him from becoming immortal. It was then that Demeter revealed her true identity as a Goddess and a temple was built in her name at Eleusis.

Meanwhile, with Demeter away from her homeland, her domestic and agricultural duties were neglected and a famine ensued that threatened the survival of the townsfolk and Gods alike, and so Zeus, unable to sustain the growth that he had seeded without the skills of Demeter, bargained with his brother Hades to restore Persephone to her mother.

During her underworld stay, however, Persephone had eaten six pomegranate seeds and had assumed the title of Queen of the Underworld, making it impossible to return back into her mother's care as if she were still a child. And so a deal was struck, where she would reside six months of the year in each domain, spending half with her husband and half with her mother. Consequently, each spring heralded Persephone's return as the flowers bloomed and the crops fruited to mirror her mother's happiness and fulfilment. But as the days grew shorter, with the first chills of autumn she would again depart, retreating to her Underworld kingdom for the duration of winter when all was bleak and desolate above.

Further facts

Demeter was worshipped in the ancient world as the 'Goddess of Grain' as she presided over bountiful harvests. She was said to ripen harvests with her warmth and the ancients celebrated her each year when they harvested their crops late in summer. She governed the cycles of nature and all growing life forms, particularly the gestation and birth of new life. As a deity she represents the feminine power that's within the Earth herself. She was said to have taught men the art of ploughing and tilling the soil and women, the arts of grinding wheat and baking bread, which led to people settling and creating permanent homes in exchange for their previously nomadic lifestyles.

The Moral

Demeter's tale is one of seasonal change, highlighting the need to accept the individuation of those who grow from our nourishment but must eventually be released to follow their own destiny. Her myth illustrates how she can never permanently protect her young from seeing and experiencing the darker side of both their own and other's natures. It is her grief that matures her, as she learns to accept loss as the opposite of her ability to birth and create. It is only time which heals this wound, during which she must learn to accept her own dark side, that of the resentful, bitter and barren mother who has neither the energy nor the inclination to nurture herself, let alone anyone else. It is only when she accepts the opposite polarity in life that the seasonal cycle can start again, heralding in new growth and opportunities.

Persephone is on a parallel journey to that of Eve where she must eat the dark fruits (symbolized by the pomegranate seeds), to find her own womanhood, her queenly aspect. The shifts from both maiden to mother and mother to wise woman are often heralded in by a sense of loss and betrayal and a period of aloneness so we may release the previous chapter (and identity) and germinate the seeds of the new.

Historical Appearance

Demeter is a woman in full bloom. As such, she is curvaceous with a natural beauty that emanates from her acceptance of herself. She has an aura of a woman who is centred, grounded and dependable.

She has been portrayed in various Tarot decks as having golden or auburn hair and wearing full smock-like clothes as if to suggest pregnancy. She is often surrounded by fruits, flowers and grains of the harvest such as sheafs of wheat.

Her hair is usually lustrous and may be plaited or covered in a handkerchief scarf as if to suggest that she needs it out of her face to do domestic or farmyard chores. Her cheeks are often rosy and there is a general plumpness about her character, indicating her love of the sensual abundance the good Earth has to offer. Similarly, she may be depicted wearing an apron, with an ample bosom and a lap wide enough to invite children and animals to a comfortable seat.

Earth Empress Profile

Note: The following profile also includes a detailed description of Persephone, the archetypal daughter who must also be understood if we are to heal our mother issues.

Demeter connects us inwardly with the universal energy of the Great Mother. This reconnection enables us to rediscover our body as something valuable and precious that deserves care (which is needed desperately today when you consider the widespread epidemic of eating disorders, cosmetic surgery, genetically modified food and substance abuse). Demeter also helps us to reconnect with Mother Nature, allowing us to appreciate the simple pleasures nature has to offer with the same reverence and wonder seen in the eyes of children who discover the natural world for the first time. Without this reverence for the natural world we become insatiable in our thirst for 'the next big thing', never content with what we have and in our ego-driven quest to create and possess forget we are custodians of the Earth.

When we lose our connection to the Universal Mother we lose the ability to work with the natural cycles to bring our ideas to fruition with ease and grace. The more we reject the notion that all valuable items demand their own natural cultivation time (such as diamonds and pearls), the more we will create items of an inferior quality which may cause harm (such as plastics which leak chemical toxins on to most of our foods). For everything there is a season and a reason, this is the wisdom of nature, an inherent acceptance that all things move and ripen at their appropriate time.

Through our mentoring by our Earth Mother we learn as children to love and care for our physical bodies, teaching us as newly arrived souls that we are creatures, not only of Spirit but also of Earth. The mother is the first spiritual teacher each soul encounters and for the first seven years of our life we focus on the lessons taught to us by our Mum, who is the blueprint for our developing inner feminine. (The following seven years, we turn our attention toward the masculine and focus more on skills learnt outside the home environment.)

Demeter's role is to teach her offspring how to attend to their physical, emotional and spiritual needs. A job which receives little validation within our culture, despite the tools she grants us with becoming our most essential life skills. A role which requires extreme patience and understanding as we slowly learn through ritual, the cyclic repetition of each given task.

The mother phase usually begins with what is referred to in astrological terms as your 'Saturn return', which is when the planet Saturn completes its twenty-nine year orbit around the sun to position itself in the same place it was at your time of birth. This translates as a time in your life when, as you approach 30, the traditional age of the mother in the ancient mysteries (double the age of the maiden at fifteen), when the ego is confronted with all that needs to change for your future growth and sustainability.

This creates a rebirth when your chickens metaphorically come home to roost and you find that you literally can't get away with what you used to, such as abusing your body with substances and living beyond your means financially. It is a time when criminal activity may result in a conviction or unhealthy relationship choices may result in total heartbreak or an unwanted pregnancy.

Throughout this period of time, the repercussions intensify, pressuring us to reflect upon our choices and take responsibility.

Saturn, the archetype of the father, teaches us by imposing boundaries and limits so we can slow down and reflect upon our actions. This opposing energy is needed to balance the energy of the mother who is often all-allowing and limitless in the possibilities she presents to her offspring. Ultimately, this transition heralds in the thirties when many of us start to consider whether we want to have children, purchase real estate or start our own business, enabling us to ground our energy.

The Demeter archetype makes itself known in three stages to prepare us incrementally for the life phase of the mother (regardless of whether or not we decide to have children). The three lessons she presents us with are...

Learn To Nurture Ourselves

By healing childhood issues, taking responsibility for our own expectations, beliefs, choices and actions we learn to stop blaming our parents and in so doing, internalize the mother archetype so we can complete the individuation from our own mother.

Give Birth To Our Creative Children

We learn to take responsibility for carving out the life we want instead of just childishly getting annoyed that it hasn't been handed to us on a silver platter. We then commit to our goal and apply the necessary consistent effort to create our own security so we don't feel like we need to be taken care of indefinitely by others.

Learn To Nurture Others

This stage presents as the urge to create and nurture, whether it's having our own children, fostering or sponsoring others, doing volunteer work, counselling, healing, and creating projects or social networks that support the greater community.

That said, whilst the traditional age for embracing Demeter is close to thirty, if the Demeter archetype is very strong within a woman, she may easily choose to have children much earlier. For example, when Demeter was the expected life path for women up until the 1970s, the number of women having children in their late teens and early twenties reflected this societal expectation.

If on the other hand, Demeter surfaces from within rather than as a projected expectation, her energy can rear its head as a deep physical and emotional need to procreate. If this impulse to procreate is not fulfilled, a woman with a strong Demeter archetype can feel incomplete and compare herself unfavourably with other women who are mothers.

Demeter dominant women often have a very close bond with their own mother as little girls and enjoy playing with dolls and emulating their mum doing the ironing and burping dolly. They often have a strong urge to nurture others and are happy to be in a more supportive role than adventuring across continents with the spirit of a pioneer. These women typically find motherhood supremely fulfilling as they have a nurturing and patient temperament that is tailor-made for the job.

If our Earth Empress is particularly developed we are happy to extend our hospitality far beyond our own nuclear family, creating an open-door policy for those in need of some home comfort and TLC, a true community service. (Note: The best gift you can buy a true Demeter is a new welcome mat!)

Our inner Earth Empress thrives when she feels helpful, whether it's by providing tangible assistance such as food, shelter, medical aid or helping others psychologically or emotionally. For this reason you will find her in service positions such as nursing, teaching, social work, healing, counselling, and childcare or as an aid to the disabled or elderly.

She ideally loves to see herself as the endless 'Goddess of Abundance'. Unfortunately this can harbour dependence from those around her, who drain her resources rather than take responsibility for their own actions. As a result, many shadow Demeters need to learn to set boundaries so that they can sustain their ability to give to themselves and others without becoming tired and resentful. This is evident in Mothers who can't say no to their kids and end up being worn out by the demands of their little monsters whose egos they continue to feed for fear they will lose their child's approval if they attempt to set a boundary. This in turn creates sociopathic children who expect life to revolve around them in the same way their Mother did. (Note: This urge to make their children's lives 'perfect' is also often subconsciously driven by a need to heal the wounds of their own inner child.)

Demeter's ultimate lesson is to honor herself first, so she can avoid the martyr complex known as 'the burnt chop syndrome' – giving the best to others and denying her own needs. She also does well to remember that the more she is responsible for others, the more they will complete the dance by becoming increasingly irresponsible, so she would do well to dispel any feelings of guilt that she alone cannot nurture the world.

Just as in the myth, Demeter's issues focus as much on death and loss, as they do on birth and gain. It is impossible to experience birth without first experiencing death psychologically. A woman giving birth to a child spends nine months shedding her maidenhood as she gestates the new life within her. This transition, known as the 'Death of The Maiden' is often helped significantly with psychological preparation in the form of ritual. This enables the changing woman to consciously acknowledge what she will lose and what she will gain, and in so doing, diminishes the likelihood of post-natal depression, which is seen in countless young mums who have not received adequate support and wise counsel.

Such rituals need not be elaborate but should include the acknowledgment of all that she has learnt in her maiden stage, as well as providing her with an opportunity to express her gratitude to her own mum, an action that signifies her willingness to consciously step over this threshold and embrace the change. Rite of passage ceremonies of this kind were commonplace in ancient cultures but have been lost, much to our detriment. Rite of passage ceremonies, art therapy, sharing circles and rebirthing (a form of breath-work therapy that releases latent fears and emotions) are all incredibly helpful during pregnancy to help women integrate this momentous life change and shift in identity.

Demeter teaches us that we need a balance of the creator and destroyer to grow. It is a sign of maturity to accept each loss as an opportunity for further growth, rather than clinging to the past like the maiden who has not learnt to trust the cyclic nature of life. So our inner Earth Empress does well to familiarize herself with the endless cycle of loss, gestation, birth and harvest, as well as the stages of grief needed to be passed through before the next gestation cycle can commence. Otherwise she is working against the greater cycles and becomes impatient and discouraged with her efforts.

Her stages of grief are: shock, denial, depression, anger and acceptance. These will vary in length and intensity, depending on the significance of the change, but each stage must be passed through in order to access and integrate the next. An interesting side effect one may experience during periods of grief is an aroused libido. Although not acknowledged as it is deemed 'inappropriate' by onlookers to see a widow hitting on guests at the funeral, it is natural to want to experience a 'little death' or orgasm to change one's mental and emotional state, albeit temporarily. As a comforting and cathartic experience, sex can provide a much-needed emotional and energetic release when one needs life affirmed through direct union with the Divine. The powers of such a healing should not be underestimated, let alone judged by the intellect. This is symbolized by Baubo's appearance in the myth when she is able to reignite Demeter's life spark by reminding her of the joys of sexual contact when she is in the depths of personal despair, her tears having drowned her inner fire.

The Dark Mother

This brings us to the shadow aspects of Demeter in her destroyer phase, the 'Mourning or Dark Mother'. Just as the seasons have their life cycle, so too does Demeter, as she cannot remain forever the jubilant harvest queen and needs to honor her desire to lie fallow periodically and replenish. Often this coincides with her children entering puberty and needing to individuate from their mother, during which time they will naturally rebel and learn through personal experience what the darker side of life has to offer. Consequently, Demeter feels unneeded and may retreat from her nurturing duties, preferring to draw the curtains, neglect housework and focus on her own inner needs. (This inner journey is her personal gestation and period of depression that enables her to embrace Hecate, the Wise Woman.) This aspect of the Mother is considered taboo in our society and many women feel incredibly empowered just having this experience validated by others in the same position. It is important therefore that women reach out to others to gather the support needed to make this life transition and I would also encourage women in this situation to express their anger in a healthy way rather than sink into a long period of life-crushing apathy.

The Dark Mother has recognisable symptoms. She often withholds emotional, physical or psychological support as a way of asserting passive aggressive punishment on those she holds responsible for her pain and is recognisable as the 'silent treatment' that engenders subtle manipulation through guilt.

There is often a significant event that triggers the emergence of the Dark Mother. It may come in the form of a divorce, her children rejecting her influence in favour of their dad's approval, a child being molested, kidnapped or dying, her child choosing a partner who she strongly disapproves of, a project failing that would've helped others or her children leaving home. This external event, although painful, is universal in transforming Demeter from a trusting, generous and optimistic nurturer into a victim/martyr depressive recluse, albeit temporarily until she, like Persephone, has learnt to integrate both aspects of the mother in equal measure. Knowing the inevitability of this Underworld event can help diminish overwhelming feelings of guilt from a woman who has tried her best to be the 'perfect mother'.

Persephone, the Eternal Maiden

It is important that we look at the issues encountered by Persephone, the eternal maiden in order to comprehend the polarity of mother/daughter. Persephone, the archetypal daughter needs to take responsibility for her own choices, rather than continually reacting to what life throws at her. Commitment is also another challenge for Persephone, as she often has a perfectionist streak that tells her nothing and no one is up to her standard, creating a pattern of sabotage and unfinished projects instead of applying humble persistence, the trait that enables Demeter to sustain her harvest.

Many Persephones are afraid of having children. This is because they know instinctively that they are still unable to successfully nurture their own needs and would not cope emotionally or psychologically with the added responsibility of a child. Their inner mother must be reawakened and anchored through self-nourishing behaviours as a preparatory step to this life-altering commitment. To do this, our first step is to face our fears and heal them, so self-destructive behaviours aren't created as a form of escape from unresolved pain.

Our inner Persephone matures when we realize that our fairy-tale ideals needed to be shattered by the Hades men we encountered. These are the Underworld lads (or lasses!) that she associates with in her journey to explore the shadow, both within herself and others. She may view these peers as exciting or charismatic but needs to reflect upon her own needs, rather than her wants before she is free to choose a mate (and friends) who have re-emerged from the Underworld and are therefore mature enough to enter into sustainable relationships. Each of these partners who break her projections of the 'perfect mate' are bringing her closer to embracing reality, although the lessons are emotionally painful to endure. Ultimately, she does well to look for the lesson and move on.

Age alone does not make a Demeter as there are many Persephones who are still caught up in needing to individuate from their mothers despite being over the age of thirty. The following is a list of ways in which this tendency can manifest:

- Being critical of your mum's faults whilst failing to appreciate her strengths in the same measure.
- Finding 'surrogate mums' who will listen to your endless dramas, providing the insight needed to break your negative patterns.
- Duplicating your mum's choices in order to win approval and on-going affection from her.
- Rebelling against what your mum has taught you by indulging in junk food, casual sex, drugs, alcohol, lack of sleep, petty crime or associating with people who don't honor you.

Similarly, what our inner Demeter may find hard to accept is that she cannot protect her children from experiencing the Underworld. This may lead us to become over-protective, damaging our children's self-esteem as they interpret this interference as a message that they don't have what it takes to cope on their own. Our inner Earth Empress therefore needs to find a balance between protecting the interests of our children and not stifling their need to experiment and grow. Demeter's process is one of continual letting go. Every time her children become more confident and autonomous in their own right, she has to release them with love knowing it is a sign that she has done her job well.

If she is unable to do this she will unconsciously live through others, her children in particular. (I have read the Tarot for women desperate to have children who lack the self-esteem to pursue their own dreams and so unconsciously want a child who'll live out their dreams for them. Some patient incoming souls will stall their conception time until their would-be mums take responsibility for their own potential and take the steps necessary to realize it.) The alternative is the classic 'stage mother' or overachieving parent who obsesses about 'little Tiffany's current performance and future achievements', often robbing their child of a carefree childhood. This is another reason why mums do well to nurture the expression of their other archetypes so their own personal life is full and rewarding, freeing their children to be themselves. If this dynamic is not consciously understood, one-dimensional full-time Demeters may be confused as to why their adult children are distant both emotionally and geographically. Alternatively, this behaviour may produce a child who feels guilty whenever they take steps towards being independent, unaware that they are being unconsciously manipulated by their mother to stay by her side to keep her happy.

This is the stereotypical 'Mummy's Boy or Girl' whose allegiance to their mother is caused by emotional incest, which unconsciously sabotages the child's efforts to form healthy relationships with other people. Unfortunately in some cases, this can even jeopardize a child developing a healthy relationship with their dad or grandparent as Demeter is threatened that any other bond will reduce the one she shares with her child.

Generally, our inner Earth Empress enjoys the company of other women. Within extended families there may be an active matriarchal social network amongst the women or if this is absent, she'll bond closely with other mothers who take turns surrogating the Persephone/Demeter role within the friendship.

Demeter dominant women are easy to spot. They love children and combine the qualities of patient teacher with the mother who provides consistent emotional security and support. They are mature enough to relegate their own needs behind those who are defenseless and dependent on their care. They also value children for their honesty and purity and so children often gravitate towards them.

Ultimately, the mother gives us a sense of safety and trust in life, so the more we allow ourselves to connect with our own inner Empress, the more we gift ourselves with an inner feeling of security and safety in each present moment.

The following are examples of Demeter as an archetype if she is not balanced by the other feminine selves:

Alice

Alice was a super-Demeter. She would rise at 5am to make her children fresh juices and hot breakfasts using organic produce. After school she ferried them around to music lessons and martial arts classes. She lived in a beautiful rustic home surrounded by native flora and fauna and assisted on many community causes as a key player. To the outside world, Alice looked like the perfect mother.

Alice was in fact, a perfectionist. Her house was always spotless and her children were high achievers who hardly watched television but her marriage was painful to witness and she was always in a high state of anxiety. Increasingly, her children became her emotional partners as her resentment grew toward her husband and their intimacy decreased.

Sabine

Sabine was a woman whose children still lived at home, despite being in their mid-twenties. Every morning she would leave home at 6.30am to drive her adult children to university and their place of work before going to the flat that she rented to work as a day care mum, taking care of other people's babies.

Although a natural Earth mother who was well-suited to her profession, when she was ill neither her husband nor her grown-up children were able to nurture her needs as they had never learned to cook. This illustrated a woman who was so accomplished at her nurturing role that those around her became increasingly dependent and were, therefore, not confident enough in their abilities to do for themselves or others when the need arose.

Earth Empress Strengths

The following is a description of how we behave when our inner Earth Empress archetype is appreciated and positively expressed:

- I am resourceful with what I have so I can provide more efficiently.
- I appreciate life's simple pleasures so I always feel blessed and abundant.
- I am connected with and observe my body's cycles and the cycles of nature
- I am patient, accepting that lasting results are worth the time and effort.
- I nurture both my own potential and the potential in others.
- I am down-to-earth, natural and honest in social situations.
- I am practical and possess a solid understanding and appreciation of material matters
- I am humble and will sacrifice extraneous wants for both my own and other's needs.
- I provide emotional counselling and spiritual insights for others. I am consistent and persistent in building my dreams.
- I will defend those too defenseless to protect themselves.
- I value the gifts inherent in the process, rather than just the results.
- I can commit to enjoying an 'ordinary' existence as I'm no longer bound by youthful perfectionist ideals.
- I listen to others and am accepting of their faults.
- I consider people's intentions, as well as their actions.
- I take good care of my health and my home as my foundations for life.

Earth Empress Shadow Traits

The following is a description of how we behave when our inner Earth Empress archetype is suppressed or misunderstood:

- I tend to view men as boys who need to be mothered.
- I unconsciously make my children into my emotional partners, instead of facing fears and blocks I have around being intimate with adults.
- I often choose partners who are immature so I can unconsciously mother them or as an attempt to retain my inner Persephone and remain an eternal maiden.
- I often martyr myself by putting my own needs last and later resent others for having their needs met.
- Sometimes I give to others out of a sense of guilt, obligation or a need for approval, rather than giving what and when I choose.
- I tend to hold on to situations, beliefs, people and possessions when they need to be released in order to grow.

- I am not really interested in what other people say or do, instead I tend to talk incessantly about my children and their achievements.
- I am competitive with my children or on their behalf.
- I often put pressure on my kids or staff to not embarrass me and make me look bad.
- I unconsciously need approval from my kids so I give in to them instead of standing firm.
- I exclude or negate my partner's attempts at childrearing in an effort to unconsciously bolster the importance of my maternal role and bond I share with my children. When my partner stops trying to parent, I then resent them for not pulling their weight.
- I am not generous to others beyond my own family.
- I focus obsessively on the health of others as it makes me feel needed or, alternatively, I don't look after my own health.

Earth Empress Lessons

To balance your Earth Empress's strengths and weaknesses, try the following suggestions:

- Give your other archetypes expression so you don't lose your identity when looking after others.
- Take steps to fulfil your own dreams to avoid living through others.
- Try not to project your own fears on to your kids, as this gives them the message that the world is unsafe and they will not cope with new experiences.
- Be patient in deciding when to have children so you afford yourself as much support as possible: financially, emotionally, intellectually and spiritually.
- Allow yourself to express any feelings of grief at the loss of your eternal maiden so you can embrace your womanhood fully.
- Thank ex-partners for the roles they have played in destroying your eternal maiden's idealistic expectations, helping you to mature.
- Find a balance between enjoying adult company and caring for children.
- Delegate some of your chores, where possible, and relinquish the need to have a home that is always 'neat as a pin' so you can enjoy a balanced life of give and take.
- Accept the inevitable individuation process of your children, students and clients, enabling you to enjoy an equal and mutually enriching adult relationship with them where you relinquish all your authority.
- Become involved in creating community, be it locally, nationally or globally.
- Abandon the idea of being a 'Supermom' – an all-abundant nurturer to everybody, instead be authentic about your limits.
- Seek replenishment and support from Mother Nature when you are tired and emotional.
- Where possible, simplify your life and review your priorities.
- Heal your inner child through conscious self-parenting so you don't feed your own inner child's desires through your own children or dependants.

Earth Empress Relationship Patterns

Personal

Often a woman with a strong Earth Empress aspect may bond with her children at the expense of emotional intimacy with her partner. A mature inner Demeter will choose a partner who is also mature and generous enough to be a good father, as well as a supportive partner with whom to raise children. If, on the other hand she projects her need to mother everyone, including her spouse, she may choose a partner who is immature and resents the children (and pets) for distracting her from his inner child's needs. When shopping for a mate, Demeter-dominant women need to resist the urge to rescue men who they feel sorry for and instead look for a man who takes responsibility for meeting his own emotional needs.

This dynamic is evident when dad is the biggest kid in the family, competing with his children and draining Demeter with his dependence and irresponsibility. Alternatively, he may recede from the family and become increasingly uninterested in their growth and achievements or in a worst-case scenario, become abusive and lash out physically, psychologically or emotionally as his childish needs aren't the priority of her focus. This is particularly noticeable in a relationship between a father and son if the father unconsciously blames the son for replacing him as the recipient of the mother's affection. Similarly, mothers have to be careful not to project their need for emotional intimacy (if lacking in their primary partnership) onto their child, which puts unfair expectations on the child to fulfil their mother's needs.

Demeter, as an archetype, will not choose a partner because of the social status it may afford her, nor will she choose a man who wants her to forever remain the maiden so he can show off her physical attributes to his friends. She may, however, be tempted to choose a younger man who is somewhat immature and self-absorbed but displays some special talent, wound or quality which wins her heart. She may make continual excuses for his selfish behaviour every time he fails to take her needs into account, repeatedly making allowances for his 'mistakes' just as a mother would forgive a young child, often forgiving him instantly when he tells her he loves her or bestows on her any small token of affection.

This pattern often leads to a long and painful string of broken promises before Demeter learns to say no (and mean it) to this psychological sociopath who honestly believes his needs are more important than anyone else's, because that's the message he received from his own mother. These men unconsciously seek out a maternal woman who will take over where mum left off — cooking, cleaning, organizing medical appointments and social engagements, whilst constantly bolstering their self-esteem. But should she make demands on him or worse still, fall pregnant, this Peter Pan type will punish her by becoming angry, withdrawing his affection or disappearing into fantasy land until Demeter is remorseful and ready to pander to his needs.

Similarly, many lesbian Demeter women may choose partners who play out the Persephone role in a similar way to their Peter Pan counterparts. This may be exacerbated if the Demeter woman's urge to mother has been thwarted and her need to nurture attracts a younger or emotionally immature woman who is unsure of herself and therefore unable to commit, causing uncertainty and a fear of betrayal from her partner.

When it comes to physical intimacy, women with a strong inner Earth Empress love time spent cuddling and expressing tenderness. Their greatest joy is to constantly receive the demonstrative affection they so freely give out to others as being earthy, sensual women they appreciate the need for human touch more than most and will thrive with a pet for company and affection if they are single. They also appreciate time spent together with a partner that is sensual for its own pleasure, rather than as an expected precursor to sexual activity. Happy to be in their bodies and savour the treats of the sensual world, Demeter-dominant women make great breast feeders, relishing the special physical contact shared between a mother and her child.

As a friend, those with strong Demeter archetypes are dependable, loyal and generous with their time and resources. Often they will go out of their way to accommodate those who they sense may have trouble assimilating such as new parents, newly-arrived immigrants, and children from broken homes or those who are painfully shy.

Famous Earth Empresses

Mother Theresa is the first global Demeter icon who springs to mind, rescuing babies from rubbish bins in Calcutta and nursing them back to health. Roseanne Barr also made a huge impact by redefining the public face of motherhood with her portrayal of a housewife in the suburbs of Middle America, warts and all. Another TV mum who has helped to air the shadow side of Demeter is Jennifer Saunders as Eddie in the sitcom 'Absolutely Fabulous', where the roles are reversed and her on-air daughter, Saffy plays out Demeter to her immature, rebellious Persephone-driven mother.

In Australia, we have also been fortunate to have the comedic stylings of Jane Turner and Gina Riley in their hit series, 'Kath and Kim', a suburban satire of a mother and daughter who turn emotional manipulation combined with ignorance into an art form, which is seen through Kath's unrelenting attempts to project her 'Slim Is In!' dogma onto her offspring.

Another notable Australian sitcom that aired the laundry of the dark mother archetype was 'Mother and Son', where Ruth Cracknell played a mother who wafted in and out of dementia as a way of tightening her apron strings, which were firmly placed around her live-in son's neck! The series illustrated the darker side of a woman who defines herself only as a mother and cannot bear her young to fly the coop.

Earth Empress Makeover Kit

The following pages include practical ways that you can coax your inner Demeter to stand proud as the fertility Goddess that she is, ranging from foods to sample and places to visit. Use this makeover kit as a tour guide to embrace all that she has to offer.

Suggested Styles

Clothes are not the ultimate priority for Demeter, who is happy to wear anything that allows her to get on with the task at hand. That said, you may find it helpful to know her preferences to help integrate your own inner Demeter.

- *Earthy, Autumnal colours are great such as olive green, chocolate, bronze and red (the colour of the mother phase).*
- *Smock-like clothes, often because of pregnancy but also out of comfort, as Demeters often prefer clothes that drape the curves of the feminine form rather than cut them into tailored lines that mimic the masculine appearance.*
- *Head scarves that keep the hair out of one's eyes and artfully cover a bad hair day.*
- *No make-up usually because there's no time and if you kiss your baby you will cover them in lipstick.*
- *Peasant blouses, gypsy style romantic clothes.*
- *Sandals, slip-ons, scuffs and slippers. (The rule is anything comfortable and easy on your back.)*
- *Plaited hair, hair dyed with henna or cut into something more manageable than the maiden's long locks, but soft enough to express one's feminine nature.*
- *Long skirts (befitting more mature women who prefer to contain their flesh rather than advertise their physical assets).*
- *All-purpose, comfortable pants (you can put on in a hurry and drive children to their destination without thinking).*
- *Wraps, shawls and cardigans – articles of clothing that enfold and nurture you.*
- *Little or no jewelry (preferring a simple, natural appearance often dictated by chores and little hands that threaten to yank anything that dangles).*
- *Sensible singlets, thermal tops, skivvies and big cotton undies that will accommodate a Mama-sized booty.*
- *Larger bra sizes for lactating mums or just because you've put on a few pounds. In fact larger sizes in general, as you become more grounded and less flighty.*
- *Hand-knitted, woven or home sewn items – because when you wear them you are wrapping yourself in love.*

Earth Empress Colours

Green

Just as in Mother Nature, Demeter represents the evergreen, renewable quality of growth. Green is also the colour of the heart charka, so it has a calming effect upon us when we wear it or use it as a shade in our home décor.

Earthy Colours

Autumnal colours such as auburn, gold, red and all shades of brown reflect the colours of the Empress and her down-to-earth nature.

Earth Empress Associated Chakra

Heart

The heart is the balance point between the upper and lower energy centres. To reside in the heart is to love all with compassion and without judgment, expressing true unconditional love. To assist this chakra in clearing energy blocks, consider having energy healings or something that is physically nurturing such as massage, yoga, pilates or aromatherapy. The colour resonance of the heart chakra is both green and pink.

Earth Empress Essential Oils

Neroli

This is a calming antidepressant and enhances feelings of happiness, as well as strengthening one's health.

Rose

Rose Bulgar and Rose Maroc are both pregnancy-safe and assist us in being heart-centered.

Earth Empress Minerals, Crystals and Stones

Green Apophyllite

This helps one to face and integrate new perspectives towards oneself and life in general. It promotes growth and openness, as well as calming and balancing the heart.

Lolite

Also known as water sapphire, it facilitates the acceptance of new responsibilities and eliminates discord, confusion and toxicity.

Jade

This strengthens heart, kidneys and the immune system. It Increases longevity and fertility, assists female reproductive problems, dispels negativity, creating peaceful, nurturing feelings towards self and others. It radiates unconditional love and balances emotional well-being.

Labradorite

This is helpful during times of change, strengthening self-reliance, patience, inner knowing and perseverance. Reduces anxiety and assists digestion of foods and new experiences.

Stone, Wood and Mud

Demeter represents tangible foundations and creations that are built from sustainable natural resources.

Earth Empress Flower Essences

The following are vibrational essences which Distil the healing properties of various plants. When taken orally they promote emotional balance and wellbeing.

Elm

Elm is good when feeling overwhelmed and having self-doubt in relation to responsibilities.

Oak

This assists one with the stamina to keep going when the going gets tough and demanding.

Heather

Strengthens the ability to 'be there' for others, emotionally and energetically.

Red Chestnut

Helps to decrease martyr tendencies and lessen overprotective worry for others.

Pine

May be used to minimize feelings of guilt and over-responsibility for others.

Earth Empress Food

Milk

Demeter is full of 'the milk of human kindness', literally in that it is her feelings of love and nurturance that allow the milk into the ducts whenever a mother thinks of her baby prior to a feed.

Fruits and vegetables

In Demeter rituals (such as baby showers), it is nice to make an altar of harvested fruits and vegetables in honor of Mother Earth's continuing abundance. Many fruits and vegetables have the procreative symbolism of yoni and lingam in their appearance (the Tantric terms for genitalia).

Cereals

(Such as corn, wheat, grains and seeds.) As the Goddess of agriculture, Demeter was worshipped as the ancient Corn Mother.

Honey

As a fertility symbol, honey is a product of those who diligently work for the Queen Bee. Honey is unrefined (like processed sugar), is a natural antibiotic and sweetens our experience of life. Demeter was known as The Pure Mother Bee, who governed our life cycles and her followers baked honey cakes in the shape of yonis to celebrate her gift of life. (Beeswax is therefore also sacred to her and candles or sculptures fashioned from beeswax are ideal for Demeter altars or gifts.)

Earth Empress Flowers

Dandelion

Unlike the rose (Aphrodite's flower), which looks exotic but has thorns and is hard to cultivate, the dandelion is humble, grows easily and is very resourceful, providing many gifts from dandelion wine to dandelion coffee (a great liver tonic).

Sunflower

In the Tarot, the Empress is often portrayed with sunflowers surrounding her to illustrate her radiant full bloom as a woman, with the warmth of the full sun, which she readily offers, bringing cheer to all.

Rose

Roses are symbolic of a heart opening.

Earth Empress Hangouts

Home

It used to be considered that a woman's place was in the home. That was because the Earth Empress archetype was the one that the patriarchal mind-set saw as the life path for a woman. And yes, women with a strong inner Demeter are happy spending a larger portion of their lives in the home, creating a warm and loving hearth for children, pets and loved ones.

Rural Settings

Demeter is very content living close to nature. If she doesn't have fruit trees and a veggie patch in the back yard, she'll at least tender some flowers. Her ideal setting is living in a country cottage preserving jams and pickles, doing home handicrafts and counselling others on the back porch.

Childcare Centres

Often women with a strong Demeter archetype will be found working in childcare, whether they have a large nurturing bosom and a waddling gait like Mother Goose or a strong inner child that can crawl on the floor with the best of them. They also work in hospitals and aged homes. Many Demeter women have an insatiable need to give (that is until the public health care system burns them out), so many opt for early careers as nurses or health care professionals.

Earth Empress Astrological Sign

Cancer

This is the sign of the crab, a creature that reverts into its shell when it feels threatened. Similarly, our personal vulnerabilities are often powerfully evoked with hormonal changes that occur during pregnancy, childbirth and breastfeeding which further anchor the nesting tendencies of our inner Demeter archetype. Cancer is a water sign, and is therefore emotionally sensitive and places a high value on emotional security. Cancerians are also prone to nostalgia and love to nurture others.

Earth Empress Symbols

Below is a list of the Earth Empress's symbols. Should you encounter any of these on a regular basis, take note, for your inner Demeter may be knocking at your door and asking you to look after your health and rest or consider the likelihood of an imminent new project or pregnancy.

The Cornucopia of Abundance

This is also known as the Horn of Abundance as it originally signified the sacred cow Goddesses' horn and all the bounty that flowed forth from her generosity. It's used as a decoration to invoke fertility and abundance from the Mother Goddess.

The Sheaf of Wheat

The Roman name for Demeter was Ceres, from which we derive the word, cereal. As a Goddess presiding over golden harvests, health and nutrition, all grains are symbolic of Demeter, the most common icon being a sheaf of wheat. Mother Earth was honored as the one who gave birth to all grains and the sheaf of wheat represented her son, the dying and resurrected God, whose reaping brought life continually as he was planted in the Underworld for the following harvest.

(Hence, the grim reaper as a harbinger of death.) The Egyptians considered wheat to be the plant of truth and baked it into communion cakes to commemorate the dying God.

Bread

Prior to the inclusion of 'Give us this day, our daily bread' in the Christian Lord's Prayer, Demeter, the patron Grain Goddess to all bakers, mills and ovens, was honored with ceremonial breads such as woven loaves. This practice was invented by Germanic tribe women who had previously plaited and offered their woven hair to the Goddess.

Eggs, Seeds, Babies, Children and Baby Animals

As the creator and protector of all young and defenseless creatures, Demeter is synonymous with all growing things, plant, animal and human in nature. Her nurturing abilities ensure each of these embryonic life forms live to fulfil their potential.

Mother Nature, Earth/Soil

The Mother, Mater, Material, Matter... all things come from the Earth and return to her. It is this reverence for the Earth as a conscious, living cosmic entity that causes great suffering amongst the ancient races who have witnessed colonials cause her such long-term damage in the name of short-term gain. The astrological symbol for Earth is Wotan's cross (see Rabbit under her Animal Totems), which according to Pueblo legend, is the result of Spider Woman's first act of creation, spinning a web from East to West, then from North to South to locate the centre of the Earth.

Pomegranate

Traditionally the Mother Goddess was depicted with a child in one hand and a pomegranate in the other. The pomegranate was known as the 'Apple of Many Seeds' and was the fruit of wisdom that Demeter's daughter Persephone ate during her time in the Underworld.

The Astrological Mandala

As a symbol of the changing cycles, the astrological mandala can also be considered as a totem of Demeter.

Earth Empress Totem Animals

The following is a list of domestic animals that like the Earth Empress, have all given both their creations and their bodies in service to the continual life cycle.

Just as the buffalo was worshipped for its generosity by the Native Americans for providing them with meat and skin for clothes and shelter, try taking the time to honor the presence and gifts of the following brothers and sisters from our animal kingdom in your life and you will be a true domestic Goddess in your heart and soul. (Since breastfeeding I have looked at cows with incredible reverence, gratitude and sadness that their offering is so often taken for granted).

Hen

Similar to Mother Goose, the hen is a symbol of the Mother aspect who patiently nurtures her young, by tending the nest and waiting for her eggs to hatch. Hence the terms hen-pecked, chick (maiden) and hen house – all derogatory colloquialisms that subtly denigrate the Earth Empress archetype in our culture as a subject of mockery whose input is not to be taken seriously. Our modern 'Hen's Night' can be interpreted as the rite of passage where a woman goes from being a spring chicken to a mother hen.

Cow

The cow has long played the role of wet nurse to the human race, supplying milk on which we wean our young. The Goddess in India has always been worshipped as a sacred cow, and within many other cultures, such as the ancient Egyptians, Scandinavians and Greeks, the cow has been revered as a sacred feminine symbol.

Pig

The classic Greek term for pig, 'cunnus', was interchangeable with the word cunt and both were revered as holy by followers of the Goddess. (Incidentally, the word, cunt, comes from the Latin, cunnus, which innocently means vulva. It was only puritanical Christian priests that referred to cunts as 'devilish' that over time demonized this word). As such, the pig was considered a meat that should be set apart and only eaten at sacred feasts, hence the custom of buying a leg ham at Christmas. Pigs as a farmyard animal with many teats upon which their young can suckle are another animal associated with the Goddess of agriculture, Demeter.

Rabbit

As a symbol of fertility, the hare or rabbit is synonymous with Demeter in her aspect as the fertility Goddess, Eostre. Her totem was the moon hare, the earlier version of the man in the moon who was said to lay eggs once a year for good children to eat. It is from this spring celebration of birth and renewal that some Easter customs have derived, with the moon hare now being known as the Easter Bunny.

Earth Empress Relative Parts of the Body

Womb, Ovaries and Fallopian Tubes

Often women who have problems with the health of these areas need to resolve some of their Demeter issues. For instance, they may need to nurture their needs, forgive their mothers for not fulfilling all of their own needs or reconnect with and heal their relationship with their inner feminine, which is demanding their urgent attention through physical pain.

Breasts

Breast cancer has been steadily increasing in the West with the growing toxicity of our food, air and water, which is then stored in our lymph nodes and fatty breast tissue. If we continue to not heed this warning to nurture the planet and ourselves with responsible and sustainable cultivation and production of our food, air and water, our mammary glands will continue to sound the alert.

EARTH EMPRESS INNER MAKEOVER ACTIVITES

It's time to roll up the sleeves, grab your journal and a comfy possie on the couch (and maybe a cup of tea) and get down to some inner housework with your inner Demeter.

I am not my Mother!

This activity is particularly good for women who find their mother extremely annoying (or perhaps their mother-in-law). Similarly, women who have a strong Persephone (rebellious daughter) or Athena (career woman) archetype will also benefit by positively anchoring the blueprint of their inner mother.

Step One: Write down ten good traits or strengths of your mum's.

Step Two: Stop and reflect on each trait and ask whether you see and value that trait in both your mum and yourself or, alternatively, whether you deny or denigrate it in any way.

Step Three: Make a check-list of traits your dad valued in your mum and whether or not he sees and values those traits in you.

Step Four: Write down ten of your mum's flaws or fears and consider how these traits in your own psyche affect you.

Mary, Mary, Quite Contrary, How does my Garden Grow?

It stands to reason that we emulate the role models that life has given us, be it conscious or otherwise. This following activity will enable you to see what thought and behavioural patterns influence the way you nurture your own needs.

Step One: In your journal, draw ten circles large enough to write in. Label the circles with the following headings:

- *Spiritual*
- *Social*
- *Intellectual*

- *Financial*
- *Health*
- *Physical Exercise*
- *Emotional Sexual*
- *Relaxation*
- *Creative*

Step Two: Under each of the following headings write down how your mum nurtured her needs in each of those areas. (To the best of your knowledge.)

Step Three: Write down how you nurture or neglect yourself in each of these areas in your own life. Note any similarities and write down any suggestions as to how you can improve upon the current status quo.

The Four Seasons

Designate four pages in your journal and mark them: Autumn, Winter, Spring and Summer. Now choose four different pieces of music, one for each of the seasons. (If you can't find four different tracks just put on some relaxing music to complete the exercise.) Starting with Autumn, allow the music to evoke feelings of loss and draw how this makes you feel. It may bring forth what it is you need to let go of in your life for further growth. Then progress on to Winter – focusing on what it is that you are gestating, Spring – what you wish to birth and bloom and finally Summer – a picture of what you hope to harvest in this annual cycle.

What's in a Name?

As meter is the Latin root for mother, *Demeter*, the mother Goddess was referred to as *Mother of the Grain, Mother of the Maiden, The Grain Goddess, The Empress, Grain Mother and Queen of the Harvest*. Germanic tribes worshipped Demeter as the Goddess, Berchta or Perchta and used to braid both their hair and breads in honor of her.

You may wish to take the opportunity to reflect upon some of the names that you've encountered that denigrate the mother archetype and how that's affected your willingness or reluctance to embody and integrate this archetype in your own life. After all, sticks and stones may break your bones but names will subconsciously affect your choices if you don't acknowledge how they've altered your perspective! Here's a few I could think of:

Big Mamma, Mommie Dearest, Mother-in-Law from Hell, Monster-in-Law, Evil Stepmother, Matriarch, Silly Cow, Fat Cow, Stupid Woman, Barefoot and Pregnant, Daggy Mum, Suburban and *Breeder.*

Put Yourself Front and Center

Make a list of all the ways you prefer to live through others rather than embrace your own reality, for example reading about celebrities, watching drama or reality TV series, living through your children/partner or reading fantasy novels. Commit to beginning one thing that you'd like to do such as learn piano or life drawing. You may wish to consider what skills you have to barter.

Art Therapy: Make a Harvest Map

Grab as many great magazines as you can find, particularly home interior and personal development periodicals, and cut out all the pictures of what it is you would like to manifest in your life. Then take a piece of card and divide it into quadrants of your life, such as home, family, creative projects, adventures and glue the various pictures and words on to make a collage. Next new moon, take your manifestation map out and ask Grandmother Moon to assist you in clearing blocks and creating opportunities to manifest all that is depicted on your map if it is for your highest good.

Embracing your Earth Empress: Further Suggestions

- Before you go to sleep each Sunday night, lie in bed and write down a list of all the things you have to be grateful for. (Don't forget the simple pleasures like sunsets.)
- Educate those around you to respect your needs. Take time out on your own to see a film, have a bath or relax in a hammock with a good book.
- Take yourself out into the garden and spend some time with your fingers in the earth, weeding during the two weeks after a full moon or planting new seeds or seedlings in the two weeks leading up to a full moon. Even just walking around bare foot will strengthen your Earth connection and your physical immunity, as will lying on the grass.
- Start honoring your physical body by doing a simple daily practice such as juicing in the morning or stretching in the afternoon. Start gently.
- Get in touch with your natural cycle by learning to chart your fertility levels.
- Purchase a moon-planting poster so you can regularly check what astrological sign the moon is in every two and a half days. Great for gardening and planning all manner of activities. For example, rest at dark moon, party at full, start new projects at the new moon and celebrate or meditate at the Equinoxes and Solstices.
- Be resourceful. Find creative ways to improve your quality of life. Consider clothes swaps, making jams, sauces or chutneys with friends, having a garage sale or market stall, altering your clothes by adding braids, or making homemade gifts or cards.
- Try going out without make-up and wearing clothes that are comfortable.
- If not a mum, consider offering to babysit for a friend or family member or register with a local hospital to nurse new-born babies of drug-affected parents who need love and physical

touch for their survival. Alternatively, you may wish to consider sponsoring a child or volunteering at your local school or kindergarten.

- If you are a mum, make a date to have the kids babysat so you can pamper your needs with a good book and a bath, a lunch with friends or a night at the cinema or theatre on a regular basis.
- Detoxify by drinking water with lemon every day, eating natural yoghurt and massaging your breasts to help drain the lymph nodes of toxicity, a contributing factor in breast cancer. Consider a juice fast every Spring Equinox. (See the Wise Up section for details.)
- Allow your inner child some playful activity each week to keep you light-hearted and balanced. For example, crayon drawing to music, totem tennis or a board game.
- Get Earthy! Compost your veggie scraps, give egg cartons to a kinder, take canvas bags or a shopping trolley to the market, buy free-range eggs or visit a community farm or garden.

Get Wise

Here is a list of book titles you may wish to check out for further Earth Empress insights and advice. The first few focus on the psychological archetype of the mother and the rest are practical handbooks for health, fertility, community-building, baking and gardening.

Earth Empress Non-Fiction

Goddesses in Everywoman by Jean Shinoda Bolen

The Goddess Within by Jennifer Barker Woolger and Roger J Woolger

The Goddess Path by Patricia Monaghan

The Mask of Motherhood by Susan Maushart

Natural Fertility by Francesca Naish

Eve's Wisdom – Traditional Secrets of Pregnancy, Birth and Motherhood by Deborah Jackson

The Body is the Barometer of The Soul By Annette Noontil

The Good Life in the '90s by Mary Moody

Diet for a Small Planet by Frances Moore Lappe

The Different Drum by Scott Peck (The Creation of True Community)

The Moosewood Cookbook and The Enchanted Broccoli Forest by Mollie Katzen

The 3 Day Energy Fast by Pamela Serure

Casting the Circle by Diane Stein (rituals for yearly cycles)

Fitonics for Life by Marilyn Diamond and Dr Donald Burton Schnell

Topics for Discussion

Below are a few conversation starters that you may like to share with your female friends regarding the relationship you have with your mum or as a mum yourself:

- How have you tried to emulate your mum and how have you tried to do the opposite of what she would do?
- What qualities and actions do you think make someone a good mum? How have you been pressured to have children and, if so, by whom? How do you cope with your own inner dark mother?
- What personal rituals or celebrations could you weave into your family life to mark the changing seasons, years and life changes?

Questions for Personal Reflection

So much of our day-to-day behaviour happens on auto-pilot so it's helpful to do a little internal digging to review some of the core beliefs that stop us from positively anchoring our own inner mother to ensure our own emotional and physical needs are met. Consider the following:

- What belief do I hold true that stops me from prioritizing my need for regular self-nurturing?
- When people give to me, do I feel uncomfortable like a debt needs to be repaid as soon as possible? If so, why?
- What do I honestly think would happen if I didn't try to be everything to everybody?

Secret Woman's Business:
Best Times to Celebrate Demeter

The 'Eleusinian Mysteries' was the major religious festival celebrated by the Ancient Greeks for over 2000 years. It was held over seven days during the Autumn Equinox each year and worshippers would re-enact the abduction of Demeter's daughter, Persephone, and her triumphant return from the Underworld amid much feasting. It is believed that through this festival, her followers experienced a sense of the continual renewal of life. More than a million people were said to be initiated at the 'Eleusinian Mysteries which finally came to an end in the 5th Century AD when the invading Goths destroyed her sanctuary at Eleusis. The Autumn Equinox falls on March 21st (Southern Hemisphere) and September 21st (Northern Hemisphere).

Lughnasad is the ancient harvest festival celebrated on February 2nd (Southern Hemisphere), August 2nd (Northern Hemisphere). Alternatively, choose the closest new moon to these dates. This is a great time to make pasta sauce with friends using fresh garden tomatoes. Also a good time to make pickles, preserves or bake a loaf of bread, plaiting in your wishes for the coming year ahead which you could either eat or varnish and hang as a wreath of abundance. (I once lived with German women who made bread in the shape of the men they were hoping to marry!)

Earth Empress Rite of Passage Ceremony

The following is a seed planting ritual, which can be done annually. (I once did this ritual with some Russian women and the pumpkin seeds planted took off like the sequel to Jack and The Beanstalk!)

You Will Need:

Rich soil

Flowers

A small pot or patch of

Garden Seeds

Please Note: Check it's the appropriate time to sow them, both on the packet and on a moon-planting calendar. A good rule of thumb is to plant in the two weeks leading up to full moon. Note: I particularly like to use bulbs for this rite because they're nice and big to hold.

Step One: Letting Go

Place your hands in the Earth and take a scoop. Then sit, holding the soil, charging it energetically with all the things in your life that you wish to let go of with grace. (You may wish to play some background meditation music to assist in consecrating your ritual space.) When you are ready, declare what you are letting go of as you place the soil in the pot, composting the old energies to nourish the new.

Step Two: Planting the New

Now hold your seed and meditate on what it is you wish to plant and nurture in your own life. Declare what you are going to nurture in your life as you plant the seed in the pot. (Be sure to give it a drink of water immediately.)

Step Three: Invoking Demeter

Sit on the ground and create a magic circle around you using flowers that you individually bless by speaking all that you have to be grateful for. Now close your eyes, take your awareness into your heart and breathe in three deep green breaths, silently asking Demeter to anchor within you her acceptance of all that is.

Earth Empress Act of Beauty

Consider now creating your green mandala depicting all the symbols and images that your inner Earth Empress suggests to you. You may wish to draw, paint, sew or create a collage of the cycles of Mother Earth or the bounty of her harvest. Next, create your personal green altar to honor the blossoming gifts of your inner Earth Empress over the coming month.

ARTEMIS: THE INNER MEDICINE WOMAN

The Inner Medicine Woman is the fifth soul sister we encounter on our journey through the seven feminine selves. She is the part of us that needs space from our everyday concerns to attend to our wounds be they emotional, spiritual, physical or intellectual. In befriending our Inner Medicine Woman we learn to use gentleness as our greatest strength and to forgive those who have taught us our most painful life lessons.

How I Discovered My Medicine Woman

When I was seventeen, I moved to another town twelve hours away from home to study performing arts at university. Whilst my Dad was driving me there, my Mum called a removalist and cleared out our family home. Disturbed by her secrecy, I didn't speak to her during the three years I was at uni. During this time, my father (who I'd never been close with) met his second wife and my brother was sent to live in foster care as a result. This chain of events, coupled with the societal pressure put on young girls to appear sexually alluring and available left me looking for love in all the wrong places (as the song goes!). With no female guidance or support my personal esteem and boundaries weren't accessible so I repeatedly found myself in dangerous and humiliating situations. (A trend I see amplified today with girls shaking their booty surrounded by pimps in video clips, Playboy brand clothes, bling and car accessories and highly sexualized Bratz dolls aimed at girls as young as three!)

The final straw occurred when my female housemates all brought home boyfriends one night and begged me to share my single bed with one of their male friends who had nowhere else to sleep, despite me insisting that I didn't want to...eventually I conceded. Drunk and not taking no for an answer he forced himself upon me and I ended up pregnant. Too ashamed of my predicament I then lied to both my lecturers and father as to why I needed time away to travel to a city to have an illegal abortion.

After that painful experience I went on the pill and wore men's shirts, jeans and Doc Marten steel cap shoes for seven years, unconsciously disguising my feminine form so I wouldn't receive any unwanted attention that I felt unequipped to deal with.

I then unveiled my sexuality by working in a strip club, where I felt safe on account of the visible presence of security guards. (Except on the one occasion when a patron sexually assaulted me by trying to show off to his young progeny by stuffing a soft cigarette packet into my yoni!)

As I have already mentioned, when I was twenty-six I became so fed up with the hurtful actions of others that I fled to the mountains and lived on my own for a year in a rudimentary cottage.

It was in true Artemis fashion that I learnt to chop wood, use a petrol-powered water pump and rescue native animals that had been hit by weekend motorists.

I clearly remember the day I left the city with my car packed up, as I uncharacteristically screamed at another motorist who had cut me off in traffic. I took this as a confirmation that my time had well and truly arrived to get out of the rat race for some much needed 'R and R' in the loving arms of Mother Nature.

Coincidentally, I had recently met some great mountain women, many of whom were single mothers who regularly attended Goddess circles and to my delight, they invited me to join them. I then saw a local doctor who put me on sickness benefits and for three months I cried, expressing all the emotional pain I had unwittingly suppressed in my effort to soldier on with life. I wanted someone to distract me from myself, anything to alter my uncomfortable feelings. I remember wanting to draw flowers to cheer myself up, but instead felt incapable of depicting anything pretty as my internal landscape was wrapped in a lethargic blanket of internal fear and unexpressed rage.

Just as the leadlight dragon on the door of my cottage indicated, I could not escape confronting my inner demons. The solar-powered generator, my sole source of power, was unable to run a computer or television, leaving me literally cut off from the outside world, with no newspapers or magazines at my disposal due to my isolation and strict petrol budget.

I spent time on my own, getting re-acquainted with my natural self and only socializing occasionally with other women, whom I sought much comfort from whilst tending to my wounds in my attempt to understand and heal my psyche.

In true Artemis style I did enjoy some intimacy in the woods with a lovely man. He was indeed a gift from the Gods, an Italian Adonis who had five planets in Libra (ruled by Venus) and genuinely knew how to cherish a woman. Despite the deeply healing sexual encounters we shared, I blew him off insensitively when I returned to the city to be with another man. It wasn't until seven years later that I was given the opportunity to acknowledge how I had personified the shadow side of Artemis, being so caught up in my own wounds that I failed to see how I had hurt another.

While living in the mountains I was initiated into the mysteries by a wonderful High Priestess who was serving her own Artemis apprenticeship whilst living away from the city life. A truly inspirational Earth angel, Jen Powell, mentored me on the Goddess archetypes, wiped the tears from my cheek and inspired me to surround myself with a library of books and begin my sabbatical in earnest. This new direction so ignited my passion that I eventually resolved to heed my calling as I stood on my porch and declared to the universe that I would dedicate my life to serving the Goddess. It was from that day on that I decided to only use my priestess name, Tanishka instead of my childhood name, Tania.

My second initiation with Artemis came during my eight years as a single mother when I had to learn how to provide for and protect both myself and my child. This involved numerous challenges, including homelessness which took me to the brink and demanded I expose my vulnerability and ask for help from my sisterhood. The hardships my daughter and I endured during these years strengthened my resolve to be an agent for global social change. So I could do my part to reduce the numbers of single parents raising children in poverty with little support.

MEDICINE WOMAN QUIZ

Answer the following quick quiz to find out what shape your inner Medicine Woman is currently in. (Circle the answer that most describes you.)

You break up with your partner, do you:

A. Beg them to take you back for fear you cannot live without him/her?

B. Bad mouth him/her to anyone who will listen?

C. Look forward to spending quality time with yourself?

You are driving alone when you get a flat tyre, do you:

A. Apply fresh lipstick and wait beside the car for a man to stop?

B. Call your auto club and stay inside the car until their arrival?

C. Get out and fix it yourself?

A friend suggests you join her in attending a women's weekend retreat, do you:

A. Make a joke about the sort of women who will attend?

B. Refuse? You don't do things with groups of women.

C. Accept and feel excited by the prospect?

Now add up your score. A = 1, B = 2, C = 3. *If you scored:*

1 – 3 Your inner Medicine Woman currently has an arrow through her head but won't look into a mirror to notice. This next chapter may hit a raw nerve but will help liberate you in the long run.

4 – 6 Your inner Medicine Woman is shy but wants to feel the power of flexing her own muscles. You will pick up a few helpful tips in the next chapter.

7 – 9 Bull's Eye! Your Inner Medicine Woman has her eye on the target and can't miss! Enjoy reading the following chapter.

Herstory: Medicine Woman Goddesses

In this chapter we get better acquainted with Artemis, the ancient Greek Goddess who lived alone, rescuing and healing wounded young girls and animals. Some other names Artemis is known by include Ursula, derived from Ursa Major, her constellation and Ursel, the she-bear, by the Saxons. Like many of the early Goddesses, Ursula became canonized as a Christian saint. She was also known as Diana or Goddess Anna in Latin; Saranyu, the Hindu mother Goddess of all creatures and in Sparta as Artamia which meant cutter or butcher. Another of her titles is Enodia, the divine midwife. The Helveticans (now Swiss) called her Artio, which the Celtic peoples shortened to Art, coupling her with their bear king, Arthur. (For an account of the ritualized stag hunt that coupled King Arthur with a representative of the Goddess, a priestess chosen from the ancient mystery school known as Avalon, read Marion Zimmer Bradley's novel, *The Mists of Avalon* or watch it on DVD.)

The Myth of Artemis

Artemis's mother, Leto, is believed to have hatched Artemis (a symbol of the moon) and her twin brother, Apollo (the sun), out of the cosmic world egg. As an earthly representative of the moon, Artemis was appointed to serve women of the world.

Artemis was destined not to marry, forever remaining 'a woman unto herself', dedicating her life to the service of others. She chose Arcadia as her home in the mountains (signifying her desire to gain higher insight), accompanied by her hounds and nymphs. This was also the home of the woodland god, Pan, who chased nymphs regularly to satisfy his lust, and Artemis found herself forever protecting those nubile maidens who could not protect themselves from him and his hunters. On one occasion a hunter named Acteon happened upon Artemis and her priestesses swimming naked in a river. When Artemis caught sight of the peeping tom, she used her shape-shifting powers in rage to turn him into a stag and he was set upon and savaged by his own hunting hounds.

Artemis had a twin brother, Apollo the sun God, but she had very little to do with him and men in general. The only man to capture her heart was a hunter named Orion, but unfortunately for Artemis she related to him more as a brother than a lover. Eventually she fell victim to her own competitive nature when Apollo challenged her to reach a target several miles out to sea with her bow and arrow. She took up the wager, realizing, after the successful execution, that the target was in fact Orion. She had killed him instantly.

Artemis was also renowned for her ferocious temper. One myth explains she would unleash the Calydon Boar that wreaked havoc on the countryside and its people whenever she felt offended. No male was successful in killing the wild boar. It was instead, a young heroine called Atalanta who stood her ground, waiting bravely until the boar was almost upon her before spearing it through the eye, its only vulnerability.

Although Artemis was a huntress, accustomed to a harsh outdoor life, fending for herself and teaching others to do the same, she regularly indulged in excursions to the theatre, where she would dress in her finery and attend operatic performances, classical symphonies or vocal recitals, often joining in the choir of muses and graces. To protect her softer side, Artemis studied the creatures she cohabited with and could literally take on their likeness, camouflaging herself whenever necessary to outsmart her enemies. She was a *now you see her, now you don't* Goddess, who could literally disappear into the forest like a wild animal.

The Moral

Having attempted and destroyed her only possible partnership with Orion, Artemis illustrates that if we wish to have a harmonious and sustainable union with our opposite, we need to connect with our receptive feminine energies rather than attack the masculine principle in a spirit of competition and war. Her destructiveness toward others, symbolized by the ranting boar that was unleashed every time she lost her temper, indicates that when we haven't resolved our own wounds, we unconsciously react, attacking and wounding others. (Artemis therefore reconnects with her disowned vulnerability through the gentle art of music.)

Further facts

Although considered a virgin Goddess, Artemis did take lovers and usually preferred to make love in the woods. Often she took female lovers, who mirrored the feminine part of her that needed to be healed and embraced. She only took male lovers who proved to her that they respected her boundaries and need for seclusion.

Artemis was an Amazonian moon Goddess, the Amazons being a tribe of female warriors who removed their right breasts to make it easier to draw a bow when hunting and fighting. The Greeks claimed that the Amazonians mated with men from other tribes but only kept and reared the female children. Historically, the Amazonian army was a feared force whose female soldiers fought in the lands of Libya, Anatolia, Bulgaria, Greece, Armenia and Russia. One of their most famous battles took place during the Trojan War when they fought against the Greek army. This conflict resulted in the death of the reigning Amazonian queen, Penthesilea, who was slain by the Greek hero, Achilles who was rumoured to be infatuated with her.

The fact it took another woman to kill the Calydon boar suggests that no man is able to appease the temperament of a woman on the war path. This can only be done by another woman, who can mirror her soul and understand the core wound that is the cause of the problem. This explains why women find valuable insights when discussing their relationship issues with other women, rather than just going head to head with their partner and why traditional cultures always valued single sex spaces and ceremonies.

Historical Appearance

Being an active Goddess, artworks of Artemis depict her with a muscular physique. Many sculptures of Artemis show her wearing a chiton (a type of short dress tied at the waist), often with one breast exposed. In fact, one image of her unearthed at Ephesus showed her entire torso covered in breasts, indicating her ability to nurture many others simultaneously.

As a moon Goddess the crescent moon is also synonymous with Artemis, revealing her status as a virgin, rather than a matron, which the full moon would suggest. This is why she is often represented wearing pale blue, the colour of cool moonlight that indicates the receptive quality of her reclusive nature. Blue is also the colour ray of healing. Sometimes she is portrayed wearing wings or feathers that signify her preparation for flight, either fear-based or transcendent, depending on her degree of acceptance and healing.

One of the earliest Artemis statues to have been uncovered is dated 6000 BC and was found in the ancient region of Catal Huyuk in Anatolia. It depicts her sitting on a throne or birth stool, which is supported by leopards or lionesses, with a new-born head crowning from her vulva. Hence her title, Mountain Mother – she who forms the world by flinging rocks from her apron.

Further facts

The myth of Artemis can be traced back to the sacrificial rites of the Neolithic peoples. In the ancient town of Taurus, priestesses of Artemis led by their High Priestess, Iphigeneia, nailed the head of any man who landed on their beaches to a cross. Similarly, in the Greek city of Hierapolis, her worshippers killed and hung their male victims on artificial trees in their temples and in Attica, Artemis was regularly honored with blood spilled from a man's neck. (So ladies, let's not point the finger at men as the only ones capable of needlessly spilling blood.) Later rituals replaced men with bulls, hence Artemis was honored by the title, Tauropolos meaning 'bull slayer'.

Medicine Woman Profile

Artemis represents our need to discover our true identity. This is ultimately a passage we must all undergo to understand our past choices and form new ones that will serve us better in the future.

As an archer, she indicates our need to first understand ourselves before setting our sights on what we want, otherwise we seek out that which may do us harm. Integrating Artemis involves contemplating what our inner needs are, for unless we understand our choices and what drives us to make them, subconsciously we will be destined to continually repeat our past mistakes, becoming bitter and less trusting with each wounding.

The inner Medicine Woman represents a need to honor, respect and give time to ourselves in order to strengthen our commitment and principles, heralding a voyage of discovery to reclaim the strengths of the feminine, to heal our inner wounds and celebrate who we are as a unique woman. Travelling is often a great way for women to connect with their inner Artemis, seeking out an adventure where they will have to rely on their wits and inner resources to get by.

Many young women now spend considerable time on their own before settling down with a life partner, affording them the psychological space to develop their inner Artemis. However, women who married before the sexual revolution of the 1960s, are currently walking away from marriages and discovering Artemis for the first time in their middle-age. Alternatively, for those serial daters with a strong Aphrodite archetype who secretly feel worthless when single, Artemis time is a tonic best taken before they become so disillusioned they give up on men altogether.

Often a catalyst such as separation, divorce or bereavement initiates our inner Artemis. During this time we can feel an inner desire to express our fierce individuality and reclaim our independence by living on our own, changing back to our maiden name or changing our appearance. Often we make a conscious choice to set ourselves apart for a time, particularly from the world of flirting with and dating men. Not surprisingly, Artemis is often a patron Goddess for women who actively seek out the company of women as companions and lovers.

Artemis time allows us the opportunity to reconnect with ourselves, enabling us to call back scattered energies, re-group and gain a fresh perspective on our life whilst residing far away from the madding crowd. The inner Medicine Woman reminds us of the value of solitude and the gifts and hidden strengths we can find within ourselves if we make the time. As a patron of wild, unprotected places, Artemis leads us psychologically into those old, frightening places that bring healing as we journey through our fears. So it is understandable when our vulnerability surfaces to be healed that many of us feel the urge to head to the hills and seek sanctuary in the quietude of nature.

The Artemis archetype was highly visible during the feminist liberation movement of the 1960s and 70s which sought to gain external female power by focusing on the exterior conflict often at the expense of their own individual healing journeys. Forty years later with the gift of hindsight we are learning to replace this outward rage with a more holistic outlook as we seek to understand ourselves and our own shadow. This shift of focus will ultimately allow women to reclaim empowerment first internally, then externally with grace and wisdom by understanding and embodying the strengths of the inner Medicine Woman.

When our inner Artemis is not consciously understood we can disown our feminine sensitivity for fear of appearing weak. This is apparent in teenage girls who display a tough confidence similar to the bravado of young males. This is common in girls who have older brothers or who have been sexually abused.

Adolescents with a strong Artemis archetype are often quick to embrace rallies and protest campaigns in their earnest desire to right wrongs and usually can't wait to leave home and embark on their own adventure. These are the girls whose mothers will watch from afar, proud of the convictions of their feminist daughters who are attempting to right the injustices that inhibited them culturally as girls.

In the fairy-tale, Little Red Riding Hood, a parable which outlines a young girl's attempt to navigate her way through life to reach the safe psychological destination of the inner Wise Woman, obstacles came in the form of wolfish men who wished to deflower or devour her and pull her off her path at a time in her young life when she can't see the wood for the trees! In this example Artemis represents our need to activate the inner protector (the huntsman in the story) who can speak up and defend us by naming perceived enemies and setting appropriate boundaries on our behalf. I recommend renting the DVD/video 'Into the Woods', a musical by Stephen Sondheim which is a tapestry of several fairy tales and their inherent psychological messages.

Medicine Woman Strengths

The following is a description of how we behave when our inner Medicine Woman is appreciated and expressed:

- I choose to live in an environment that truly honors my inner needs.
- I value my solitude and only spend time with people who demonstrate they are worthy of my trust and friendship.
- I try to find compassion for those who offend me, trusting life will exact its own justice.
- I create and value sisterly and brotherly friendships that give me emotional intimacy.
- I constantly challenge myself by learning new skills, increasing my independence and confidence.
- I like to invest energy in a cause that has great meaning and is personally rewarding.
- I allow myself to discover that the love and trust of another special person is very precious and worth exploring.
- I confront my flaws and own my rage and pain.
- I express outrage on behalf of those who are too intimidated to represent themselves in the face of an aggressor.
- I am loyal to my loved ones and consider their feelings.
- I educate others to 'pick their time' when approaching me and not to interrupt my work without good reason if they want to avoid an abrupt response.
- I don't judge people and their actions as black and white, but rather, appreciate the complexities of each person's path and outlook.
- I connect with and accept my vulnerability, helping me to understand others.
- I try to forgive myself and others for making mistakes.
- I trust myself to discern what is best for me and I then act accordingly.

Medicine Woman Shadow Traits

The following is a description of how we behave when our inner Medicine Woman is not consciously understood and integrated:

- I opt for a life of doing as little as possible for fear of failing or getting hurt by life's disappointments.
- Unable to find adequate self-expression, I feel frustrated or depressed.
- I am fiercely competitive, reactionary and impetuous and I unconsciously hurt others in my desire to create a better life.
- I am sometimes cruel, vengeful and insensitive towards others but only see myself as a victim instead of a perpetrator.
- I tend to react fearfully with a 'fight or flight' response to situations I don't fully understand.

- I can be hot-headed, rash and impatient when a cooler, more sophisticated, creative approach would be more fruitful.
- I sometimes enjoy pursuing men but if they are vulnerable, I quickly distance myself to avoid feeling uncomfortable.
- I deny my own vulnerability and my need for intimacy with someone special to my heart.
- I may rebuff a lover and treat him like an intruder if I lose interest.
- I may see men as the enemy and be blind to the faults of the feminine.
- I may 'trash' women who have taken on more traditional archetypes, such as homemakers and mothers.
- I sometimes lack mercy in my attempt to right perceived wrongs.
- I have a pattern of giving my trust too easily and then swinging completely to the other extreme and mistrusting others completely when hurt.
- I demonise those who hurt me, rather than owning my own lesson.

Medicine Woman Lessons

To balance your inner Medicine Woman's strengths and weaknesses, try the following suggestions:

- Pay attention to the soft thoughts that remind you of your inner needs.
- Ensure you have a time and space to retreat.
- Identify the missing pieces unacknowledged within your psyche and begin recognizing and accepting them.
- Know you have the right to meet your own needs.
- Set clear boundaries with yourself and others so your needs are met.
- Think for yourself instead of always deferring to others for advice.
- Trust yourself that if you set your sights and aim your bow, your arrows will always find their mark through trial and error.
- Learn to rely on yourself to take care of your own needs by attempting to perform tasks that are out of your comfort zone.
- Allow others to care for you when you feel vulnerable.
- Learn to use discernment and trust your intuition when making decisions that affect your wellbeing.
- Develop trust in the divine plan by beginning to trust yourself to handle whatever experiences life offers you.
- Take full responsibility for healing yourself, your expectations and your life.
- Seek solace to reflect and heal temporarily when you need to rather than hiding indefinitely from life experiences.

Medicine Woman Relationship Patterns

Personal

The most important relationships we encounter when activating and integrating our Artemis archetype are those we experience with other women. You may notice a stage in your life when you feel the urge to seek out female company, live alone or live in an all-female household. I remember breaking up with a partner and needing to find a new residence and the only mantra running through my head was, 'Get thee to a nunnery'. Sure enough, I moved into a house with three other priestesses, all of whom were single and doing their inner Medicine Woman healing journey.

During this intense time of re-evaluation and self-reflection, other women tend to act as valuable mirrors, validating our strengths when we need to reaffirm our individuality.

Many women feel instinctively they need their female friends around them when they need to connect with their inner Artemis, even though they have no conscious understanding of the Medicine Woman archetype. Those with a more dominant inner Artemis may renounce people in general, preferring to commune with wildlife in order to hear themselves think. Since Artemis is not a pin-up role model employed by the patriarchs to emulate, many women feel extremely uncomfortable at even the thought of being on their own and so miss healing and learning from their wounds. They then run the risk of diving into another relationship only to repeat past mistakes.

Although Artemis is the first to champion society's underdogs, she is often the first to inflict wounds upon others, albeit unconsciously. Artemis women who have disowned their femininity for fear of experiencing vulnerability may lash out at another to unconsciously defend their emotional wounds should their vulnerability be exposed.

Often Artemis dominant women who have been sexually abused by men or experienced a dysfunctional mother/daughter relationship find lesbian relationships can be valuable in healing their disowned vulnerability. But regardless of our sexual orientation, when forming intimate relationships, our inner Artemis only feels safe to commit when we first establish a solid foundation of friendship so trust can develop whilst honoring our need for personal space.

If we fail to do our 'Artemis Journey' to find ourselves, we unconsciously fear committing to someone else for fear of losing ourself or making the wrong decision. Whether you are intimate emotionally and/ or physically with other women, a reconnection with the universal Great Mother, female friends and mentors all play a significant role in our journey to reclaim our feminine essence.

If the Medicine Woman is a strong part of your psyche you may be immune to falling in love, preferring to take care of yourself without the responsibility of caring for others. This decision is particularly liberating for women who have grown up with the traditional expectation that their purpose in life should be to take care of one man. However, beware that shunning a relationship can become a justification for women who are afraid of experiencing intimacy for fear that others will impose upon them their values and decisions, rather than respect their own independence. It is important for women with strong Artemis energy to maintain their identity in a relationship, even though such symbolic means as maintaining their maiden name or insisting on being addressed as Ms instead of Mrs after they marry. Many women who identify strongly with Artemis won't feel compelled to have children and will lead a less domestically-demanding life.

Some Medicine Women prefer to evade possibilities for true intimacy by having casual sex, using others as they themselves may have been used in the past, unconsciously acting out what has been done to them in an effort to understand it. They may appear fierce as a means of screening potential partners, rather than expose their vulnerability. Other Artemis dominant women retreat so far into their intellect that they become emotionally unavailable both to themselves and others, for fear of being hurt and losing control. All of these scenarios are pictures of women who are denying their feminine vulnerability and who often display the same cold indifferent characteristic of commitment-phobic men.

In the fairy-tale Snow White, Artemis as the young maiden runs to the forest to take refuge from those who pose a threat to her survival. But as she runs further into unfamiliar territory she becomes more consumed with fear, until she must face her greatest fear, the realization that she is alone in the world. This is in fact her opportunity to embrace her 'all-oneness' with the universe, understanding her interconnectedness with the plant and animal kingdoms. Snow White does this by befriending the mice, the birds, the deer and the Earth elementals, known as dwarfs.

Famous Medicine Women

Women who display the archetype of Artemis have been ridiculed in the past for daring to undertake traditional male pursuits such as hunting and fishing. Characters such as Annie Oakley and Calamity Jane were two such caricatures displaying one-dimensional portrayals of the Lone Wolf archetype in the mid-fifties, both being celebrated when they conformed to a more conventional apron-wearing feminine role.

Thelma and Louise were the 1990s answer to Artemis, with Hollywood creating two heroines who left their unfulfilling relationships to find themselves and walk on the wild side. Unfortunately, it was too confronting for Hollywood to have these women succeed on their lawless mission so the patriarchal arm of the law was enlisted to send these women 'over the edge', and they literally careered over a cliff face to their death as a warning to like-minded women not to buck the system in the wild west. Fortunately, we have seen gutsy Amazons take to the silver screen such as Jennifer Lawrence in 'The Hunger Games' and Angelina Jolie, who embodies Artemis off-screen as a philanthropist and UNICEF ambassador.

As a society we don't often get the chance to honor the life and work of Artemis women as they are often quiet achievers, content to stay out of the limelight and get the job done. It is interesting to note, however, that Lady Diana, Princess of Wales, played out a very public portrayal of Artemis on the world stage. (Diana being the Roman equivalent of the Greek Goddess, Artemis.) First as a virginal young maiden she married Prince Charles (himself a hunter), only to be repeatedly deceived as she placed her naive trust in men who publicly betrayed her. She eventually became a lone public figure, working as a patron for the disadvantaged. She was hunted down unmercifully by the media, intent on capturing her photo for magazines and newspapers.

Other modern day Artemis heroines include Gloria Steinem, Germaine Greer, Barbara Walker and Naomi Wolfe – all of whom have spoken out on the rights of women and the need to address the oppression of the feminine within our patriarchal society.

Medicine Woman Makeover Kit

The following pages list a wide range of suggestions to help you heal and embrace your inner Medicine Woman.

Suggested Styles

Artemis is not a vain Goddess as she values practicality above image, as you would if fending for yourself in the hills! So you may wish to rethink any decision to slip into a ra-ra skirt with pink frills. Chances are, if you find yourself entering into an Artemis stage of your life, you may well find yourself being attracted to the following sorts of apparel:

- *Animal hides.* Look for suede, leather, fur and buckskin. Artemis is after all a warrior and a huntress so if you are not inclined to hunt and skin an animal, consider imitation fabrics or bless second-hand items that come your way.
- *Bones, teeth, claws or wings.* Often when Artemis calls to us we feel drawn to wear the totems of the animals whose medicine will assist our healing journey. Use your intuition and work with what the universe offers you. You may wish to make a medicine pouch for the bones, teeth or claws of animals whose souls have bestowed upon you a personal and timely gift.
- *Boots.* You may find yourself with a sudden hankering for boots. Do not fight it, go with it – because those boots were made for walking and this signifies you have some travelling to do – both inner and outer.
- *Short hair.* Often women going through their Artemis time feel the urge to shave their head or reduce their feminine locks. Our hair contains the vibrations of our past experiences and this often allows one to reset the clock and enjoy a fresh start. It should also be noted that some women hide behind this butch exterior indefinitely.
- *Tattoos.* Body scarification is an ancient tradition used to mark initiations passed by the seeker on their journey home. Rather than merely getting a tatt because you like the look of it, consider the symbolism of the chosen totem so that you are fully aware of this new addition to your skin. You may wish to mark yourself with henna as a temporary substitute for permanent ink.

When I was embracing Artemis while living in the mountains I came across a freshly-killed kookaburra. His mate was still by the side of the road watching and I grieved with her, crying for the life that had just crossed over the veil. I then took the warm body home and removed the wings with an axe, which was extremely confronting but empowering. I then hung them above my fireplace and noticed the silhouette of an Indian chief on the underside. At the end of my period of seclusion I ran my first Goddess workshop and the totem above the door of the institution was a stained glass kookaburra wearing a mortar board. (An emblem which I was told symbolized the laughing teacher.) I loved this explanation as it has long been my mission (inspired by Sesame Street) to use humour as a tool to educate, a philosophy touted by ancient Taoists.

Medicine Woman Colours

Wearing any of the following colours will help soothe any issues that may be surfacing for your inner Medicine Woman. Similarly, take note if someone you know tends to always dress in these colours – chances are they are an Artemis woman who may need some tender loving care, so approach with caution.

Pale Blue

Artemis was often depicted wearing a pale blue chiton (a mini dress tied at the waist). Pale blue is also the colour of the throat chakra so wearing this colour, particularly near the throat, can help you to assert yourself, protecting yourself and your interests.

Brown and Green

Being a woman of nature, Artemis-dominant women tend to favour earthy, practical colours that reflect their down-to-earth nature.

Medicine Woman Associated Chakra

Throat

This is the energy centre that represents our ability to personally express ourselves. Often women experiencing Artemis need to clear their past emotional hurts to regain their inner strength, allowing them to speak freely from this power centre. In addition to speaking your truth and expressing your emotions, singing and chanting are a great way to clear energetic blockages in the throat. The colour ray of healing and of this chakra is light blue. You may wish to also consider additional healing modalities such as rebirthing, toning and sound healing.

Medicine Woman Essential Oils

Petit grain

A nurturing oil that is both protective energetically for the wearer and empowering.

Cypress

This oil eases grief and feelings of loss. It is also purifying and healing, and calms feelings of jealousy.

Citrus oils such as Lime, Lemon and Grapefruit

They uplift, purify and stimulate healing.

Medicine Woman Flower Essences

The following are vibrational essences which distil the healing properties of various plants. When taken orally, they promote emotional balance and wellbeing.

Walnut

Walnut calms feelings of uncertainty and argumentativeness. It assists in determining clear life direction and inner calm.

Water Violet

This is good for when you feel emotionally withdrawn from life. It helps to overcome feelings of self-righteous superiority and false pride.

Olive

Olive is ideal for overcoming complete exhaustion and reconnecting with inner strength and vitality.

Medicine Woman Minerals, Crystals and Stones

Azurite

This crystal is great for assisting personal transformation. It calms the nervous system, cleanses thought and enhances meditation.

Lapis Lazuli

Lapis energizes the throat chakra and dissipates tension and anxiety. It assists mental clarity and psychic connection with the Higher Self and guides. Lapis is a real power stone that helps you to anchor your Higher Self, and was popular with the ancient Egyptians.

Medicine Woman Food

Camping Foods

Trail mix, damper, billy tea and dried fruit are all foods that our inner Medicine Woman can take with her for sustenance when she needs to escape the city and breathe in the fresh air of the wilderness.

Vegetarian/Vegan Foods

As an active campaigner for animal rights, many Artemis women choose meat substitutes such as tofu, tempeh, seitan and miso, as well as a wide variety of nuts, legumes, pulses and sea vegetables. Organic and genetically-modified free foods are also a top priority to ensure the food you are eating actually contains a vital life force. Water that is oxygenated and filtered is also vital. Visit the following websites for more info: *www.hado.net* and *www.earthsoulscience.com*

Cleansing/Fasting Foods

Freshly squeezed vegetable and fruit juices are great for detoxifying your body, which in turn release past emotional blocks that have been suppressed with fats, sugars and alcohol. The raw enzymes found in fresh fruit and vegies also give you an energy boost and assist in both the prevention and cure of disease as they rebuild healthy cells.

Medicine Woman Flowers and Trees

Native Wildflowers

Any growing wild flowers are symbolic of the Goddess of the Wilderness. It is said that if no natives are found in an area, the healing power of that region is lost. Hence the need to repopulate our environment with native plants that reinstate the healing energetic blueprint of the Deva (nature spirit).

Willow and Cedar

Although natives are sacred to Artemis, willow and cedar trees are particularly symbolic of Artemis. As a healing agent, cedar is useful for assisting focus and relaxation and is used as an antiseptic. Willow helps us to access our deepest emotions and is used in ritual to signify the element of water.

Goddess tip

Pay attention to your dreams, Artemis might make a house call! When I was healing some old wounds I had a very vivid dream where I was taken in as an initiate into a circle of older women on a very remote mountain. I remember swimming in a hot spring overlooking the most breathtaking 360-degree mountain top view and I woke up feeling very refreshed and nurtured.

Medicine Woman Hangouts

If you are recently single or need a break from the rat race, consider seeking out some of Artemis's haunts to restore your soul to sanity.

The Wilderness

Artemis is synonymous with the wild places that need to be explored within our psyche for us to find inner peace. It is fitting then that she seeks out those untamed and natural landscapes where she is unlikely to be disturbed or judged while she carries out this important work.

Mountains

The mountains represent the higher perspective that we access when we are elevated above our daily concerns. Mountainous areas, because of their high altitude, are naturally conducive to meditative and altered states that can offer us clarity and insight. This is why traditionally many mystics ranging from Rip Van Winkle to Moses have spent time in solitude 'on the mount' convening with the Divine.

Women's Refuges, Rape Centres and Self-Protection Classes

As a protector and healer of women, Artemis is present as an archetype in shelters and resource centres for battered, raped or abused women who need respite to come to terms with their experience. You will often find women with strong Artemis energy who had an initiation by fire and healed themselves working in such environments.

Animal Sanctuaries and Shelters

Women with significant Artemis energy are often drawn to work with animals. They may work in conservation, veterinary clinics, zoos or they may provide medical aid to sick, injured and neglected animals. These women might have had a fascination with horses as adolescents or worked as a volunteer at animal shelters.

Environmental Protection Authority

Often Artemis women will be found working as an advocate for the environment, this may be in a government bureau such as the Environment Protection Authority or as an activist, researcher or writer.

Girl Guides, All Female Sports and Women's Support Groups

Basically anywhere that's a male-free zone.

Medicine Woman Astrological Sign

Sagittarius

As a fiery sign that focuses on a new direction in life, the sign of Sagittarius best represents Artemis. Also known as The Archer, this sign represents the need to learn through life experience, to become the intuitive philosopher and teacher of higher wisdom later in life. The lesson of Sagittarius is to remember the big picture and rise above trials and tribulations. This helps us to avoid executing a lower tribal form of justice known as 'an eye for an eye' which usually only serves to escalate potential conflict. Like Artemis, people with Sagittarius strongly influencing their natal charts often have a love of freedom and the great outdoors. Coincidentally, the opposite polarity of Sagittarius is Gemini, the sign of the twin – represented by Artemis's twin brother, Apollo. One of the lessons of Sagittarius is not to create harm on the physical plane through thoughtless words and actions so next time the moon is in this sign, be mindful not to sling your barbs insensitively at others. Similarly, when we experience Artemis in our life we need to be mindful that we don't verbally lash out at others before we've taken time to consider and understand our own reaction.

Medicine Woman Symbols

Should you happen upon any of the following imagery – in advertising logos, films, books or in your day-to-day life, consider it a gesture from the Medicine Woman Goddess herself. If this happens repeatedly, try to get some time on your own to heal any unresolved hurts.

Bow, Arrow and Quiver

Arrows were the preferred weaponry for Artemis in her hunt, the arrow being a phallic symbol, as she takes responsibility for her own masculine energy and the direction in which her life is headed. Sometimes the crescent moon is portrayed as her bow.

Crescent Moon

As a virgin Goddess, Artemis is often depicted with the crescent moon. This is because her burgeoning feminine potential hasn't been fully realized as she focuses on developing her masculine side in an attempt to become self-reliant. The light of the new moon indicates her need to illuminate the fears that lay within her subconscious so that she may heal her psyche.

Feathers

Artemis is sometimes referred to as Feather Woman, indicating her affiliation with the wild and free spirits of the skies. She may leave some in your path or you may wish to collect some and make a feather fan for smudging (burning sacred herbs to cleanse ritual areas), or alternatively wear some in your hair.

Medicine Woman Totem Animals

Should you dream of any of the following animals, know that you are being afforded the blessing and protection of the Shaman Goddess, Artemis.

Bear

Artemis is sometimes referred to as the Great She-Bear, the constellation we know colloquially as the Big Dipper. Its official name is Ursa Major, which reflects her role as ruler of the stars and protectors of the axis mundi, the poles of the Earth. (Its seven bright stars were also known as the Seven Sisters.) Artemis was a shape-shifter who could transform herself into many forms, the bear being one of her most popular. The word beserk comes from the bear shirt known as a bear sark which Artemis bestowed upon warriors who demonstrated great courage. At her annual festival in Ancient Attica, priestesses were dressed as bear cubs whom Artemis would fiercely defend.

Dogs and Wolves

Artemis was usually seen accompanied by her hounds, whose instincts and loyalty she trusted implicitly. Artemis was often referred to as The Great Bitch and her priestesses as The Hunting Bitches, signifying their close affiliation with their dogs.

(Hence the slanderous term 'Son of a Bitch', which meant a son of the Goddess, which has long been equated with evil in patriarchal theology.) It was because of the female dog's affiliation with the ancient Goddess that the word bitch has become an insult in modern culture instead of a term of reverence that it once was.

Lioness

The lion was often synonymous with Artemis's twin brother Apollo. In the Major Arcana Tarot card of Strength, a woman is shown taming a lion with the gentleness that comes from possessing true inner strength. It is this characteristic that we need to develop when incorporating Artemis, instead of trying to force others to concede to our will. The lioness and the deer are representative of the two opposing sides of Artemis.

Deer

The deer is also sacred to Artemis as a symbol of the gentleness needed to win her trust and heal her wounds. The male deer or stag was the sacrificial consort of the Goddess. In the myth of Artemis, this was played by the hunter Acteon who stumbled upon her bathing and was consequentially torn apart by his own hunting hounds. The phallic horns on the stag's head represented potent masculine life force and sexuality which Artemis fears until she has healed her earlier wounds. As a result, venison was often served at Artemis feasts.

Medicine Woman Relative Parts of the Body

Throat

When we have a sore throat or lose our voice there is often something we need to speak but are afraid of the consequences if we do.

Neck

This is the bridge between the heart and the head. When we have a pain in the neck we are often caught in indecision between the two.

MEDICINE WOMAN INNER MAKEOVER ACTIVITES

It's one thing to know you're nursing some old wounds, it's another to know how to heal them. Like the word 'patient' suggests, healing takes time and patience, whether the wound is physical, emotional or psychological. So give your inner Artemis the gift of time to focus on completing the following processes to help lighten the load she is carrying.

Create a Timeline

Step One: Draw on a large sheet of paper or in your journal, a line that runs across the width of the page. (I like to draw this as an arrow.)

Step Two: Travelling backwards in time from right to left, mark the major incidents in your life that have caused you to feel hurt or wounded. Write your age and the cause of your hurt.

Step Three: Select one that stands out to you the most.

Step Four: Close your eyes and visualize yourself moving up a spiral into the celestial realms. See yourself as an angelic entity and ask that the soul of the person who wounded you also be present as their Higher Self.

Step Five: In your mind's eye, say whatever it is that you need to say to this person then invite them to respond.

Step Six: See yourselves exchanging scrolls and unravel the parchment you receive. This is the sacred contract that you agreed to complete with this person prior to incarnating. On it is written the lesson that you agreed to learn through this encounter. Now thank this soul for playing out their role on the physical realm for your higher learning.

Step Seven: Repeat this process with the other wounds on your timeline. You will often receive a free flow of insight into the other incidents now that your intuitive channel is open. To save time, you may wish to gather all of the people on your timeline together on the inner plane and thank them collectively.

Reconnecting with the Gentle Doe

Write down ten things about yourself that you feel vulnerable about people seeing or knowing. Go through each point on the list and accept that it's a part of you and forgive yourself for any shame you may feel.

Target Practise to set Boundaries

Step One: Draw on a sheet of paper or in your journal three concentric circles (a target), being sure to leave enough space in each to write.

Step Two: Label the inner circle, Intimate; the middle circle, Friendship; the outer circle, Acquaintance.

Step Three: In the Intimate circle write the names of those people in your life whom you trust to see your vulnerabilities, without fear that they might shame you. (Don't worry if this is only your cat.)

Step Four: Write in the Friendship circle those people whom you trust to see some of your vulnerabilities.

Step Five: In the Acquaintance circle write the names of those whom you don't feel safe to expose your vulnerabilities.

Note: In my workshops many women were surprised to learn that often family members end up in the acquaintance circle. It is important to honor these indications by your inner self so you know where to set your boundaries and with whom, in order to avoid further humiliation or pain due to external pressures to oblige others socially.

Your Fateful Tale

Just as all the old fairy tales are parables of wisdom for the trials and tribulations we encounter on the path, understanding your 'fateful tale' holds the key to unlocking your future happiness. Consider writing your life story to date. You may wish to set yourself a word limit or write it in a particular genre such as rhyme, sleuth or song. By recording your experiences sequentially it is easy to see how your choices have affected the twists and turns in the road you have travelled, making it easy to see repeated patterns that need to be changed.

Coming Back to Yourself

If you have recently become single or widowed, write down the parts of yourself or the pastimes you have given up whilst in a relationship. Make a commitment to yourself to reconnect with those aspects again to feel whole and fulfilled.

Casting the Burden

Think of a fear or burden that has cast a shadow on your faith in the Divine Plan. (Such as an instance when you were generous and it wasn't appreciated or reciprocated, creating a fear that the Divine will not support you in meeting your needs.)

See your fear as a thought form, whether in your body, in your mind or in your energy field and ask telepathically to be assisted by one of your guides, an angelic entity or one of the ascended masters that resonates with you such as the Christ, the Magdalene, Buddha, Shakti or Allah. See the thought form that is your fearful belief being given over to their presence and transmuted back to the light from whence it came.

You are now free to be in peace and at one with the Divine.

You are now free to move where the current of your life takes you, knowing that you are always divinely led and protected. It is only when you view yourself as separate from the creative Divine life force that you will feel afraid. When you take the time to reconnect with the Divine peace of all, you will again surrender into a blissful state.

Know that your life is both a blessing and a teaching.

What's in a Name?

Artemis was commonly referred to as *Mistress of the Beasts,* which refers to her ability to inhabit inaccessible regions of wilderness, surrounded only by the nature kingdom. Her other names include *Magna Mater, Cybele, Rhea, Anath and Artagatis.* The Greeks called her *Meter Theon,* which means Mother of the Gods.

Consider now some of the nicknames that your Artemis archetype has heard or received to date. To get you started I've listed a few I could think of: *Bitch, Butch, Dyke, Tom Boy, Recluse, Man Hater, Snap Dragon, Woman in Army Boots* and *Spinster.*

Art Therapy: Release the Hounds!

Followers of Artemis, called Alani (meaning 'hunting dogs') wore the mask of hunting dogs when they followed Artemis on a nocturnal hunt. Make yourself a shaman's mask, utilizing the medicine and totems of the animal that is assisting you in your healing process. You may find the medicine cards listed in the Get Wise section helpful. (There is also an Australian set of medicine cards available.) When you have finished, consecrate the mask by wearing it in the wilderness under a crescent moon and calling upon Artemis to guide you in finding your inner strength and self-acceptance.

Embracing your Medicine Woman: Further Suggestions

- Go to the wilderness, especially the mountains for a full moon, and notice the effect the lunar light has on the animal life. Animals hunt and sing and run and call out to the moon – join them or perform your own ritual.
- Do something to protect and defend the wild and her creatures. Join the World Wilderness Fund, meditate on their behalf or boycott companies who are destroying natural habitats at an alarming rate. For more info visit *www.AnitaRoddick.com.au*
- Join a choir, chant in the bath or sing whenever you can and if possible arrange a night out at the opera or concert hall at least once a year.
- Organize a day or evening to spend with only female company, nourishing your feminine through the reflection of others.
- Get out of the city on your own or with some other women and enjoy a nature walk or, alternatively, visit an animal sanctuary or fall asleep under the moon and stars.

- Learn to rely on yourself by learning new skills and trying new things, such as changing an oil filter in your car or hang gliding!
- Be a support person at a birth, help out a pregnant friend or spend time mentoring a young girl. (For thousands of years, Artemis has been invoked as a spiritual midwife to protect women in childbirth. The word mid-wife when translated means, with woman.)
- Do an assertion course to assist you in setting boundaries clearly with others or enrol in some self-defense lessons to feel better equipped to protect yourself.
- Look at where you have hurt men, not just the other way round.
- Set up a time or space for yourself where you can retreat regularly to centre yourself, whether it's time to write in a journal or a place to sit and contemplate.
- Give yourself permission to be a recluse. If there is an unresolved hurt from your past, now is the time to heal and resolve it. Allow any tears to flow. Read books on forgiveness; see a spiritual healer or counsellor to help you release any old pain.
- Spend quality time with animals for unconditional love, be they your own or a friend's. Talk to any birds that cross your path.

Get Wise

The following is a list of books that you may wish to check out to assist you in working through your inner Medicine Woman issues.

Medicine Woman Non-Fiction

The Life You Were Born to Live by Dan Millman

Buffalo Woman Comes Singing by Brooke Medicine Eagle

The Body is The Barometer of The Soul by Annette Noontil

Intimacy and Solitude by Stephanie Dowrick

Goddesses in Everywoman by Jean Shinoda Bolen

The Goddess Within by Jennifer Barker Woolger and Roger Woolger

Women Who Run With the Wolves by Clarissa Pinkola Estes

Medicine Cards and Sacred Path Cards by Jamie Sams and David Carson

Topics for Discussion

- One of Artemis's main challenges is to feel her vulnerabilities without needing to attack the person who has revealed her sensitivity. Next time you meet up with your female friends try naming what you see as your vulnerabilities (these being the weaknesses, insecurities and wounds that you sometimes feel ashamed of).
- Dare to share as many as you can with a trusted friend and invite them to do the same. Afterwards compare how many you had in common. This act of witnessing allows you to dissolve and release any subtle feelings of shame or embarrassment as you afford each other the same amnesty. Remember, every person has sensitive areas they carry within themselves, regardless of how confident they may appear.

Questions for Personal Reflection

The following questions are for your personal contemplation and to ascertain how healthy your inner Medicine Woman aspect is:

- Do I fill my days up to avoid spending time alone?
- Do I spend more time fighting for causes rather than resolving my own fears?
- What is my greatest fear and why? What does that represent symbolically? (For example, I fear being eaten by sharks or bitten by snakes and rats. On reflection I realized this represents that I fear unforeseen fateful changes that could jeopardize my best laid plans.)

Secret Woman's Business: Best Times to Celebrate Artemis

New Moons are the traditional times to honor Artemis, particularly out in the wilderness. Consider going bush with your sisters, build a bonfire and howl at the moon!

During childbirth invoke Artemis or as a patron during pregnancy, asking for her protection and assistance during your birthing process.

Diana (the Roman Artemis) was honored on August 15 (northern Hemisphere) in **Nemoralia** by torch-bearing women who brought their leashed dogs to the grove for the blessing of the Goddess. They then returned to the city to wash their hair ritually while praying for ease in childbirth. (Calculate six months hence for the Southern hemisphere equivalent.)

In Athens, they celebrated **Mouichion**, a procession in her honor with cakes decked with a circle of lighted candles, celebrated on the Spring time's first full moon. (This is where we get our modern tradition of lighting candles on a birthday cake.) In **Brauronia**, a ritual was held for prepubescent girls where they'd dress in yellow and dance as the bear mother before her statue, bringing her power within themselves.

Medicine Woman Rite of Passage Ceremony

Animal Totem Healing Journey

It is important with the following rite of passage to complete steps one and two without looking ahead to step three, so grab a book and cover step three before you begin.

Step One: Write three animals down on a piece of paper. Be sure not to edit your first thoughts.

Step Two: Write words best describing their character, their movements, their appearance, their strengths and their weaknesses.

Step Three: Peruse your list and reflect on the following information. The first animal is how you see yourself currently. The second animal represents how others see you now and the third animal symbolizes what you aspire to embody.

In their oracle, Medicine Cards, writers Jamie Sams and David Carlson describe 'Medicine (as) anything that improves our connection with the Great Spirit.' It is for this reason I ask you to now set aside some time to work with your third totem animal, the one you most aspire to be like, for this animal holds a key to your wholeness and healing at this time. You are about to call upon the power of your healing animal.

To gain the understanding they have to offer, you must approach your totem animal with reverence. Reverence guarantees receptivity. Light a candle, take the phone off the hook (and the mobile) and sit in silence under the moon or within its gaze if possible. For in the silence of the quiet mind you are fertile and open to receiving the spirit of the animal teacher who has chosen to work with you. If you have difficulty quieting your mind, try putting on some transcendental music to take you into an altered state of consciousness.

Ask the spirit of this animal to be present with you. You may visualize it, sense it, smell it or hear it. Merge inside its skin energetically and feel its heart beating within you. Feel the energy of your animal and their physical strengths and characteristics. Now sense within yourself its inner qualities as you become one with your healing animal. Move as one. See through the eyes of this magnificent creature. How do they see the world? How do they see you?

What advice do they have to give you? Thank your power animal for its gifts of wisdom.

Talisman Charge

Plan a trip to a wild area in the coming weeks. Ask Artemis to guide you in choosing a destination and pay attention to signs and synchronicities. Ask her to provide you with a healing talisman from this area. When you arrive, be sure to spend some time alone walking in the wilderness, keeping an eye out for your talisman. It may be a certain stone, a feather, a leaf, seed pod or set of cicada wings. It will grab your attention and you will have trouble putting it down. If you can put it down easily this one is not for you. Accept what is being offered to you, even if it seems a humble totem.

The next step is to charge your talisman with the wisdom, guidance and healing energies of your power animal and the Goddess of the inner hunt, Artemis.

Close your eyes and visualize both your power animal and Artemis sitting with you, touching the talisman. Visualize yourself in a column of pale blue light and take three deep breaths breathing this energy into your throat chakra. Ask Artemis to anchor within you her inner strength and healing gifts. Place both your hands on the talisman and ask to be a clear channel for both her and your healing animal's energies to charge your talisman. Bless the animal, earth or tree spirit that has delivered this gift unto you for your healing and empowerment journey. Bless your power animal for their love and healing. Bless Artemis for her inner strength and assistance.

Medicine Woman Act of Beauty

Consider making a light blue mandala to further assist the healing of your throat chakra. You may wish to depict your healing animal or feathers in some way or even glue treasures from the natural world on to it. Then create a shrine to honor the inner journey you have taken to unveil Artemis within your consciousness... perhaps even in the backyard.

HECATE: THE INNER WISE WOMAN

The inner Wise Woman is the sixth aspect of our feminine psyche that I have the pleasure of introducing. She has long been belittled as a withered and frail granny whose mercurial faculties have eroded to a fine dust beneath her church-wearing hat but make no mistake she is powerful in her ability to discern all that lies beneath a given situation or person and is a wise ally for any heroine needing counsel, healing or insight. In a culture that fears the natural process of ageing, it is a powerful act for all women, regardless of their age to embrace the inner Wise Woman.

How I Discovered My Wise Woman

Although I have not yet reached my crone years I have experienced inner descents to commune with my archetypal Wise Woman in the form of memorable bouts of depression and seclusion trying to make sense of it all. Looking back, most of these periods were triggered by a sense of failure, betrayal or rejection causing me to become insular and insecure, culminating in sleepless nights, tears, self-criticism and a general feeling of apathy.

When I was younger I was terrified of feeling this way as I feared becoming like my mother who suffered from depression for what seemed like all of my teenage years.

The positive side of my Mum's sensitivity is that she is very psychic but I never saw her value or develop her inner Wise Woman gifts or speak openly about them with other women. I have since discovered this state of isolation and depression was an epidemic amongst psychically sensitive women of my mother's generation which was tucked away neatly behind suburban brick veneers. A phenomenon summed up beautifully by my spirit guides who told me that without like-minded circles of support our growth is destined to be stunted and dysfunctional, illustrated by the fact that even trees in a forest instinctively know to grow in circles so they can remind each other to grow straight and tall. When I became a mum I fully grasped how dangerous it is for our mental health to expect that we should be able to constantly care for others 24/7 whilst keeping up with the endless cooking, cleaning, washing, shopping, bill paying and errands (not to mention, working outside the home to bring in enough income to survive) in total isolation, rather than share our load by living in communities as used to be the norm before the industrial age.

Whilst I still get depressed from time to time, now when I experience Hecate, the archetypal Wise Woman with her symptoms of depression and lethargy, I honor them by retreating, analysing dreams and oracle cards, spending time in nature, performing rituals and sharing social time with supportive friends. I make a concentrated effort to bring to light my shadow aspects so I may experience a psychological death to bring about a shift in consciousness. Easier said than done of course, depending on the depth of despair I have found myself in and the responsibilities of survival and parenthood that continue on regardless. But by approaching these inner descents shamanically I have found that I move through them much more quickly compared to when I was in my twenties and endured longer periods of depression, which were clouded and prolonged by the use of marijuana and Prozac.

Today, I am continuing to learn the value of my sensitivity and develop my inner gifts by spending time with various Wise Women for healings, counsel and guidance. When I was pregnant I was fortunate enough to have an encounter with a woman who was Hecate personified. She was the tour guide in an underground cave complete with dripping stalactites. Earth spirit entities stared at us from every nook and cranny and a central pool for crying was lit like a scene from Lord of the Rings. Stooped with her hunch and limp she walked up to me, commented on my pentacle and pregnant belly and advised me to return to this location in my mind's eye when I gave birth. Outside there was even a wishing well, a cultural relic from our European Goddess worshipping ancestors.

I also recently had the privilege of witnessing a Wise Woman friend of mine enter into her Hecate aspect when I read for her two days before her hysterectomy. Rather than go hysterical internally, she consciously began her descent into Hecate's labyrinth and embraced the process as a powerful death of the Mother phase and birth of the Crone. Although a hysterectomy was her journey, I do not advocate this as a necessary introduction to Hecate, just as one need not wait until menopause to embrace the wisdom of the witch.

WISE WOMAN QUIZ

Answer the following quick quiz to find out what shape your inner Wise Woman is currently in. (Circle the answer that most describes you.)

You see yourself in a photograph and look older than you expected, do you:

A. Call a plastic surgeon?

B. Complain to a girlfriend?

C. Meditate on what that means to you?

You find yourself feeling depressed mid-Winter, do you:

A. Make an appointment to request anti-depressants?

B. Seek out the counsel of a Wise Woman for insight or a reading?

C. Write down and draw in your journal to process what shadow emotions are surfacing?

You are asked to share your life's wisdom in a magazine article, do you:

A. Laugh and say that they've asked the wrong person?

B. Research other people's wise thoughts and perspective?

C. Enjoy writing whatever comes from the wellspring of your heart?

Now add up your score. A = 1, B = 2, C = 3. *If you scored:*

1 – 3 Your inner Wise Woman is veiled both to yourself and the world. This next chapter will enable you to see and own your pearls of wisdom, regardless of how you see yourself now.

4 – 6 Your inner Wise Woman thrives on the wisdom she receives from others. The next chapter will help you to develop your own intuitive insight.

7 – 9 You are a big Kahuna! Your embodiment of the Wise Woman will be a shining light for others to follow. Enjoy reading the following chapter.

Herstory: Wise Woman Goddesses

The Wise Women Goddesses were those hooded elder women seen and often feared by the common folk as a meeting with them represents change, such as the meeting Macbeth has with the three witches, who were also known as the three Fates, Morai or three Sisters. It is human nature to fear the unknown due to a deep mistrust in the Divine Plan because it is beyond cognitive understanding. For this reason many messengers, prophets and oracles have historically been punished or ridiculed for the truth they imparted, such as the Greek princess and priestess Cassandra who saw and foretold the Trojan War only to be disbelieved by her own family and people. Other names given to the aspect of the inner Wise Woman include the Norse Goddess, Hel (from where the Christian term Hell was derived); Morgan le Fay, also known as Morrigan or Mara from the famous Mystery School at Avalon; Brigid the Irish triple-Goddess (who embodied the aspects of Maiden, Mother and Crone); and Cerridwen, Welsh Goddess of death and rebirth. It is the ancient Greek Crone Goddess, Hecate, however who will light your path through the misty labyrinth to meet your inner Wise Woman.

The Myth of Hecate

Hecate was an ancient Greek Goddess who lived in the Underworld (the realm of our shadow aspects). She is the archetypal crone or (more fashionably) elder woman, a stage which marks the third and final chapter in a woman's life. As such she is often portrayed as a hag, stirring up brews in her large black cauldron, a receptacle of magical transformation and accrued feminine wisdom.

The story begins when Hecate was a young girl. She was said to have stolen a pot of rouge to give to Europa, the Holy Cow Goddess. Fearing the wrath of her parents, Zeus and Hera, she fled, stopping en route to seek sanctuary at the house of a woman in childbirth. The Gods, fearing her involvement as a midwife, superstitiously plunged her into the river Acheron, in an effort to cleanse away her supernatural powers. She was then carried away by the current, which delivered her underground into what became known as the Underworld. It was here she learned much about the art of alchemy and became an Underworld Queen who presided over purifications, magic and enchantment.

Hecate was the Wise Woman all the Gods and Goddesses consulted when they needed insight. The most well-known myth in which she features is that of Demeter and Persephone, which outlines the abduction of a daughter whose innocence is destroyed so that she may take her place as a fertile woman and embrace the second phase of womanhood, as a mother. Hecate is the link that guides women across their respective rites of passage.

In the myth she does this by accompanying the naïve Persephone as a protective guiding spirit into the dark recesses of the Underworld and secondly, by assisting Persephone's mother, Demeter (who has the maturity and awareness to consult her directly), to gain insight into the circumstances concerning her daughter's disappearance. Like most of us, Demeter panics, experiencing what is commonly referred to as a 'dark night of the soul' — a loss of all hope, faith and understanding — before calling upon Hecate for help. In fact, Demeter raged uncontrollably for nine days before she thought to visit Hecate, who gave her the clarity she needed, telling her it was Hades who had indeed abducted her daughter.

Hecate was a seer. She was not concerned with the external goings on of Mount Olympus but rather the inner planes of existence, making her a respected ally to all. The one lover she is reported to have taken was Hermes, the God of Wisdom, who was also a keeper of knowledge and served as a guide alongside her at the crossroads of life and death.

Whilst residing in the Underworld, Hecate also befriended The Three Fates (sometimes referred to as the Erinyes, Moirai or Furies). These were the women who continually spun the wheel of fortune, exacting punishment in the form of karmic occurrences upon those who failed to observe the natural laws. As their affiliate, Hecate is also associated with the ancient Goddess Fortuna, who has since been referred to as Lady Luck.

In fairy tales, Hecate is illustrated as a kind and generous Fairy Godmother who has just what protagonists need to overcome any obstacles in their path. Similarly, she is commonly portrayed as a spinster who lives alone in a cottage deep within a forest, teaching secrets to those who prove they are true of heart and purpose. Unfortunately, the later version of Hecate saw her demonized in modern adaptations of sacred and folkloric texts, transforming her into a malevolent and nasty old woman whom children were subsequently taught to fear.

Further facts

In ancient societies Hecate was a female shaman, a tribal matriarch revered as a 'Holy Woman' or 'Wise Woman'. She understood the processes of nature, enabling her to heal, read oracles and protect seekers from doing harm when exploring supernatural realms.

The Moral

Although the portrayal of Hecate is questioned by modern academics who claim her character has been slandered by patriarchal writers projecting their own fears about midwifery, the tale as it stands suggests that her own youthful lack of judgment which led her into the seedier side of life at a young age was also the initiation required to develop her depth of understanding. Ultimately, her time in the shadow lands has caused her to reflect rather than act (on both her own actions and the actions of others).

Further facts

During the middle Ages nine million healers were burned or drowned (1% of whom were male). This backlash came after a popular resurgence of feminine wisdom and healing arts amongst the peasant classes which threatened the high financial and social status enjoyed by male physicians. A fear campaign ensued, claiming that any woman who was a healer was evil and should be murdered, which successfully eradicated all competition and kept the knowledge of healing amongst the noble classes who continued to profit at the expense of the poor. The number one crime cited was midwifery.

Historical Appearance

Hecate is often depicted riding her female horse through the night sky, which is where we derive our modern term for a frightening dream, a nightmare. In this capacity Hecate brings to light our innermost fears that need to be consciously understood. Nightmares are therefore said to be important dreams that hold the key to that which we are battling in our waking life (which is why they are especially vivid so we will remember them).

Further facts

Hecate was the patron Goddess of the healing arts and as such assisted practitioners to act as midwives in guiding others through times of personal metamorphosis. This included shamans, such as those who use herb lore, prophecy, divination and dream analysis to assist clients, as well as more conventional practitioners who today use various modalities of physical, emotional, spiritual and psychological healing to help alleviate suffering and confusion. In fact, so revered was the contribution of women's spiritual wisdom under her patronage that the Ancient Greeks and subsequent royal lineages would not make either personal or political decisions without first consulting an oracular priestess.

Often the howling of black dogs announced her approach and she was usually seen accompanied by Cerberus, the three-headed dog who guarded the Underworld and whose appearance often shocked (much like her own), but was no deterrent for those seekers who were committed in their intent to discover her mystical secrets.

Other illustrations of Hecate show her wearing a hooded cloak, which suggested her affinity with all that is hidden. She would also carry a scythe (like the grim reaper), which gives her the ability to cut away all that is no longer needed. Alternatively, she is shown with three faces, indicating the triple phase integration of her maiden, mother and crone phases. More colloquial images, such as those in children's fables depict her as a witch on a broomstick, sporting stripy tights, black clothes and boots, a conical hat and a generous smattering of facial moles and warts.

Wise Woman Profile

I like my mentor Jen Powell's description of Hecate's presence in our lives as the times when we feel we are being enfolded in a cloak of lethargy. This may manifest as depression, general apathy and tiredness toward life in general, a nervous breakdown, exhaustion, chronic fatigue or an episode of mental illness. Unfortunately, the mainstream way of responding to these soul sicknesses has long been to medicate the symptoms and return the sufferer back to outward productivity as soon as possible.

But it is these very symptoms that are our soul's way of asking us to sit down, journey inward and await some intuition. For when we truly surrender to how we feel and express it, we then clear our ability to channel the insight needed to integrate our past experiences, giving us renewed energy to continue forth with our quest.

Symbolically this is shown in most heroic tales where the protagonist enters a dark place such as a cave, swamp, dungeon or poppy field and is temporarily impeded from further activity until they solve a riddle by coming to terms with the darker side of human nature. This is how spiritual wisdom is possessed, through the conscious seeking of higher truth or meaning. Often grief and loss of our ego's desires mark the beginning of this stage of the journey – the death phase which precedes each psychological birth.

The test at this time for the heroine is to find and maintain hope in the darkness, to literally learn to see in the dark. Just as the hero's journey is motivated by a need to venture outward to find one's life purpose, the feminine journey is by contrast, one of surrender. We must therefore allow time and space to spiral inwards to the depths of our own subconscious so we can discover our ultimate truth and regain a sense of reverence for the synchronicity and mystery of the Divine Plan (as well as a deeper appreciation of our own soul gifts).

It is important to add that the light cannot be reached without first venturing into the unknowable darkness. This process happens periodically throughout our lives, usually in accordance with the seasons, i.e. turning inward during Autumn and Winter. Although we may return to this place of despair on a regular basis, each successive return grants us with a deeper understanding of ourselves and of life in general. In other words, if you are feeling despondent, it's important that you give yourself full permission to express your negative feelings through mediums such as drawing, dancing, chanting, crying or swearing like a trooper in the back yard.

To express your dark side in a creative and safe way keeps you from imploding or exploding when the pressure becomes too great to handle. Depression is therefore the result of suppressing those negative thoughts and feelings that we feel uncomfortable acknowledging and expressing for fear they will overwhelm us. The result usually means that we remain stuck in that dark polarity until we allow the energy to shift by venting it.

Traditionally women have met regularly to express their collective 'madness' through sound and movement, to free their body of negative energies under the light of the moon. I used to meet with a few girlfriends in a church hall where we would do this to Gabrielle Roth's Five Rhythms CD – trance music designed to take you through five different emotional states. No doubt to innocent passers-by we sounded like an insane asylum, but we would all leave feeling refreshed and liberated, ready to face the unacknowledged madness in the world with renewed vigour. After all, madness is merely the result when our wild, free and instinctual nature is given no voice. It is this part that acts as a release valve when our rational mind is overwhelmed with the irrationalities that life has shown us.

If you have experienced the darker side of human nature in any way, shape or form it is imperative that you set aside the time to revisit it in order to fully comprehend its impact and lesson in your life. 'The dark night of the soul' is a stage we must all undergo when we feel that life is meaningless and experience complete disillusionment with all that we know to be true. When we feel this way, all we can do is surrender to our grief.

It is interesting to note that the death and rebirth process a butterfly undergoes within its chrysalis involves a trinity of energies where the caterpillar is reduced to liquid before reforming as a winged creature. This dissolving of one's original form into water is also the symbolism of baptism and re-birthing ceremonies, where a person is submerged in water signifying the surrender to one's one grief which will in turn soften our rigidity and make moist and fertile the foundation for new growth. Just as in each Spring season we need the rainfall to fertilize new growth, so too we need to release our tears in order to lubricate the process of internal alchemy otherwise we remain detached from our heart and emotions, rationalizing how we feel instead of moving through it.

This tendency to rationalize our feelings instead of expressing them can occur in long-term counselling which often fosters a dependence on medical professionals who are paid to listen to the incessant problems of their clients. The holistic model by comparison, encourages experiential processes which then enable us to shift the emotion and gain direct insight. Acknowledging that once someone has returned from their own Underworld journey they can then act as a guide for others who may need to navigate their way through the dark.

Hecate represents the power and wisdom we can attain in times of solitude (which is why in Tarot readings if someone pulls the Hermit card, I consider it a calling card from Hecate and a strong suggestion that they spend time away from the madding crowd in order to reconnect with their inner light).

Hecate is the phase of the Crone – the final aspect of womanhood. Cyclically we experience her during the dark moon at the end of each lunar month (between the waning moon and the new crescent moon when we can't see the moon in the night sky). Seasonally, we feel her pulling us inward during Autumn and Winter, culminating in the Winter Solstice (the longest night of the year) when we just don't have the energy to spread our light out into the world at large.

Being ruled by the moon Hecate is a powerful creative force, however her work is unseen and therefore often difficult to validate. In our 'material' world which values only what it can tangibly taste, smell, touch, hear and see, Hecate's gifts are viewed with suspicion as we feel uneasy about what we can't easily affirm. Ironically, it is usually when we are not seen to be doing much in the physical world that we are often really moving forwards internally. It is by really trusting the process that we allow it to continue uninterrupted, which is vital to enjoying the breakthrough that we so desperately crave. Often the breakthrough heralds not only a new personal approach to life that is more mature and void of less struggle, but it often ignites great inspiration, manifesting as profound new works of art, literature, philosophy or scientific discovery.

Once we know how to honor the Wise Woman within ourselves, we are bestowed with countless gifts of inspiration, vision, magic and regeneration. However, if we reject her process out of a closed and cynical mind-set, we are denied understanding and may experience a shadow manifestation such as psychosis, obsessive compulsive disorders, violent or vindictive tendencies towards ourselves or others and creative stagnation.

Trance-formation means literally to enter into a space between the worlds, the abyss of Great Mystery, allowing its energy to forge you into a new shape with an expanded consciousness. Without this ability to surrender to and accept the changes brought about by the Higher Power's will, we are unable to truly appreciate the miracle of birth and rebirth. In other words, the more we can learn to celebrate and honor each death within our own life, the greater our appreciation and gratitude of life and its inherent gifts. We must experientially know each polarity to appreciate its opposite. Which is why when we truly understand how natural the ongoing death/ rebirth cycle is in our own life we can then learn to accept change rather than fear it. This is why I believe we need to confront our societal taboo around death. After all, if we are able to embrace death as a natural release from this form into another, we will in turn lessen our fascination with violence in the media and perhaps even reform the treatment of animals in the meat industry, honoring all life as part of the great cycle of life and death. When we appreciate that all that dies will be returned to us in a different form, understanding that matter itself cannot be created or destroyed but is merely changed, we will then not cling desperately to the status quo of resisting change at a cost to our spiritual evolution.

Ultimately, death is our greatest teacher. For when we lose all that we hold dear we reflect upon what is truly valuable and discover not only who we truly are, but also the nature of all things.

Below is a case study that illustrates how Hecate can play out in her shadow aspect if we are unable to face and reflect upon our fears:

Suzette

Suzette was a woman who spent the majority of her life healing others in mainstream medical facilities and by the time she had reached her fiftieth birthday she was burnt out and wanting to retreat. She retired, citing chronic fatigue as her reason for leaving. Two years after her decision to take sick leave, her children grew concerned at her lack of social interaction as they couldn't understand the enjoyment she now derived from her own company. This was compounded by her eccentricities, which became more obtuse the longer she shunned the outside world. Eventually she developed obsessive compulsive behaviours towards everything that she couldn't outwardly control. This in turn gave Suzette more reason to stay behind closed doors where she could resist all change, despite the limitations this confining lifestyle imposed upon her.

Wise Woman Strengths

The following is a description of how we behave when our inner Wise Woman is acknowledged and honored:

- I regularly cleanse myself and my environment energetically using sacred smoke, healing symbols, Feng Shui, aromatherapy and crystals. (Not all at once unless you want to charge money as a performance artist!)
- I stay grounded by gardening and ask for intuitive assistance from the resident Deva and nature spirits with whom I share space.
- I regularly meditate, do yoga or experience hands on energy healings to maintain a healthy equilibrium between my mind and spirit.
- I light a candle, meditate or perform a simple ritual at times of seasonal change, such as the Solstices and Equinoxes and cross-quarter seasonal festivals known as Samhain, Imbolc, Beltane and Lughnasad.
- I note when it is a dark moon (two weeks after a full moon) so I don't push myself to be active.
- I study myths and symbolism so I have a framework through which to understand my intuitive insights.
- I help others to unveil their wisdom and invite Spirit to use me as a channel for the good of all.
- I try to maintain good health so my body is a clear channel for Spirit.
- I often go consciously into trance to journey inward for insights.
- I regularly look at what I need to let go of in order to grow.
- I give myself equal time reflecting and doing.
- I embrace change with trust and gratitude, knowing that I am supported by Spirit.
- I stay tuned in to changes in cosmic energy, moon phases and planetary shifts knowing that 'dis-aster' means to go against the stars.
- I try to become self-aware of my spirit, seeing myself as a winged spirit in a mortal body.
- I value the process of ageing and own my accrued inner power and wisdom.
- I open myself to understanding new dimensions of being.
- I know my life experience is invaluable to others and I am happy to offer support and guidance to others.
- I value my insights by recording them in a journal.
- I only speak my insights and otherworldly experiences to those who are interested and open to hearing them.

Wise Woman Shadow Traits

The following is a description of how we behave when we have denied our inner Wise Woman through fear or ignorance:

- I fear the occult sciences and those who study and practice them.
- I try and avoid feelings of depression by using drugs or indulging in quick comfort fixes such as drinking alcohol.
- I value the spiritual realm but neglect my needs in the material realm.
- I only see the wisdom and power to heal in others and not myself.
- I don't take the time to bless meals, friends, seasons and life experiences.
- I use magic to serve my will without respecting the free will of others.
- I think I need special 'ritual tools' and a 'how to' manual to do magic the 'right way' instead of using my intuition and creativity.
- I suppress my inner hag and madness to appear 'acceptable' to others.
- I risk psychosis by using mind-altering drugs for adventure rather than in vision quests supervised by experienced shamanic elders.
- I resist all change, doubting the process of my life is unfolding in accordance with Divine Will.
- I hold onto my previous identity as an earth mother well into my elder woman years rather than embrace my wisdom and power as a crone.

Wise Woman Lessons

To balance your inner Wise Woman strengths and weaknesses, try the following suggestions:

- Validate your intuition, gut feelings and visions by acting upon them.
- Consciously embrace periods of lethargy and depression as opportunities for insight and growth.
- Go easy on yourself when feeling 'dark' and accept your shadow side.
- Work with your dreams by taking time to analyse their symbolism.
- Take time in solitude as much as possible (especially when menstruating) to connect with the wisdom of the unconscious.
- Gift yourself with meaningful rituals to celebrate your moonpause (menopause) as an initiation into your Wise Woman years.
- Read life symbolically by interpreting everything you experience as a lesson.
- Strengthen a practical relationship with your guides by meditating and take note of synchronicities and act upon them.
- Surrender to all change, calling upon Hecate to guide you.

- Incorporate natural magic, ritual and astral journeys to lessen the need for escapism.
- Try not to hide your magical self away for fear of persecution or ridicule.
- Practice self-healing methods before reaching for pain-killers where possible.
- Revel in your 'hagginess' and eccentricity regularly.
- Embrace your ageing process as a gaining of power, grace and wisdom.
- Try not to impose your truth on to others who are travelling on a different path. Try to connect regularly with elementals, fairies and devic energy in the garden.
- Consciously bless activities such as cooking, cleaning and bathing.

Wise Woman Relationship Patterns

Personal

The inner Wise Woman's primary relationship is with Spirit, although she also enjoys mentoring young maidens and cackling with other wise woman over copious cups of tea. Hecate is quite content to spend time on her own, as this gives her the tranquillity to hear her inner perceptions and journey to the unseen realms undisturbed. So regardless of your age, learn to trust your own intuition as your prime source of authority and continue to seek out higher understanding and you will be granted a serenity often seen only in the wise elders who have seen every scenario life has to offer.

Often women with a dominant Hecate archetype will be drawn to work with the elderly, those who are dying or with birthing mothers. Alternatively, they may work as healers or as channels for guidance. On a personal level, their strong connection with the spirit world gives them unseen companionship when their adult children may be busy leading their own lives. They also tend to be bookworms who enjoy living alone with just an animal for intimate friendship. Ritual work with other light workers is also supremely fulfilling for these women who do well to balance their tendency toward isolation if they are to avoid becoming depressed, dark or neurotic in their outlook.

Considering that one of the common initiations that heralds a journey with Hecate is the loss of a spouse or even a belief system, seeking out the company of other Wise Women is a great source of inspiration to avoid slipping into the shadow expression of our psyche, such as swinging between emotional polarities of victim/martyr.

Famous Wise Women

The first pop culture Hecate who springs to mind is Samantha from 'Bewitched', who resurrected a tongue-in-cheek positive portrayal of a woman connected with her otherworldly powers for the good of all. This was a welcome change from the earlier fairy tales where patriarchal writers like the Brothers Grimm portrayed witches as nasty old hags who should be avoided and feared, such as the witch in Hansel and Gretel, Snow White and the thirteenth black fairy from Sleeping Beauty.

The Wizard of Oz was a little more balanced with its portrayal of Wise Women, presenting both the good witch of the East and the wicked witch of the West, implying choice in all things magical.

Fortunately, young girls today have role models like Hermione Grainger from the Harry Potter series, whose immense knowledge personifies the witch as a Wise Woman with good intentions. Unfortunately, there are still beat-ups like the television shows, 'Charmed' and 'Sabrina, the Teenage Witch' which encourage teenage girls to wield their supernatural powers over others to achieve their ego driven goals.

This highlights that we need to see older women speaking their wisdom in our media, which is still dominated by patriarchal programming such as male sports and crime shows in prime time. Women's forums such as Oprah are relegated to daytime slots as they are perceived as being of interest only to stay at home mums, the elderly, sick and unemployed.

Wise Woman Makeover Kit

The following pages contain a myriad of inspired suggestions, lotions and potions to assist you in revelling in your maximum magical potential as a Wise Woman.

Suggested Styles

When embracing Hecate we often feel drawn to wearing dark colours in an effort to dim our external light so we can focus on our inner state. Another trademark of the witch is of course the conical hat, which just like a church steeple acts as a 'Cone of Power', stimulating a spiralling vortex of energy upwards, which will assist you in consciously directing your energy to manifest your desired wishes. Here are some other suggestions when fitting out your wardrobe with a few Hecate additions:

- *Purple, indigo and black fabrics.*
- *Lace and lace up bodices (purely for fetish fun!). Silver jewelry and crystals.*
- *Dyeing your hair two tones or more. (A witch was said to show her many strands of wisdom in the multi-colours of her hair.) Alternatively, letting your grey locks of wisdom out to be seen.*
- *Witchypoo Boots, particularly those that lace up the front. Long skirts and conical hats.*
- *Stripy tights, rainbow felt slippers and other eccentric handicrafts.*
- *Ponchos, shawls and woollen wraps that enfold your energy inward. A pentacle or Wotan's cross. (see Wild Woman Symbols)*
- *Ethereal clothes, such as those made out of gauze, chiffon or tulle. Wings. (Which your grandkids will love!)*

Wise Woman Colours

If you wake up in the morning and a) don't feel like getting out of bed or b) feel drawn to wearing either of these colours, know that your inner Wise Woman would like to spend a little time with you.

Black

Often we wear black when we unconsciously wish to shroud our light and not draw attention to ourselves, either because we don't have the energy to radiate socially or because our focus is on the secrets contained within. Hence our common teenage fascination with wearing black, as we begin our descent into the Underworld with an inevitable loss of innocence. Black candles are often used when invoking the presence of Hecate, although all you really need do is speak her name, as with all your conscious intentions – realize the power of the spoken word.

Indigo

Indigo represents the colour of the third eye (see below) and is reminiscent of the midnight blue sky. Wearing indigo enhances your receptivity to the inner planes of existence.

Wise Woman Associated Chakra

Brow (Third Eye)

When opened this energy centre enables us to develop our clairvoyance (clear seeing), intuition and insight. If, however, this energy centre is closed we tend toward cynicism, tension headaches and remain overly detached from life and others. The brow chakra also rules the pituitary gland, which helps activate our extra sensory perception (a function dulled by the contraceptive pill). It also vitalizes the central nervous system. The colour of this energy centre is indigo. You may wish to consider gifting yourself with regular silent or guided meditations and rituals to further assist the healing of this chakra.

Wise Woman Essential Oils

Clary Sage

Clary Sage is a great oil to burn for depression as it lifts one's spirit. It is also great to use during childbirth (but not during pregnancy). It is both grounding and protective.

Chamomile

Chamomile aids meditation as it is both calming and an antidepressant.

Lavender

Lavender balances the emotions, calms the nerves and is a great antiseptic.

Wise Woman Flower Essences

The following are vibrational essences which distil the healing properties of various plants. When taken orally they promote emotional balance and wellbeing.

Gorse

Gorse is great for dissipating feelings of overwhelming despair, loss of hope and re-energizing one's zest for living.

Gentian

Gentian is helpful for overturning pessimism and rising above melancholic lethargy.

Cherry Plum

Cherry Plum is great for alleviating emotional desolation, suicidal thoughts and the symptoms of a nervous breakdown.

Wise Woman Minerals, Crystals and Stones

Moonstone

Moonstone enhances our lunar feminine nature, magnifying intuition and subtle perception. Wearing moonstone can also assist in opening the heart, balancing emotions, accessing past lives, alleviating pre-menstrual tension and general anxiety. It is also renowned for assisting the process of birth.

Amethyst

Amethyst purifies and regenerates all levels of consciousness, aids mental disorders, assists the process of alchemy and transformation, enhances psychic ability, channelling and meditation. It is also healing, calming and protective for the wearer.

Wise Woman Food

Special Dietary Needs

Hecate-dominant women are often prone to having increased sensitivity to processed foods, chemicals and substances like wheat, dairy and gluten that have been eaten to excess in the Western diet. The more aware a person becomes, the more this is reflected in the food they choose to eat, so crones often choose to eat simple foods that are rich in nutrients and easy to digest. Often pollutants such as caffeine and alcohol are eliminated altogether.

Wise Woman Flowers and Trees

Poppy

As the source of the barbiturates heroin, opium and morphine, the poppy is synonymous with deadly sleep. Poppies were previously associated with the death aspect of the Goddess.

Willow

Wands used for divination and circle casting made of willow were used by followers of Helice, the Greek virgin form of Hecate. Willow bark was also used by the ancients for pain relief and is still used today in the form of aspirin.

Yew and Poplar Trees

These trees were sacred to Hecate as they stood at the crossroad between shadow and light. Poplars were sometimes considered to be the Tree of Life as their leaves were dark on the side facing Heaven and light on the side facing Earth.

Oak

Oak has long been used by witches and fairies for making wands as the oak tree is considered one of the wisest and most magical of trees because it takes so long to grow.

Wise Woman Hangouts

Caves and Labyrinths

Caves represent the womb within Mother Earth, the hidden tomb where creatures such as bats (which represent death and rebirth) hang upside down. Caves also signify retreat from outside pressures so that we may have the serenity to venture inside ourselves and connect with our soul needs and the universe at large. Similarly, labyrinths are sacred mazes designed as a walking meditation. One enters the maze with a question in mind and upon reaching the centre, one meditates and receives insight into their query.

Wishing Wells

Wells were sacred to Hecate as sites where one would allow a receptacle to descend and retrieve from the unseen waters of the unconscious. Pagans used to decorate and pray at these sites and make offerings to Hecate and other Underworld Goddesses.

New Age/Witchcraft Shops and Libraries

These are a magnet for Hecates of all ages with a thirst for knowledge, particularly those with an extensive range of books, herbs and knowledgeable staff, rather than those stocking overpriced giftware with dolphin motifs.

Storms

As a symphony of elements charging the atmosphere with the kinetic energy of change, storms are sacred to Hecate and represent the Tower card in the Tarot (which, as it falls after being hit by lightning, signifies the outgrowing of old beliefs and structures). Storms bring our frustrations to a head and demand that we give them expression or implode psychologically. The bolts of lightning represent the sudden shock of insight into our unsatisfying situations.

Women's Circles/Coven Meetings

Ranging from those who follow a set ritual structure to those more informal gatherings of women. Hecate loves a good dance on the full moon, making lunar wish lists in the company of her sisters and regular nights of healing or ritual followed by feasting.

'Crime' Scenes

As patron of the Underworld you will sense her presence in all dark circumstances where she is waiting to guide souls back to the light. This includes nightclubs, gothic bars and venues where drugs are taken as an entry into the world of chaos and illusion.

Funerals

At funerals, cemeteries, morgues and locations of death, Hecate is there to gather souls and guide them home to the light.

Psychiatric Hospitals

Often those who are seen as 'mad' by our patriarchal society are those whose experience of the shadow or spiritual realm has consumed their psyche in an effort to try and resolve their experience.

Wise Woman Astrological Sign

When the moon is in Pisces each month (for approximately two and a half days), we are inclined to feel like our Hecate self, so keep a check on the astrological moon phases by purchasing a moon diary or astrological calendar from a new age or health food store to make allowances for your vagueness at these times. (Not a good time for a business meeting!) Similarly, when the sun is in Pisces, our dreams and psychic abilities are more vivid so this is a great time to get a reading or do some powerful inner journeying. Take note also of Hecate on the Pisces full moon each year when the sun is in the sign of Virgo (Pisces' opposite sign).

Pisces

As the final sign of the zodiac, Pisces represents the urge to be of service to the world. Pisces is ruled by the planet Neptune, one of the outer planets that influences our connection with the netherworld (our imagination and otherworldly senses; for example, clairvoyance, clairaudience, clairsentience, telepathy and intuition). The lesson of Pisces is to reflect the light of the Divine and its symbol, the fish was a symbol of spiritual wisdom long before it was appropriated by the Christian faith. The shadow of Pisces is to fall into the polarity of victim/martyr, which occurs when our spiritual connection is tenuous, creating a self-sacrificing need to rescue others rather than seek to understand and heal ourselves.

Wise Woman Symbols

Should you encounter any of the following signs in your dreams, you can guarantee there's something in your cloakroom that needs to be aired and understood. These are the symbols of Hecate that indicate an underworld descent is in order.

The Moon

From midday onward, our shadows get longer both physically and psychologically as we draw closer to the feminine nocturnal energies. The night is ruled by the feminine energy of Grandmother Moon, the symbol of all Goddess temples the world over. Night represents the darkness of the womb, the void or place of unknowable and infinite possibilities between worlds. The moon is the light that allows us to reflect on our thoughts, actions and the greater universe.

Bones and Skulls

They represent the need to pare issues back to their basic form in order to reveal their true nature, literally getting down to the bare bones of the matter.

Wotan's Cross, Crossroads

Wotan's Cross is the symbol of an equal cross within a circle. The cross represents Great Grandmother Spider's dividing of the Earth into four directions, elements and seasons for balance. Likewise, the crossroads is symbolic of our need to stop and reflect on what new path needs to be taken in order to balance the whole. Wotan's cross was also the original symbol on the buns we now know as Easter buns, as a celebration of the crossroads of death and rebirth.

Keys and Gates

Hecate was said to hold the key to open the gate. Keys represent insight and gates symbolize the doorways to hidden parts of our psyche, which in turn enable us to access greater understanding. If one does not surrender to this ongoing process of change, one cannot be reborn, so if we are to experience the new opportunities that await, we must surrender to fate.

Fairies

Hecate is the archetype of the Fairy Godmother. The word fairy was once interchangeable with the word 'fate'. Fairies are air spirits or sylphs, elemental nature spirits that exist in the second dimension, alongside our three-dimensional realm where we have physical form. They are energetic beings that assist the growth of plants. Women who are nature spirits have also long been referred to as fairies.

Imps

Imps are playful sprites, male nature spirits who delight in making mischief in the name of fun. Robin Good fellow or Puck was perhaps the most famous imp to date. Such spirits are drawn to women who are connected with their Hecate archetypal energy as they are as playful and true to themselves as young children. Men who are connected with their magical child archetype still display this impish quality.

The 'Death' Tarot Card, Miniature Coffins and Compost

All of these signify change, the regeneration that occurs when the old returns from whence it came so new life can begin. In the Tarot, one is encouraged to embrace death, signifying change as children do, with enthusiasm, knowing it will herald in new growth. It is only adults who have forgotten to trust in the Divine Plan as they focus upon and are fearful of what they will have to sacrifice.

Cauldrons

These are receptacles of all the accumulated wisdom gathered by women within their metaphysical wombs – the place of gestating new life. Hecate is often portrayed stirring many grotesque ingredients into her cauldron in order to make something helpful for humankind.

Baskets

Basket weaving was a craft sacred to the Goddess and carried by the Moon Goddesses Artemis and Hecate. They symbolize the intertwining of all experiences to create something useful that can gather more wisdom, as well as the cultivation of crops that can be harvested and collected after nurturing their growth from a seed.

Scythe, Athame

Long since appropriated by the patriarchal Grim Reaper, the scythe was used by Hecate to cut from her life what was no longer needed and harvest that which had reached its full maturity. Likewise, the athame is the ritual knife or sword used by witches in ritual to signify the element of air, the double edged sword that represents the mind.

The old superstition that breaking a mirror will bring seven years of bad luck merely alludes to the continual errors in judgment that will be made if one is unable to reflect.

Wise Woman Totem Animals

If you have a fear of any of the following creatures, best to check in with your inner Wise Woman and see if she is cowering in a corner, frightened of all that is supernatural and reassure her that it is not only 'Super!' but perfectly natural.

Cats

Cats have long been considered the most popular animals chosen as familiars, the term given to animal spirits that assist the magical workings of wise men and women. Cats are sensitive creatures who help keep a space psychically clean by alerting their owners to spirits caught between the worlds.

Frogs

Frogs are a symbol of birth as the human foetus so closely resembles them. The ancient Egyptians commonly wore frog amulets and had frogs on their currency which said 'I am the resurrection', indicating their soul rebirth.

Hounds

There are claims by historians that women were the first to domesticate the dog in early matriarchal cultures. Dogs were said to accompany Hecate in Greece and are also helpful familiars as they are able to see and smell spirits (so they help keep your home psychically clean and bright).

Owl

As a symbol of wisdom, the owl is a nocturnal creature whose perception is razor-sharp. Owl feathers are therefore a sign that Hecate is there to guide you should you find or be given one on your travels.

Raven

Ravens represent high magic; the transformation of self and therefore of one's life.

Bats

Bats are a symbol of death and re-birth. The bat hanging upside down in the cave like the 'Hanged Man' Tarot card represents the need to experience a 120-degree shift in perspective, focusing on spirit instead of the material realm to gain a fresh perspective.

Butterflies

These are a symbol for soul transformation as they represent the transcending of selfish ego desires in order to pursue spiritual growth.

Spider's Webs

Long associated with haunted houses, spider's webs are indicative of a woman's focus on other-worldly pursuits rather than domestic chores, as well as the weaving of one's fate, originally done by Great Grandmother Spider in the Native American creation legend.

Wise Woman Relative Parts of the Body

Forehead and Temples

Migraines are often a sign we haven't been honoring our inner wise woman but getting enough 'down time' to reflect and integrate past experiences. When there is a build up of energy in the third eye we need lack of external stimulus to attune to and soothe our sensitivities.

WISE WOMAN INNER MAKEOVER ACTIVITES

So you're sitting there in your purple felt witches' hat and stripy tights surrounded by frogs and spider's webs wondering how best to spend time getting to know your inner Hecate. Try the following ideas from her jumbo activity book.

Divination

Try using a pendulum to clarify celestial guidance. Hold a crystal (amethyst or clear quartz work well) on a cord or chain perpendicular to the ground. Then establish a response for yes and no. This can be done by asking for a 'Yes' response from the pendulum, often it will spin clockwise or move right to left. Then still the crystal, thanking it and ask for a response to indicate a 'No'. Usually it will move opposite to the first response.

Greek women traditionally use a woman's wedding ring as a pendulum over her pregnant belly to get an answer on the gender of her unborn child. You can also use your body as a conductor. For example, you may be tilted forward for a 'Yes' response and back for a 'No' response. Alternatively, focus your attention on your heart centre. If you get a feeling of expansion take this as a 'Yes', a constricting sensation indicates a 'No'.

Accessing Messages from your Subconscious

Put on some trance or meditation music and using whatever colours you feel drawn to, begin drawing on a large piece of paper. Don't plan ahead what you are going to draw, simply draw whatever comes in the moment. You may wish to try drawing with your eyes closed or with your less dominant hand. (Don't worry if you draw one image over the top of another, this is about process not results.)

When you feel as if the energy is spent, reflect upon what you have drawn, analysing the significance of the colours (use the chakras as a guide), the types of strokes, symbols and the overall feeling of your expression. It may depict a story, event or relationship in your life or your feelings towards it. This activity is akin to seeing a dreamscape laid out in front of you, making it easier for your conscious mind to decipher what's going on in your subconscious.

Developing your Psychic Powers

This is an activity best done with a relative stranger. You may wish to hold a circle one night where friends bring friends so you can work with someone you're not already familiar with.

Select someone to work with as a pair and sit opposite them. Designate one of you to be the 'A' person and one to be the 'B' person. 'A' closes his/her eyes and 'B' just looks into his/her third eye and says whatever impressions or insights they receive, such as what they feel they need and any other feelings they may receive about those around them. After about five minutes, swap turns. I recommend asking the Higher Self of that person to speak through you as a channel for their highest good. (Note: it is important that you both disregard any channelled insight that does not resonate with your own inner truth.)

The Seven Signs of Ageing

It makes me laugh when cosmetic companies cite 'The Seven Signs of Ageing' in their war against facial character and forget to mention priceless inner qualities such as maturity, humour, wisdom, self-empowerment, self-reliance, humility and substance.

Write down seven benefits that you have gained with age, such as caring less about what other people think of you.

Shared Card Readings

There are many different oracle cards out there in the market place today.

Select a deck that speaks to your soul with its images. (One deck that I specifically enjoy using for this activity is the Osho Zen deck.) Then the next time you have friends over and it feels appropriate, pull out the deck and take it in turns to shuffle and pull a card.

The first person pulls a card and passes it to the person on their right who looks into the card and describes what lessons and insights they see symbolically in the card. They then pass the card onto the next person who does the same until everyone around the table has added their insights to the reading of the card.

Finally, the person who pulled the card reflects verbally on how everyone's insights relate to them at this time (as well as any other messages they see in the imagery on the card).

The process is then repeated so each person receives a reading from the entire table. Don't worry that you aren't 'psychic', trust that each person will see something in a different way from the next, this way each insight adds to the overall picture. It is important not to censor your thoughts when reading. Just look into the card and speak whatever thoughts come to you, using sensitivity and tact but not withholding the truth you receive.

Learn to See in the Dark

Next time you're in an unfamiliar location (such as a country paddock at night), practise learning to see in the dark. Simply close your eyes and ask Spirit to guide you where to walk, so that you have to develop your inner sight (the innate sense that tells you where to tread to avoid small holes, animal droppings and logs). Dark moon is another appropriate time to try this as it's near impossible to see even with your eyes open.

Shape shifting

Stand opposite a mirror in a darkened room with a candle below your face. Allow yourself to focus on your third eye so that your eyes lose their sharp focus and the shadows on your face begin to blur. Alternatively, you may prefer to stare deep into your eyes until your face's appearance begins to change. Different images will appear, changing your face to resemble the faces of those you have worn in earlier incarnations.

What's in a Name?

Here are some of the names by which the ancients knew and worshipped Hecate:

Hekat, Hekate, Nocturnal Goddess of the Moon, Guardian of the Unconscious, Queen of Witches, Prytania; Queen of the Dead, The Dark Goddess, Goddess of Storms, Patron Spirit to Midwives, the Goddess Hel (from where the Christian term Hell was derived), the Celtic version of Hecate, *Morgan*, also known as *Morrigan or Mara* (i.e. Morgan le Fay).

Consider now some of the nicknames that you have been taught to associate with the archetype of the inner Wise Woman. Here's a few I thought of:

Old Maid, Witchypoo, Hag, Hippywitch, Old Bat, Little Old Woman, Granny, Evil Sorceress, Demonic Woman, Devil Worshipper, Pagan, Bride of Satan and Crazy Old Woman.

Add any you can think of and make a note of any that carry a strong charge for you. If you can remember the person who used this term, take a moment to reflect upon how wise you now consider them to be and forgive them for their ignorance.

Similarly, you may wish to consider some of the common derogatory sayings towards Wise Women that have developed during the reign of patriarchal consciousness, such as:

'How can you trust something that bleeds once a month?' Or 'She's a bit strange and into weird shit', 'Really flaky', 'Away with the fairies', 'A bit batty', 'Not all there', or 'Crazy as a cut snake'. Repeat the same process as above if you wish.

Art Therapy: Draw your Spirit Guide

Place four clear quartz crystal points in each corner of the room and place an amethyst in the centre and a smoky quartz on the ground. Put on some meditative music and sit in the centre of your crystal grid with a candle. Now close your eyes and ask Hecate to join you. You may see her or sense her energy. Draw what you see or sense as the guiding spirit of Hecate.

Embracing your Wise Woman: Further Suggestions

- Increase your wisdom with some study.
- Buy or rent some books or enrol in a metaphysical class.
- Wear an amethyst (purple) crystal to amplify the energy of your crown and third eye chakras, enabling you to better intuit guidance.
- Embrace the magical side of life by holding a ritual for the next dark moon (the phase between waning and waxing). It may be as simple as meditating by candlelight or writing down something you want to let go of or call into your life (only in accordance with free will and for the Highest Good of all) and speak your intention aloud and burn it to release it to the ether.
- Accept any changes that are happening in your life. This is a time to let go of the past. Weed, clean, throw out old possessions and clothes. The more you can let go of, the larger the opportunities you will create.
- Surrender to the void. Often feelings of lethargy or depression surround us when our inner Wise Woman wants us to focus on the inner world instead of the outer one. Allow old grief to surface, befriend the dark, sit quietly and reflect.

- Treat yourself to a Tarot reading or healing for some additional insight when you next find yourself standing at the crossroads.
- Pay special attention to your dreams. Hecate illuminates what our subconscious is trying to tell our conscious mind. Spend time reflecting on your dreams, writing them down or discussing them with friends.
- Paint your hands or feet with henna (its red colour being associated with our life-giving 'magic blood').

Get Wise

Here are a few titles that grace the bookshelves of Wise Women around the globe. Treat yourself to some brain food for your next rainy day.

Wise Woman Non-Fiction

Positive Magic by Marion Weinstein

Green Witchcraft by Ann Moura

Pocketful of Dreams by Denise Linn

Dreams. Signs of Things to Come by Quentin Watts and Vicki Canisiu

Elderwoman by Marian Van Eyk McCain

Healing with the Angels by Doreen Virtue

The Mythic Tarot Book by Juliet Sharman-Burke and Liz Greene

The Woman's Dictionary of Symbols and Sacred Objects by Barbara Walker

The Wise Wound by Penelope Shuttle and Peter Redgrove

Witch by Fiona Horne

The Magical Name by Ted Andrews

Topics for Discussion

Invite a few friends over for a cup of tea around the kitchen table and make a brew using a pot of tea leaves (or alternatively, make a pot of Turkish coffee) and read the symbols in each other's cups when you have finished discussing the following points. (Turn the cup upside down on a

tea towel and turn it three times clockwise before returning it to the upright position to read.) In addition, you may wish to...

- Explain what you have learnt from any periods of depression you have experienced.
- Discuss some of the ways that your mother or grandmother have embodied Hecate.
- Swap some home herbal remedies; for example, for lower back pain in winter, soak your feet in a bucket of water with salt and lavender oil as hot as you can stand it. This relaxes all the muscles in our body that constrict when we feel cold.
- Any paranormal experiences you or any of your loved ones have had.

Questions for Personal Reflection

Take some time this evening before you turn out your night light to contemplate the attitudes of your inner Wise Woman by pondering the following questions:

- How do you negate your own inner wisdom?
- What fears do you have about ageing?
- How can you commit to honor the needs of your inner Wise Woman in your own life?

Secret Woman's Business: Best Times to Celebrate Hecate

Halloween

Previously known as All Hallow's Eve, Samhain or the Feast of the Dead, Halloween is the night when the veils between the worlds are at their thinnest. Celebrated in Autumn (October 31st in the Northern Hemisphere and April 30th in the Southern Hemisphere) to commemorate our link with those in the spirit world. The word, 'ghost' and 'guest' used to be interchangeable words with the same meaning. Deceased ancestors and friends were always welcome guests at these feasts, with places being set for them and their names said by way of invocation and welcome.

You may wish to observe this night on your calendar by lighting candles, cooking up a feast using aromatic and warming foods that can be smelt by attending spirits such as cloves, cinnamon, ginger and cardamom. Alternatively, you may wish to cook dishes that were enjoyed traditionally by your ancestors, make a Jack-O-Lantern or tell stories about the lives of those who have crossed over.

You may also like to take the opportunity to dress up in witch's britches, a fairy costume or as someone in a previous incarnation. Halloween is a great way to teach children to celebrate endings as much as beginnings so they value both death and rebirth processes in their own lives.

Compitalia (taken from the Roman word for crossroads, which was 'Compita') was the name given to the midnight rituals that took place at crossroads on dark moons until early Christian authorities outlawed the practice by sentencing those who were caught to a three year fast! You may wish to do your own ceremony at a crossroads on a dark moon at the witching hour of midnight (which marks the zenith of nocturnal energy). Opt for a quiet country crossroad in preference to a major urban traffic intersection with lights and speed cameras!

Imbolc (also known as 'The Quickening') is the Sabbat (one of the 8 seasonal festivals) between the Winter Solstice (the longest night of the year) and the Spring Equinox, where the yin and yang energies are balanced. It is the time when the light pierces through the darkness of Winter to herald in the further lightening of days, bringing with it fresh insight and renewed hope for the future. You may wish to take a ceremonial bath, dress in white or light lots of white candles. (Imbolc falls on August 2nd in the Southern Hemisphere and February 2nd in the Northern Hemisphere.)

Wise Woman Rite of Passage Ceremony

Since Hecate is a Goddess who presides over transformation, the following is a simple ritual you can do whenever you feel depressed, grief stricken or lost in the dark. This process will help you to ground the process of death and rebirth in your body so you can accept it more completely with grace and understanding in your day-to-day life.

You Will Need:

Meditation music to play throughout the ceremony.

A bowl of salt water (just add some rock or sea salt to spring water if you wish).

Chalk, sand or river stones to mark out a large spiral on the floor (at least three metres wide).

A candle in a holder and matches.

A burning dish such as a wok or Chinese soup pot.

A compass (if you don't know the directional points of your chosen location).

Two pieces of note paper and a pen.

Scan the following list and choose those items whose magical properties are appropriate for you at this time. (Note: where possible use dried herbs instead of fresh ones as these ingredients will be burnt during the ritual.)

Mint: To Attract Helpful Spirits

Lavender: Surrender and Relaxation

Sandalwood: To Release Fear

Pepper: To Ward off Negativity

Sage: Wisdom

Frankincense: Purification

Ginger: Success

Orange Peel: Love

Rosemary: Happiness, Blessings and Courage

Thyme: Healing

St John's Wort: Energy and Power

Chamomile: Balance

Cloves: Wealth

Cinnamon: Psychic Awareness

Mustard Seeds: Passion

1. Cleanse: Dip your hands in a bowl of salt water and flick it over your body. (This will also cleanse your energetic bodies known collectively as an aura.)

2. Casting the Circle: Stand in the centre of the room and visualize a violet flame creating a circle or orb that encompasses the room. You may wish to say or think something along these lines:

I cast this circle of power in the name of love and light and ask that I am now protected in a ring of violet flames for our magical workings. Any energies evoked within this circle are done so in accordance with the free will and highest good of all.

3. Invocation of the Five Directions: (Note: If doing this ceremony in the Southern hemisphere, proceed as written, if you are in the Northern hemisphere, reverse the direction; for example, starting in the East, then invoking in the South.)

AIR

Turn to face the East and hold up your wand (or staff) as a conduit for energy and invite in the ancestral Wise Women known as Air Crones, honoring the strengths that they bring to your circle: profound thought, quickness of tongue, eloquence to compose poetry, wit and effective words of power. You may wish to say something along the lines of:

Help me to attain mental clarity, clearing any negative beliefs that are clouding my better judgment.

FIRE

Turn to face the North and hold up your wand as a conduit for energy and invite in the ancestral Wise Women known as Fire Crones, honoring the strengths that they bring to your circle: an understanding of the secrets of fire and energy, an understanding of how to conserve, store and spend energy wisely, as well as endless creativity and joy. You may wish to say something along the lines of:

Grant me the gift of divine inspiration, assisting me with the discipline to generate it for myself by reconnecting daily with the Source.

WATER

Turn to face the West and hold up your wand as a conduit for energy and invite in the ancestral Wise Women known as Water Crones, honoring the strengths that they bring to your circle: the ability to neither repress nor deny emotional responses, the gift of balance between compassion and detachment, as well as emotional sensitivity and intuition. You may wish to say something along the lines of:

Help me to honor my heart's desires as sacred and worthy of cultivation and fulfilment, as well as the courage and commitment to reflect and act upon my intuition.

EARTH

Turn to face the South and hold up your wand as a conduit for energy and invite in the ancestral Wise Women known as Earth Crones, honoring the strengths that they bring to your circle: a love and conscious understanding of what the physical body needs, a personal connection with Mother Earth, her seasons and harvests, as well as a resourceful and wise outlook in relation to money. You may wish to say something along the lines of:

Help me to find a balance between my responsibilities and creative play, enabling me to honor my physical commitments to myself and others.

SPIRIT

Turn to face upwards and hold up your wand as a conduit for energy and invite in the ancestral Wise Women known as Spirit Crones, honoring the strengths that they bring to your circle: an understanding of the psychic plane and an ability to access appropriate guides and healers from other realms, as well as the ability to help strengthen your gifts of clairvoyance, clairaudience and clairsentience. You may wish to say something along the lines of:

Help me to channel insights for my spiritual growth and trust in the support of the Divine Plan at all times.

4. Intention of Purpose: Simply state here how you want this ceremony to assist you in your life. For example:

Help me Hecate to identify and embrace what needs transforming in my life.

5. Incantation: Light your candle and focus on the light as you repeat the following mantra continuously. (This will take you into an altered state so you are receptive to receive insights.)
Hecate, wise one – come to me. Hecate, wise one – help me see.

6. Walk the Spiral: Stand at the entrance to your spiral that is marked on the floor. Feel any fears you may have about your transformation and breathe into them as energetic/emotional blocks which dissolve with each deep breath. Begin walking slowly, focusing on the light of your candle. When you reach the centre, sit and meditate, asking Hecate for insight. When you're ready, stand and walk out of the spiral, retracing your steps.

7. Letting Go: Write down on your first piece of note paper what you wish to release, then read it aloud and light it on the flame of your candle and drop it in your burning dish.

8. Calling In: Now compose a 'Lunar Wish List'. This is a list of ten things you wish to call into your life. Don't be afraid to be specific but never interfere with the free will of another. Next, declare that which you are now calling in to your life by reading aloud your lunar wish list and charge your intention, burning the herbs you have selected to assist you, waving the paper in the sacred smoke. (After the ritual, put your lunar wish list in a place where it will be exposed to the moonlight on a regular basis.)

9. Close Circle: Thank unseen friends who have gathered to witness and assist your act of co-creation, including the crones from the five directions and then diminish the violet flames in the reverse manner as when you cast the circle. Declare that your magic circle is now open. Note: It's a good idea to eat something after a ritual to ground your energy. Placing your forehead on the floor is also a quick way to ground.

Wise Woman Act of Beauty

Consider now creating your indigo mandala for the healing of the brow chakra. You may wish to incorporate Hecate's symbol, Wotan's Cross. Now create an altar to honor the journey you have undertaken with your inner Wise Woman. You may wish to adorn it with bones, spiders, black candles and fairies.

ISHTAR: THE INNER HIGH PRIESTESS

The High Priestess is the seventh and final soul sister we meet on our feminine mysteries tour. As an archetypal energy, she has been repressed culturally for approximately 2000 years. This is largely due to the influence of religious doctrines that equated a sexually liberated woman with evil. Fortunately, Ishtar presents us with the opportunity to enter the magical doorway into our own sacred sexuality, allowing us to reconnect with the divine experientially through our own bodies.

How I Discovered My High Priestess

In 1996 I was asked to leave a share house where I was living by the guy who had been there the longest, after he lost a bet to sleep with me to our other housemate... a fact I became aware of after the event! And so I found myself determined to find a place to call my own so as not to be at the mercy of another's bidding.

Unfortunately, this decision coincided with a property boom in my then home suburb of St Kilda, resulting in the quiet relocation of local artisans as apartments were systemically renovated to justify exorbitant rent increases. So after three months of repeated application rejections on account of my occupation being 'waitress', I decided to visit the legendary Byron Bay to gain some perspective on what to do next.

To my delight, I discovered a girlfriend of mine was moving to Byron to live so we decided to share expenses. Now I was really excited... being a fan of Thelma and Louise about to embark on my first road trip. The departure date arrived and we set off wearing boots and gingham, half expecting we would see Susan Sarandon en route. Twenty minutes passed and we found ourselves sitting at a red light in Preston when my friend turned to me and said, 'Guess what I've been doing the last two weeks?'

'Stripping.' She said, smiling.

I just about choked. This was my friend who was a practicing Catholic and still dating her high school sweetheart of seven years. I discreetly retrieved my gobsmacked chin off the car mat and eagerly awaited further details. She told me she had stripped for ten consecutive nights and made two grand! (Those magic words granted an instantaneous image of myself wrapped around a pole.) And so my inner quandary began...

'Hmmmmm, I'd probably be a natural. I love to dance and I have enough Scorpion energy in my natal chart to ignite a coma patient.'

I then visualized myself performing with feather fans and long gloves a la Gypsy Rose Lee.

(Gasp!) 'What am I thinking? I was a school prefect and house captain. I was a golden girl in the regional centre of Mackay, North Queensland in the late 1980s. What would people think? I have spoken out publicly against women in pornography in my stand-up act. I am an overachiever, I am not a bottle-blonde living in a trailer park.'

(Pause) 'But the money! I'd only have to work two nights a week and I could rent an art deco apartment of my own.'

(Pause) 'What about my stretch marks?'

My friend assured me all the girls had stretch marks (and cellulite, veins and wrinkles) that were undetectable under the black lights (the ones that make your teeth glow like you've swallowed uranium). She also stressed that the men weren't allowed to touch the dancers and even revealed to me her 'designer pussy' wax job in the ladies loo at a pub where we stopped for dinner. By the time we arrived in Byron I was so desperate to find a financial solution that would enable me to keep my clothes on that I seriously considered selling Amway for a full 45 minutes.

The moment of truth came when I found myself sitting on the beach and I realized that the only thing standing between me and the decision to work as an exotic dancer was my pride. Having identified my own hubris (yet again!), my spiritual ambition kicked in and I committed to give stripping a go.

On my first shift I arrived to a dressing room filled with fifty girls applying make-up in various states of undress in front of light-bulb framed mirrors. 'Hi!' I announced and not one of them responded so I quickly found a seat and began getting dressed. Then the shift manager yelled out across the crowded room, 'What's your name?'

'Tania', I replied.

'Is that your real name?' she snapped.

This took me back as I'd never been asked that before (not having worked for ASIO), so I sheepishly said, 'Yes.' And she yelled in a broad Australian drawl, 'You can't use your real name! You've got 30 seconds to think of a new one!'

The name Nicola popped in to my head. 'Nicola!' I called out (as politely as I could). She then paused and screeched, 'Ni-COLA?' unfamiliar with how to pronounce this curve ball I had inadvertently thrown her. This was the first of many incidences when I had to laugh only on the inside, a very lonely situation in which to find oneself. Those of us on our first shift were then herded down to the sub-zero basement and shown how to strip by a woman who had never stripped (curious). When she lay on her back with her legs in the air I thought this pose a tad farcical. I had preconceived ideas of showing off my repertoire of dance moves rather than mimicking a woman in second stage labour. She then started schooling us on the three currency exchange rates we would need to understand to give correct change from our garter belts. Not being a natural mathematician I had more than a little trouble grasping the all-important information, which visibly annoyed our tutor.

We were then taken upstairs to the club to look at some 'real' strippers in action. We filed in behind our drill sergeant like nervous virgins with clammy hands, bulging bladders and palpitating thyroid glands. All around the room were naked girls on tables with their genitals two centimetres from men's noses (despite the ten centimetre rule so persistently stressed in the basement). It looked like what I imagined a brothel would look like. There was a 'Spa room' where we could be asked to bathe naked with other girls or, alternatively, paint each other's naked bodies. 'Oh, my God!' It hit me like a freight train, 'I had just joined the sex industry!'

The reality was I had already signed the lease for twelve months and had moved my furniture, so I was going to have to make this new career option work. I steeled my nerves as I watched girls throwing themselves head first down poles like guest stars from a Russian Spectacular. I would be happy if I didn't trip over trying to get my underwear off over my high heels while standing on a table top.

Before I knew it, it was my turn to get up on a one metre square table and take my clothes off seductively... a real challenge to Jimmy Barnes! That said, I got through it and got off. An adrenalin sport to be sure.

Once the initial shock and nerves dissipated I actually came to enjoy parading my sexuality for all to see. (An exhibitionist from the age of five, I used to disrobe and jump up and down naked on my bed trying to distract motorists for a laugh!) I made good money relatively fast, which I attributed to my nightly meditation to invoke the Goddess, thereby igniting my inner flame to rival that of a New York precinct on a Saturday night. This piqued the resentment of one of the hardened career strippers who couldn't understand my 'success' given my lack of cleavage. She repeatedly filed complaints about my alleged 'dirty personals' (a term used to describe lap dances where the girl touched herself or allowed the patrons to touch her). And so it became commonplace for me to be stripping for a man in a private room and for him to point out that there was a young woman, the shift manager, crouched behind a pot plant watching me. To which I would dryly comment, 'I know.' I soon moved to another club that had a Goddess statue in the foyer and needless to say, I was much happier.

What I did enjoy the most was being alone on a podium and using creative visualization to invoke the divine with whom I would dance erotically. (My favourite invocation was the dancing Hindu God, Shiva. Known as the 'Lord Of The Dance' before Michael Flatley.) Whereupon I would lose myself in an ecstatic trance state, to the point where I'd have sexual juices trickling down to my ankles, much to the bewilderment of club patrons. This gave me a taste of what it must have been like for Ishtar's temple dancers so long ago. This, however, was a constant challenge given the 'Solomon's Temple' attitude of the clubs, which honored bar takings over any allegiance to ancient deities. The other big perk was that I could eat two consecutive breakfasts and not gain weight, thanks to the gruelling twelve hour shifts.

As a result of this experience, I determined to be responsible for honoring my sexual needs. I took lovers when I was single. I regularly did dynamic meditation to release energy blocks and accessed ecstatic states through frenetic breathing techniques. And eventually (when I was so disillusioned with men that my nickname was 'Snapdragon'), I befriended my husband and negotiated a relationship built on spiritual values and emotional healing, instead of my old pattern of unconscious seduction. Before we consummated our union sexually, I vividly remember the night when Ishtar visited me and 'rode' my body for two hours. Pluto was making some transit across our night sky that was beyond my immediate comprehension but which resulted in kundalini surges that gave me physical tremors so marked I was hard pressed to keep my dinner on my fork. My dear friend and housemate recognized my need for release and kindly offered her deluxe range of vibrator attachments, which I declined as I felt awkward at the thought of them. Instead I ran a bath, using a blend of herbs and salts that had been infused with magical intention, surrounded myself with candles and exotic music and oils and invoked the Goddess, Ishtar.

First, I closed my eyes and began chanting to the music. Next the mantra, 'I am divine' began running through my head, until it increased with such intensity and rhythm that it began spilling out of my mouth as my body began to writhe, my skin slippery with oils. I literally became delirious. So heightened were my senses that I was groaning with pleasure and I wasn't even touching myself. I began speaking in tongues and sweating and turned on the shower above my head, sending fresh water cascading over my electrified skin. When the energy had run its course, I dressed myself ceremonially in a silk shift draped with a purple velvet priestess robe, anointed myself and thanked the Goddess. I remember walking back into the house from the bungalow holding the burning candelabra triumphantly like the Statue of Liberty, knowing that I was now ready for divine union.

Several years have now passed and I have written a trilogy of books on Sacred Union, assisted countless couples into states of deeper emotional and psychological intimacy as a Tantric coach and been met by my Beloved who honors all the facets of my sacred feminine and shares my passion for walking the path of Sacred Union.

HIGH PRIESTESS QUIZ

Answer the following quick quiz to find out what shape your inner High Priestess is currently in. (Circle the answer that most describes you.)

A friend invites you to attend a Tantric Love Goddess workshop, do you:

A. Laugh at her and tell her absolutely not?

B. Ask her to tell you all about it afterward?

C. Feel excited by the prospect and agree to go with her?

You're at a party with great people, music and food, do you:

A. Stick by the side of the person you came with?

B. Eat, drink or smoke more than you wish you had the next day?

C. Dance like there's no tomorrow?

Do you consider the most important relationship in your life to be:

A. With your partner?

B. With yourself?

C. With Spirit?

Now add up your score. A = 1, B = 2, C = 3. *If you scored:*

1 – 3 Your inner High Priestess has a chastity belt on that is keeping your sacred flame the size of a tea light. This next chapter will enable you to find the key to liberate your ecstasy.

4 – 6 Your inner High Priestess is feeling drawn to the flame of Divine ecstasy but is holding a fire blanket and hose just in case things get out of hand. The next chapter will help you better understand your fears so you can overcome them and shine in your full radiance.

7 – 9 You refract the light of Spirit in all colours of the rainbow. This following chapter will gift you with further tips on how to merge more deeply with the Divine Source and experience even greater levels of ecstatic rapture.

Herstory: High Priestess Goddesses

The aspect of the High Priestess or bride of the Divine was known as many names in the ancient world such as Ishtar (our tour guide), Inanna, Astarte, Ashtart, Athar, Attar-Samayin, Ishara, Ashera, Attart, Athra, Stella Maris and Esther (all of which mean star). To the Native Americans and Inuit tribes she was known as Rainbow Woman; to the Celts she was known as Iris, the Angel of Temperance; to the Hindu's she was known as Shakti, consort of Shiva who together danced creation into existence. Mary Magdalene as the sacred prostitute and bride of Christ was another incarnation of this aspect, which has long been misunderstood and shamed culturally, although her title survived, being given to nuns who took vows devoting themselves to the Christ as his symbolic bride. I also include in this archetype Lakshmi and Abundantia, ancient creatress Goddesses who embody divine pleasure, sensuality and abundance on all levels.

The Myth of Ishtar

Ishtar was the Babylonian Queen of Heaven. As a majestic feminine figure she made Cleopatra look positively drab. An exotic beauty of unparalleled proportions, she dazzled onlookers with both her charm and scintillating fashions as she sashayed about her crystal palace. A well-respected matriarch for both her leadership and love, she resided high in the Ogdoad, the eighth planetary sphere, which was symbolized by a ring of eight stars.

One day, according to ancient legend, Ishtar received word from Ereshkigal, her sister that her husband had died, so Ishtar prepared to attend his funeral rite and pay her respects.

And so Ishtar prepared to journey below, beneath the primordial ocean, to visit her pregnant sister, the Queen of the Underworld. First she fastened about her the seven meys, the crown jewels that symbolized her unearthly powers, knowing full well that Ereshkigal's gatekeepers would instruct her to remove her royal regalia as a condition of entry. (It was custom that all men and women entered the Great Below naked and as vulnerable as the next person.) Ishtar began her descent, meeting another of Ereshkigal's henchmen at each of the gates who took from her the following items:

Gate 1 – her royal crown

Gate 2 – her earrings

Gate 3 – her necklace

Gate 4 – the amulet from her breast

Gate 5 – the beaded girdle from her waist

Gate 6 – the bangles from her wrists and ankles

Gate 7 – her clothes

Ereshkigal, who was envious of her sister's station in life then called her right-hand man, Namtar, and commanded that Ishtar be thrown in her dungeon instead of attending her husband's funeral. She then summoned sixty diseases to lay waste upon every part of her sister's body, which was then hung on a stake like a piece of rotting meat and she was then left to die for three days without medical treatment.

Meanwhile, up in the high altitudes of Heaven, Ishtar's handmaiden Ninshubur grieved her Queen's descent into hell and appealed to the other Gods and Goddesses in the Great Above for help in securing her safe return. But fearful of Ereshkigal's wrath, none of the other deities would come to her aid. That is, except for the God, Ea who took pity on her and agreed to help. This he did by fashioning two beings from the dirt under his fingernails. He named them the Galatur, two creatures that would be spared the usual death rite upon entry to the Underworld as they were classified as inhuman.

Fortunately, as Ishtar hung dying, the Galatur arrived as Ereshkigal was in the throes of giving birth. So grateful was she for their ceaseless help during the birth that she promised them any wish they could name. At once they requested the release of Ishtar, who was immediately freed and allowed to return to her own celestial sphere. There was but one condition. She would have to choose another to descend into the Underworld to take her place. This was in return for her having received the gift of ultimate power and wisdom, which could only be gained through the experience of death.

Ishtar agreed and soon arrived home to find her dutiful handmaiden, Ninshubur and her two sons waiting by the seventh gate, bemoaning her sad fate. But then she looked around and noticed her husband, Dumuzi, was nowhere to be seen. Finally she reached the palace only to find him decked out in his splendour, sitting upon Ishtar's throne whilst smoking a reed pipe. Ishtar, furious at his indifference, instantly appointed him as her successor in the Underworld. Hearing this judgment he panicked and fled, only to be followed by Underworld demons determined to capture their prey. Terrified, he ran to his sister Gestinanna's house and hid.

Upon hearing of the death sentence that awaited Dumuzi, Gestinanna was moved to try and protect him by offering to share his fate. A plea that Ereshkigal considered before determining that Dumuzi would thereafter spend six months of the year in the Underworld and six months a year in the Great Above, during which time Gestinanna would serve half his sentence in the Great Below.

Further facts

Archaeologists working throughout the area once known as Mesopotamia have since uncovered figurines made of lead that depict the act of sacred sex, where the men are shown always in a standing position, whilst the women are reclining on altars. (A little different to the pressure put on women today to be pornographic circus performers in the boudoir. So don't install that trapeze unless it turns you on!)

The Moral

In order to find a partner who doesn't take you for granted, you may first have to go to hell and back to truly know yourself. To do this, one must strip back all the beliefs, ambitions and creature comforts that were afforded you by your station in life. (These are then replaced with a more mature and personal perspective after much personal contemplation.) After a woman has undertaken this rigorous journey into the shadow lands she will never prostitute herself again by staying with a man who is not mature and wise enough to honor her as his queen.

Further facts

Ishtar's temples were the central icon of ancient Middle Eastern cities. Each temple featured a processional of lions and an eternal flame (similar to our modern war memorials). The flame represented the infinite sacred flame of spirit, which her priestesses kept alight. (Interesting to note that our patriarchal western society honors the spirit of the dying God in the same way the ancients celebrated that of the living Goddess.) Her tantric priestesses were called Red Dakinis, Brides of Divinity or The Sacred Harlots of Ishtar. *The term Dakini means skywalker (indicating that these chicks were using the force long before Luke started waving his tantric wand of light about!).*

Historical Appearance

Prior to the Judeo-Christian religions, Ishtar was the most popular deity ever to be worshipped. Clay figurines that have been unearthed throughout the Middle East portray her as voluptuous, with buxom breasts and trademark large, fleshy thighs and derriere. (Mmm, bootylicious!) Her presence has been described as being as tall as the heavens and as wide as the Earth. (That's no shrinking violet.)

She is usually portrayed cupping at least one of her breasts with her hand, in what is known as The Ishtar Pose, hence her title, Mother of the Fruitful Breast (the Carmen Miranda of mammary glands!). She is often dressed in transparent veils or a robe not dissimilar to Joseph's, reflecting all the colours of the rainbow and laden with jewels and sensual Middle-Eastern finery, namely her legendary beaded girdle.

She was described as having long, dishevelled hair and an undulating, serpentine body reminiscent of the hypnotic pelvic moves performed by belly dancers. She often held a torch, symbolizing her eternal flame of spirit and liberation. The most well-known artistic depiction of her is in fact the Statue of Liberty, a gift from the French government to the United States to celebrate their newly won freedom.

Ishtar often appears winged, with bright sunbeams radiating from her image and a crown halo of eight stars about her head. Her attire and state of partial or total undress often reflects her patronage of prostitutes and her role as the Goddess of Sex.

Further facts

Uruk or Erech (now called Iraq), considered Ishtar's holy city, was called the town of Sacred Courtesans, although Ishtar was also said to preside as a patron over harlots who worked in ale houses. In fact, in Iraq today they still dress their scarecrows as brides of the Divine, in the hope their masculine deity will 'make water on her' and fertilize their crops with rain (representing semen).

Worshipped as the Queen of Heaven, she was considered one of the most powerful Goddesses in the Assyrian, Sumerian, Akkadian and Babylonian pantheons. This is because she was portrayed expressing both her warrior and lover aspects, indicating she had integrated both her masculine and feminine to become a supreme being. In her warrior aspect, she was represented by a chariot drawn by seven lions and holding a bow in her hand. As a lover, she was known for her voluptuousness and passion.

High Priestess Profile

Ishtar is the part of us that aligns our sexuality with our spirituality. This is necessary since both aspects are expressions of the same creative life force. When they are viewed as separate, we tend to sit in the polarity we feel most comfortable with and judge the other as less important. For example, many priests and nuns suppress their sexuality, seeing it as 'a lowly desire', only to preach piety (their spirituality being more about their ego's ambition than their personal connection). As a result their repressed sexual energy distorts and plays out in the shadow of their psyche, being expressed in covert liaisons that experiment with the use of power, such as the molestation of children.

Similarly, those smug folk who ridicule those who openly express their spirituality (out of fear they themselves will be ridiculed for showing their vulnerability) tend to become obsessed with sexual pleasure that focuses only on physical and emotional sensations, creating both sexual and sensate addictions. Neither example is balanced. We need to allow the natural ignition of our sexual energy and then use our consciousness to channel that energy upward to experience prolonged ecstasy with the divine.

Women with access to their Ishtar energy usually have an earthy sensuality that is delightfully unaffected. They'll eat with their fingers given the opportunity and often have a bawdy wit, possessing the ability to laugh heartily, both at themselves and with others. It is their manner, their lust for life that attracts people to them (a fact, which sadly eludes women who are manicured, bleached, pumped full of botox and silicone, whilst wearing overpriced designer clothes. Sweetie, Darling!). It is precisely this attitude that enables women to exude natural sex appeal.

Often an Ishtar woman will appear to have a fiery quality about her, which translates as enthusiasm, passion and creativity. It is these traits that fire up the spark in others, attracting more than moths to their flame. For this reason it is important that women with overt High Priestess archetypes keep a careful check on their energy levels, resisting the urge to always shine brightly even if that's what acquaintances come to expect, the quintessential party girl. To honor our inner Ishtar, it is imperative that we get adequate rest to avoid burn out. Similarly, we can avoid the shadow overtaking our inner High Priestess by not allowing financial fears or greed to prostitute our energy levels by feeling pressured to work more than our equilibrium can sustain. Burn-out can also be caused by 'Taking on too much', as lots of opportunities excite our inner Ishtar and she has a problem saying no, resulting in us spreading ourselves too thinly across the board. Alternatively, substance abuse such as drugs and alcohol that keep her feeling 'high' at the cost of her adrenals, also pose another potential threat to her divine spark. It is important to note that what re-awakens her flame is experiencing reconnection with the Divine, heightening her energetic sensitivity and charging her personal force field with a voltage that is guaranteed to ignite others. This also enhances her sensitivity so that flavours are experienced as more intense, touch more stimulating, sound more mood-altering and aromas more intoxicating. (Many shadow Ishtars use drugs for the same effect, which leave them feeling like their mental perception is clouded and their battery needs a severe jump start.)

Alternatively, if our inner Ishtar's energy has been shamed or repressed, we may harshly judge other women who express themselves sexually as cheap or profane, rather than look inwardly to release our own blocks and inhibitions. Sexual abuse can also result in the suppression of a woman's Ishtar energy, leaving her feeling ill-equipped to deal with any wolfish male attention that she may attract should she allow her inner Ishtar out to be seen. It is for this reason that Ishtar must be approached from the inside out, by first acknowledging and healing any past painful sexual experiences, so that boundaries can be set with confidence. This allows a woman to liberate her spontaneous sensual nature, instead of forever keeping it under lock and key for fear of unwanted repercussions. It is valuable to remember that our sexual energy is also our divine spark, our life force. So if we are suppressing or blocking this energy out of fearing consequences, we are only really half alive.

The following two case studies illustrate scenarios where women have suppressed their Ishtar energy and suffered as a result:

Sandra

Sandra was a married mother of three children. Although she loved her husband deeply, their sex life was ultimately unfulfilling for her. Rather than insist on addressing this with Tantra workshops or visits with a sexual therapist, Sandra repressed her inner Ishtar's needs until the day came when a man came along who lit her dormant sexual spark. Ishtar's need for sexual fulfilment overpowered her rational mind. She had a brief affair, but felt overcome with guilt, so ended the fling and told her husband of her infidelity. She then shamed her Ishtar energy further by inwardly avowing to suppress her 'better than she had before'. The result being that her previous lover began stalking her and tormenting her. Despite a restraining order, he spray-painted obscenities about her, calling her a slut and a whore on her family car. Because she felt this way about herself, she had attracted a man who was mirroring her own beliefs about her denigrated Ishtar archetype.

Melissa

Also a wife and mother, Melissa was in a similar situation where she was not feeling sexually fulfilled within her marriage. Although she had pleaded with her husband relentlessly over many years to address his lack of libido, he had never followed through his assurances that he'd address his disinterest in sex.

Eventually, the day came when her Ishtar archetype became sexually attracted to a young man who worked at her local convenience store. Although she failed to act upon her urges, feeling them inappropriate, she was emotionally distraught to the point where she was considering leaving her husband.

On a positive note, more women are consciously embracing Ishtar and reaping the rewards. Take for example the following case study:

Roslyn

Roslyn, a 58 year old grandmother and spiritual healer, decided to spice up her sex life with her conventional husband of many years by renting a five-star hotel room and surprising him by appearing in black vinyl fetish wear. Both she and her startled husband had a thoroughly fun evening and rekindled their love life.

Many maidens often unconsciously trade on their sexual appeal in their quest for true love. This can lead to a string of one-night stands, where they are unable to discern the nice guys (or girls) from the wolves in sheep's clothing. Many young girls also need to reflect on their behaviour and choices to avoid getting caught up in the heat of the moment against their own better judgment. Not so much from a moral standpoint, but in order to better protect their emotional and physical wellbeing (for example, sexually transmitted diseases, unwanted pregnancies and lowered self-esteem).

Unfortunately, in our western culture there is still a double-standard that credits boys and young men who are sexually promiscuous as 'studs' and judges young women who engage in the same behaviour as 'sluts', creating a social stigma that can be psychologically damaging. Women in general should be assured that a strong sexual drive is healthy if accompanied by empowered, conscious choices. This requires a strong sense of self which would be greatly enhanced if more young girls received adequate instruction into the love arts as part of their rite of passage into womanhood. For example; if girls were encouraged to pleasure themselves sensually and sexually they wouldn't be as likely to experiment with partners who didn't honor them. Similarly, being introduced to Tantric practices such as dance meditation and energy healings would enable them to experience energetic and transcendental union, with a bliss factor akin to great sex, lessening their dependency on needing someone else physically to take them into an ecstatic state.

After all, learning to contain our sexual energy is the first step in finding and establishing a soul mate partnership, as this allows our Higher Selves to connect and create intimacy without the lower selves' propensity for lust, need and dependency raising their head until communication and trust are firmly established. (Nana advice, but it works, 'Be friends first'.)

Unfortunately, what our commercial conditioning imprints upon us is, 'perfect the art of seduction to get the best looking person in the room' (who often turns out to be the most self-centred, unaware and arrogant!). You only need frequent any nightclub to see Darwin's survival of the fittest playing out in animalistic scenarios, with the dominant macho alpha males seeking out the pretty, but naive young girls. My advice is to find another venue in which to dance and only visit a meat market if you intend to buy a scotch fillet!

Although Ishtar is married in the myth, she is also a patron of sexual healing and as such, encourages women to take full responsibility for meeting their sexual needs within a sacred context. It is therefore very helpful for women to consider seeing a professional female Tantrika (Tantric healer) to clear emotional and energetic blocks to intimacy by reconnecting them with their breath and their bodies. It is also a key component of Tantra to develop an awareness of the inner Goddesses and the chakras they govern, enabling us to honor ourselves and our bodies as sacred so we insist others treat us accordingly. Because ultimately there's nothing as attractive as a self-fulfilled woman, who knows and sees herself as divine but more importantly, a woman who has made this transition will not compromise herself or her values in order to secure a mate.

Ishtar also knows the value of expressing all of her Divine powers; as a loving and loyal wife, a bedroom nymph, a temple priestess and a consummate businesswoman. It is for this reason that she would not enter into any union that denied her the full expression of each and any of these roles. Hence her totem animal is the lion, as it takes a King, a mature and well-rounded male, not a mere knight to match her. In fact, it is often an encounter with an Ishtar woman that marks the catalyst for a man making this transition from knight to King, which is why it was said that it is Ishtar who gives a King the sceptre to rule.

Ishtar represents the illuminating power of the full moon. As the completion of Lilith's journey to find her shadow to become wise, she reconnects us with our ultimate truth, that we are a divine being having a human experience. Knowing this, she is unashamed in testifying to the source of her inner strength, that being her spiritual conviction and devotion. It is this truth that gives her the courage to stand up for herself, knowing that she is perfect in the eyes of the Divine and is therefore beyond the judgment of mortals.

This knowing is reclaimed in her journey through the seven levels of entropy, where she discovers what illusions are separating her from experiencing her Divine being. It is this ability to see and know her own warts that enables her to transcend being controlled by her shadow nature. This entitles her the status of 'Magician', as she now has the ability to consciously transform her external world through conscious thoughts, words and actions (rather than reacting to life's experiences as a victim who seeks to blame others for her sometimes naïve choices).

High Priestess Strengths

The following is a description of how we behave when our inner High Priestess is appreciated and expressed:

- I use my energy creatively, especially when I'm celibate so I don't become desperate for someone else to 'come and light my fire' sexually at the pub on Friday night.
- I see my body as a vessel through which to channel celestial spirit.
- I clear my emotional blocks through dance, singing, drawing or self-pleasuring.
- I choose partners who are my equal instead of those I can dominate out of my fear of true intimacy.
- I use my sense of humour to include and uplift, not exclude and put down.
- I let my bawdy wit out to be witnessed by all, including my partner and in mixed company. (People who say, 'Too much information' are afraid of honesty and fun!)
- I feel comfortable both initiating and receiving sexual contact, knowing I deserve to be pleasured.
- I value my sexual expression as natural, healthy and divine (both my primal lust and my sacred sensuality).
- I enjoy sexual exploration set at a pace I feel comfortable with (so I don't feel like crap in the morning waking up next to a stranger).
- I have the spiritual maturity to establish a celibate courtship with potential partners so I can discern their genuine interest and commitment to a sacred union.
- I am able to explore deeper levels of emotional and energetic intimacy with myself, spirit, friends and my partner, which helps keep my sexuality alive and connected.
- I set aside regular time with myself and/or partner to honor our sacredness sexually, sensually and energetically.
- I regularly clean and protect my energy field with white light.
- I honor my spiritual truth by anchoring and integrating my inner and outer self in all that I do.
- I respect my body as Divine by adorning it and treating it lovingly.
- I value my energetic bodies by experiencing and giving energetic healings such as Reiki.

High Priestess Shadow Traits

The following is a description of how we behave when we have suppressed the inner High Priestess within our psyche:

- Sometimes I view sexuality as cheap or dirty or think of vaginas as unclean.
- I fear my sexuality so I suppress feelings of arousal rather than heal past traumas and set clear boundaries, using discernment when choosing partners.

- As a result of cutting off from my sexual energy I inadvertently suppress my life force.
- I sometimes use seduction to secure a mate and then resent them for not valuing the sacredness of our union.
- I can unconsciously flirt to get my material needs met.
- I can seduce, but later scapegoat the role of 'seducer' on to 'the other' not owning my part in the mutual conquest when it's over.
- I can use my sexuality as a weapon, withholding sex to exert power.
- I can sell out my personal ethics for short-term material gain because I am driven by survival fears.
- I can compulsively use substances to avoid feeling dissatisfied, rather than face and change my reality (i.e. cigarettes unconsciously create a literal 'smoke screen').
- I don't appreciate what I give others, so I often feel indebted when others reward me materially.
- I can be demanding and expect people to give me energy instead of containing and regenerating my own energy.
- I can burn too brightly, then burn out because I have an ego attachment to being seen as a shining light at all times.
- I can take on too many projects and social events because they all excite me rather than be realistic about my time limits and energy.
- I rebel to pursue external freedom rather than do a spiritual discipline to experience inner freedom.
- I can suppress my spontaneity for fear of being out of control.
- I can deplete my energy reserves because I become greedy for money and overwork myself.
- I can choose partners who don't comprehend or value my spirituality, which reflects my internal lack of commitment to my own spiritual path.
- I want to marry for status or financial security because I fear putting my trust in the Divine Plan.
- I tend to denigrate myself with self-deprecating humour.

High Priestess Lessons

To balance your inner High Priestess's strengths and weaknesses, try the following suggestions:

- Pursue inner adventures such as creative visualization and meditation to avoid needing drugs that give an inner adventure at a cost to your body.
- Consecrate your body by honoring it as a temple for Spirit instead of using it purely to serve ego desires without reverence.
- Consecrate sexual unions by first connecting with Spirit, granting you abundant energy to share sexually with your partner.

- Nurture your sensual and sexual needs without guilt or judgment.
- Educate your partner in both sensual and energetic pleasuring to enhance sex. Explore a balance of primal fornication and Tantric union with partners.
- Unblock any energy centres that are constricted with fears or past hurts.
- Reassess any beliefs that your family and society gave you and see if they resonate as true for your soul's life path.
- Pay attention to when you feel drained by a situation or a person and remove yourself.
- Top up your energy daily from Spirit so you don't need to unconsciously steal it from others by demanding attention.
- Learn to identify how you and others you know are 'energy vampires'.

High Priestess Relationship Patterns

Personal

Sex has long been considered taboo for a woman to enjoy and express on her terms. The contraceptive pill certainly played its part in liberating women sexually in the 1960s, limiting the likelihood of unwanted pregnancies, should women dare to act on their libido. However, this has since contributed to us being collectively less discerning with our potential sexual partners, heightening the risk of emotional, mental and physical health abuse, and further highlighting our need for the positive integration of Ishtar within our personal relationships.

Another indication that the archetype of the High Priestess is sorely needed within our relationships is the fact that half of all marriages now end in divorce. I don't see this as altogether bad, but rather as a phase of natural progression as we move beyond co-dependent wedlock into more mutually empowering conscious unions.

Another contributing factor is that our preparation for the great rite of sacred marriage has become more about what shoes, flowers and cake to have than a thorough understanding and training in the love arts, Tantra and our human potential. It is my personal wish that each woman has access to these ancient feminine gifts prior to joining with another, enabling her to positively anchor the archetype of High Priestess both for her own and her beloved's conscious enjoyment.

Ultimately, the inner Ishtar aspect is vital to the survival of a marriage. If a woman suppresses her Ishtar energy within a marriage, fearing her lusty self may be off-putting to her spouse as 'cheap', she is vulnerable to becoming so erotically attracted to another man who does spark her sexual energy that she has an affair against her better judgment. Likewise, if 'the whore' is not present in the marital chamber, a husband is more likely to be seduced by it elsewhere or pay for professional services. This is particularly prevalent in traditional European cultures where the Mother is placed on a pedestal and revered as holy whilst she is expected to serve her family as a martyr. A falsehood both men and women rebel against by seeking out the harlot archetype elsewhere. (For instance, girls seeing boys behind their parents' backs and husbands who keep a mistress on the side or visit brothels.)

The popularity of medications, such as Viagra, further indicates that Ishtar is in need of more recognition within our relationships. Treating the symptoms of impotency and frigidity without addressing the root cause (excuse the pun) is indicative of our reaction to all manner of soul sicknesses – mask it with drugs and then act righteous when our kids use illegal drugs to do the same.

Famous Wise Women

Fortunately, Ishtar has been stepping out of her closet inch by inch this century with notables such as the bawdy actress, Mae West, the breast baring Italian politican, Ciccholina and famed sexologist, Annie Sprinkle lighting the way for others to follow.

Other lesser-known Ishtars include the Statue of Liberty (see Historical Appearance) and Snow White. The latter is an adaptation of the Ishtar myth, with Snow White meeting the seven dwarves (representing each of what also became the Christian seven deadly sins) in her journey to become whole, wise and prepared for sacred union with her beloved.

High Priestess Makeover Kit

The following pages include a treasure trove of exquisite items guaranteed to help unleash your Ishtar energy. From crystals, aromatic oils, jewels and finger licking aphrodisiacs... what follows is a Pandora's box of sensual bliss.

Suggested Styles

Although this is primarily an inner makeover, clothes play an important part in influencing our behaviour. So if you wish to activate your Ishtar energy, try experimenting with a few of these fashions from Ishtar's closet. Basically, anything exotic is the rule of thumb here. But below you'll find a few more hints.

- *Wear big dangly earrings, also try toe rings and anklets (a la 'bells on her fingers and rings on her toes!'). Adorn yourself with belly rings, nose rings, bindis, body jewelry and glitter so you sparkle from head to toe (stick-on ones are a good alternative to piercing).*
- *Paint your toenails red and apply aromatic oils to your skin.*
- *Seek out belts that draw attention to your yoni and hipster clothes that reveal your curvaceous pelvis.*
- *Drape fabrics that have luminescent qualities like silk, lurex or sequinned garments.*
- *Use soft, translucent scarves in brilliant colours that are great to break hard lines and are also good for furnishing your boudoir.*
- *Treat yourself to a pair of ornamental jewel-encrusted dress thongs.*
- *Dare to wear clothes that reveal your midriff and belly, no matter what curves or caesarean scars you're sporting. If you love them, so will others.*

- *Outline your eyes with kohl pencil and accentuate your erogenous neck and collar bone with a choker.*
- *Wear suspender stockings that reveal your fleshy thighs just to feel like a minx no matter what the occasion.*
- *Decorate a bra with beads or purchase a brassiere or bodice that packages your buxom breasts like a serving platter.*
- *Style jewelled belly laces and gold, silver or diamante strands about your forehead and hair.*

High Priestess Colours

If you're feeling drawn to wearing these colour combinations, Ishtar is in the house! (Using this as an indication you may also be interested to learn which of your workmates is a Tantric Goddess behind closed doors!)

Crimson

This is the combination of red and purple, representing the base and crown chakras, which your inner High Priestess aligns. Crimson signifies passion, in that it mimics the shade of a blood-engorged vulva and is both intense and deep like Ishtar's affections.

Colours of the Rainbow

Ishtar was said to wear the colours of the rainbow around her neck, signifying that she had earned her royal regalia by journeying across the rainbow between the Great Above and the Great Below, integrating all of her energies and becoming whole and aligned with Spirit.

High Priestess Associated Chakra

Crown Chakra

Located at the top of the head, this energy centre is our portal to the Celestial realms. Its function is to vitalize the upper brain (cerebrum) and unify our ego with our Higher Self, channelling forth Divine inspiration, guidance, union with the Infinite and heightened consciousness. Its colour is violet.

High Priestess Essential Oils

Patchouli

Patchouli calms the nervous system and enhances feelings of love and passion.

Ylang Ylang

A reputed aphrodisiac, ylang ylang also gives one a feeling of inner peace as it slows a rapid heartbeat while stimulating the senses.

Bergamot

This is a stimulant oil that assists in the expression of creative energy.

Jasmine

Mix a few drops with avocado oil for an aphrodisiac massage oil blend (or wear a sprig of fresh jasmine in your hair to welcome Spring).

High Priestess Minerals, Crystals and Stones

Diamond

Diamond dispels blockages in the crown chakra, assists one in accessing master healer energies, and enhances and purify the mind, body, spirit connection. It also strengthens faithfulness.

Amethyst

Amethyst assists channelling abilities, cuts through illusion and transmutes the lower energy centres into their highest potential, divine love.

Carnelian

Carnelian is a highly evolved healing mineral which assists in the purifying of the blood, liver, kidneys, gallbladder, pancreas and lungs. It also enhances soul connection.

High Priestess Food

Chocolate

In ancient Egypt only royalty were permitted to enjoy drinking chocolate. The Mayans, another ancient and highly advanced civilization, also brewed it with chilli powder for use in ritual.

Wine

Wine has long been used in fertility rituals to relax and release inhibitions. Try mixing red wine with ginger, cloves, vanilla and sugar for a potent aphrodisiac ambrosia.

Spices and Herbs

Nutmeg was used by both the Indians and Europeans as an aphrodisiac and to prevent premature ejaculation. Cumin, coriander, cardamom, chilli, basil, ginger and garlic are also known for their aphrodisiac properties.

Exotic fruits

Quince was traditionally eaten at weddings and dedicated to the Goddess. (Great with gruyere cheese!) Grapes are associated with Dionysus, the God of sexuality, food and wine. One Tantric exercise is to put a whole grape in your mouth and take twenty minutes to peel it with your teeth inside your mouth and explore its tastes and textures completely before swallowing. Many other fruits are suggestive because of their visual association with genitalia, for example banana (masculine) or oven-dried roma tomatoes, known as love apples (feminine). Other fruits, such as mango are great for their texture and luscious juice, which is best eaten with the hands.

Honey

Honey is often used as an ingredient in aphrodisiac dishes. Try mixing with almonds, pepper and ginger. In Arabian bridal showers, the bride would be bathed ritualistically by her new mother-in-law and presented with a pair of honey-filled slippers symbolizing her new journey of sweet wedded bliss.

Nuts

Nuts, particularly pistachios, are suggested in Arabian love manuals. Almonds and pine nuts are also recommended as well as walnuts, which were used in ancient Roman fertility rites.

Rice

Symbolically rice was thrown at weddings to represent the groom's sperm showering the newly-weds with fertility!

High Priestess Flowers

Lotus

In many ancient traditions (Chinese, Egyptian, Indian and Middle Eastern), the lotus was the flower of the mystical quest, which later became known as the Holy Grail throughout England and Europe. In Persia, the King's sceptre was in fact a stylized lotus, representing his union with the Goddess, the lotus resembling her sacred doorway to the great beyond, her yoni.

Orchid

Although this flower resembles the female genitalia, its name comes from the Greek word for testicle, orchis, as its twin bulbs resemble a set of man's balls. It has long been used as a love charm to enhance virility, being given to rams and goats that were reluctant to mate and as an ingredient in love potions. In the Arthurian language of flowers, a gift of an orchid was an intention to seduce.

High Priestess Hangouts

The following is a list of places where our inner Ishtar is more than happy to hang out. Feel inspired to pay them a visit or create your own.

Goddess Temples

Although most were destroyed when the patriarchal religions surfaced, many are being rebuilt to reflect the growing interest in the Divine Feminine. You may wish to create an area in your home or garden that honors the Goddess. Suggestions include water features, ferns, statues or pictures of female angels, fairies, Goddesses, crystals, flowers, draped fabrics, candles and incense.

The Sacred Marriage Chamber

Give your bedroom a makeover in honor of your inner High Priestess. Create a canopy, invest in some decadent cushions, have candles ready to light either side of your bed and smudge the room regularly with incense or sage to clear old stagnant energies.

Bordellos

As their patron, Ishtar is a Goddess readily evoked in all sex industry venues. Hopefully we will see more of these venues honoring the Divine Feminine and elevating the love arts back to the consecrated position they deserve, introducing men and boys to both the mystical and sensual realms instead of merely prostituting women's bodies and energy for profit.

Harems

Thankfully not prevalent, with polygamy being illegal in most countries, as the reality of harem life for women is one of boredom and subsequent competitive dramas as a result of being kept in captivity for sexual service. That said, creating a harem as an Ishtar fantasy is a fun way to reconnect with your sacred sexual priestess. I regularly host bridal showers in an exotic harem setting with all invited guests attending in full Goddess regalia! You may wish to have your own Harem party with your best gal pals by simply decorating your lounge or sunroom with a silk parachute, draping soft fabrics, creating aesthetic water features with lotus flowers and floating candles and arranging large velvet cushions on a Persian rug. Prepare a sumptuous banquet or each bring a plate and share your sexual secrets and hot tips! Hiring a hot tub and serving an aphrodisiac ambrosia is a great addition.

Chai Tents

Named after the delicious, spicy, milky tea, chai tents have long been popular in the Middle East as a gathering place for conversation, peace pipes and live music. Now gaining ever-increasing popularity in the West, many alternative gatherings such as folk festivals and weekend markets are incorporating them regularly with great success. Try serving a brew of the aromatic and sweet chai tea at your next party whilst sitting under a translucent canopy so you can still see the stars. (Chai tea can be purchased at most health food stores.)

High Priestess Astrological Sign

Take note whenever the moon is in Virgo (for approximately two and a half days each month), as your inner Ishtar may want to come out to play. This may be felt more intensely when the full moon is in Virgo or the Sun.

Virgo

Virgo is the sign of the priestess so those with strong Virgoan energy know the importance of sacred space, of needing to contain and distil their energy and use it wisely. Most people with Virgo prominently in their natal chart have an innate understanding of Tantric principles. As Scorpio represents the bottom half of the Shekinah, the serpent's primal lust, Virgo represents the top branches of the Tree of Life that transmute and refine those same energies as the Goddess extends heavenward, joining with the infinite and allowing her individuality to dissolve. Virgo qualities include skepticism, tact, neatness and energetic sensitivity. Virgoans need cyclic routine to thrive and as such often enjoy the cyclic rituals celebrated by the Goddess on her seasonal calendar.

High Priestess Symbols

To live as a Goddess is to invite the magic of serendipity and synchronicity along with you every time you venture out the front door. For example, if you are unsure if your inner High Priestess wants to get better acquainted with you, just check to see if any of the following icons cross your path and you'll know it's a sign that Ishtar is giving you the nod.

The Rainbow

The rainbow is traditionally the bridge between Heaven and Earth, hence its popularity as the road home used by famous seekers such as Dorothy and Kermit the Frog. All ancient mythologies incorporated the rainbow as a sacred emblem. From the Australian Aboriginal rainbow serpent, to the Haitian Maman Brigette, the Cuban Olla and African Oya. As a symbol it represents all colours and creeds together in harmony. (It is by no mistake that our gay and lesbian brothers and sisters walk beneath this banner.) Scientifically, a rainbow is the outcome when light is refracted through a prism, similar to the diffusion of white light through our etheric bodies, resulting in the seven coloured chakras or energy centres. Just as all matter consists of vibrating energy particles, items such as skin, hair, plants and stones when viewed under close inspection in strong sunlight are said to reveal millions of tiny rainbows. Crystals in particular are said to radiate rainbow energies. Oriental mystics considered the rainbow as the symbolic union of opposing masculine and feminine energies, which they called, 'Tai Chi' or 'The Great Ultimate'.

The Temperance Card

In the Tarot, the Temperance card is the last of the four moral lessons the Fool must undergo. It depicts Iris, the Greek Rainbow Goddess, also known as the Temperance Angel, pouring water between two goblets, indicating the balancing of emotions through the alignment of our human and spiritual natures.

The Seven Pillars of Wisdom

This was the name given to the seven states of awareness that Ishtar received in her vision quest. The number seven symbolizes the surrendering of the ego's will to the soul's wisdom, illustrated in the myth by her physical torture. The seven pillars of wisdom were later adapted to become the seven sacraments.

The Dance of the Seven Veils

This is a sacred dance once performed by priestesses of Ishtar who had undergone the stripping of the seven veils of illusion, as part of their spiritual initiation. Salome is the most famous heroine to have performed this dance, appearing as a priestess of Ishtar in the Bible. The Native American Indians also have a similar tradition called 'La Mariposa' (meaning 'Butterfly Woman'), where a large elderly woman dances, wearing the transformational rainbow wings of a butterfly (the symbol for soul). In Tom Robbins Book, *Skinny Legs and All*, there is also a beautiful depiction of the Dance of The Seven Veils which is well worth reading.

Veils

The word 'Revelation' comes from the Latin *revelatio* meaning 'to draw back the veil', which is why in our modern day wedding ceremony, the groom unveils the bride. The veil traditionally was worn by the representative of the Goddess and it was thought that a man was unfit to rule if he couldn't look beneath the veil to view his fate or dark feminine (soul). Likewise, a woman was first expected to reveal the Goddess within herself to herself before she could reveal it to her partner and initiate him in the ways of the feminine.

The Eight Pointed Star

Represents Ishtar's home in the Great Above, the Ogdoad or eighth planetary sphere. The star is symbolic of her ability to herald the way home to the angelic realm. In numerology, the number eight represents the empowerment and abundance received after surrendering to the spirit during the lesson of the number seven. Which is why Ishtar was said to be 'mistress of the eight bright ways', having survived the journey through the seven states of illusion. Mary Magdalene was also said to have cast the seven demons out.

The Seven Chakras

Because Ishtar is associated with the conscious use of energy, her first initiation is to reconnect with and clear blocks in each of her energy centres, known as chakras. Although there are many chakra points throughout our light body, the main seven are...

Base Root: Representing survival issues, fear, fight or flight instincts, anger, lust and passion. Located at the base of the spine, it is red in colour.

Sacral: Representing creativity, sexuality, procreation, desire. Located in the centre of the pelvic region, it is orange in colour.

Solar Plexus: Representing self-confidence, personal will and self-authority. Located above the navel and below the chest, it is yellow in colour.

Heart: Representing unconditional love, compassion, forgiveness, balance and acceptance. Located in the centre of the chest, it is green in colour.

Throat: Representing inner truth, honesty and clear communication. Located in the throat area, it is sky blue in colour.

Third Eye: Representing vision on the inner planes, intuition, insight, perception and imagination. Located between the eyebrows, it is indigo in colour.

Crown: Representing the portal to the Cosmos, alignment with one's Higher Self and inspiration. Located at the top of the head, it is violet in colour.

The Full Moon

The nocturnal hours are ruled by the feminine forces, which heighten our connection with the spirit realm and the allure of Great Mystery. The full moon is a time when our lunar or feminine nature is overpowering, which is why hospitals and police stations record higher admissions every full moon as people have an increased tendency to act like lunatics.

The Morning/Evening Star

Traditionally Ishtar's followers looked to the morning star or the first star of the evening to address their thoughts and prayers, the star being her symbol. Hence the origins of the children's rhyme, 'Star light, star bright, I wish I may, I wish I might that all the stars come out tonight.' It has been said that the morning star was her maiden voyage across the sky (Aphrodite) after which she disappears and then reappears in her mature transit as the evening star (Ishtar).

The Wedding Ring

As a symbol of unity and wholeness, the wedding ring represents the commitment between two people to honor the Divine in each other, creating a temple for their spiritual growth. Diamonds have long been used as the gemstone for the marriage band, which coincidently carries the vibration of the crown chakra, the doorway to our spiritual consciousness.

The Tree of Life

Also referred to as the Shekinah (the Divine Feminine principle), Ishtar is often depicted sitting atop in the Tree of Life's branches as the cosmic Queen of Heaven. Meanwhile her counterpart, Lilith is shown amongst the roots, as the grounded Earth angel, the opposite feminine polarity.

High Priestess Totem Animals

Although the likelihood of one of these creatures crossing your path is small, should you meet them in a dream or constantly stumble across iconography that depicts them, be on the lookout for the opportunity to assert your own regal powers.

The Lion

The lion indicates her royal stature and her divine partnership with the ruling king. A partnership which was enacted each Spring Equinox (New Year's Day in ancient Persia) by the serving the High Priestess of the Goddess Temple with the reigning king to ensure he was humble enough to concede to her spiritual wisdom.

The Dove

As with Aphrodite, who has similarities with Ishtar as a love Goddess, both were synonymous with the dove as an emblem of peace and goodwill.

High Priestess Relative Parts of the Body

Top of Head

Often when our crown chakra is being stimulated we will find our head feels very itchy. This is common when there are solar flares which stimulate our kundalini.

HIGH PRIESTESS INNER MAKEOVER ACTIVITES

You've read the myth, you've painted your toenails, now it's time to incorporate some sassy, sensual techniques to spice up your next communion with your beloved. (Be that yourself, your partner or both!) These first few processes are great for resolving an argument or to connect soul to soul before lovemaking.

Creating Intimacy (in-to-me-see)

True intimacy is about allowing yourself to be truly seen, both your divine essence and your personal vulnerabilities, enabling you to see your beloved equally and openly. To experience this soul to soul connection try the following.

Sit cross-legged facing your partner or looking into a mirror. Look into each other's eyes for two minutes without breaking contact. Allow laughter or any emotions to surface and be experienced without judgment. Simply breathe into them and let them pass whilst maintaining eye contact.

Third Eye Communion

Sit cross-legged facing each other with your hands in a shared prayer position. (This is done by alternating your hands.) Sit close enough to have your brow chakras touching (forehead to forehead), with your eyes closed. After approximately two minutes in this position, take it in turns to kiss each other on the forehead honoring the Divine God/Goddess in each other respectively, for example by saying, 'I honor the Goddess in you'. A nice variation is to breathe in white light for six breaths and send it down into the Earth where you visualize it expanding out to encompass the earth and all her inhabitants.

Resolving an Argument

Sit cross-legged facing each other (as in the third eye communion activity), but remain in silent communion for as long as feels appropriate. Then take it in turns to say everything that's weighing upon your heart and mind. Keep the emphasis on trying to own your own behaviour. This also creates a helpful forum to share any insights, feelings and fears. Be mindful of using 'I' statements, in preference to more accusatory 'You' statements, for example 'I feel frustrated that it gets left up to me to organize household chores and parental responsibilities.' instead of 'You make me feel frustrated when you don't think of what needs to be done around the house and with the kids.'

Be sure to also first set clear ground rules, i.e. no interrupting and that eye contact must be maintained and be non-judgmental.

Giving and Receiving Divine Love

If you are not doing the following activity with a lover, be sure to first ascertain what physical boundaries you both wish to put in place (such as 'no touching' genitals and breasts). It is important that 'no agenda' touching is observed to ensure that energy is flowing from the heart and not used unconsciously as a seduction from the lower chakras.

Step One: Put on some celestial background music to create a loving and healing space. Choose who is going to give and who is going to receive.

Step Two: The Giver places their hands on their heart and visualizes a stream of Divine light entering down through the crown of their head from the celestial spheres. Feeling it flow down into their heart, allowing it to cascade down their shoulders and arms (where your heart meridians are located), until they feel the energy enter and 'turn on' their hands with a tingling sensation.

Step Three: The Receiver stands with their eyes closed, weight evenly distributed, arms down by their sides awaiting their healing.

Step Four: The Giver places their hands on their partner with the reverence you would afford a deity, honoring the divine being that they are. The Giver may wish to consciously ask Spirit to use them as a conduit for divine love. They may also wish to intuitively be guided to try different strokes, holds, colours and caresses. After five to ten minutes, swap turns.

Mimicking Baubo

Baubo was a female clown Goddess known as 'The Laughing Pelvis' on account of her lewd, crude wit. In Japanese mythology she was known as Ame-no-uzume-no-mikoto, 'The Alarming Female'. Both portrayals of this archetype were responsible for relieving female fear and sadness with sexuality, joy and laughter.

Have a slut party with your girlfriends and turn up wearing the trashiest ensembles you can find underneath trench coats. Or alternatively you may wish to draw Baubo's face on your navel. Create rude food offerings such as sausages and meatballs, mussels and chocolate-dipped bananas. Play games where you share your hottest sexual tips and perform stripteases to bump and grind music such as 'The Stripper' the classic olde time stripping track. For an alternative game, play some provocative music and ask your guests to stand in a circle. Then one at a time, take turns running into the centre of the circle and performing some crude motion, which everyone in the circle mimics amidst raucous laughter.

Devotion VS Addiction

If what is at the centre of your focus doesn't have the power to nourish you it will poison you from the inside out. That central focus may be a belief, an unavailable person, money, alcohol, an eating disorder or a drug of dependence.

Try making a list of your addictions, followed by a list of creative/devotional activities you could try to substitute them with to experience as many natural highs as possible.

Below is an example list. Please Note: The Goddess smiles on hedonism, so don't exclude all of those wonderful pursuits listed under addictions, just be mindful of over-indulgence.

ADDICTIONS	NATURAL HIGHS
Fantasy Novels	Dance Meditation
TV	Bush Walking
Videos	Chanting
Food	Drumming
Shopping	Charity Work
Sex	Tantra
Cigarettes	Breath Meditation
Alcohol	Fresh Juices
Work	Yoga
Coffee	Superfood
Other Drugs	Gardening

Love Objects (people, pets, cars etc)	Self Pampering
Travel	Astral Travel/Guided Visualization
Socializing	Star Gazing
Nail Biting	Inspirational Tapes/Books
Cleaning	Creative Writing/Automatic Writing
Gossip (i.e. magazines)	Dream Analysis

What's in a Name?

Below is a list of some of the titles by which Ishtar was known in the ancient world:

Light of the World, Star, Mountain Shaker, Leader of Hosts, Creator of People, Lady of Heaven, Guide of Humanity, Shepherdess of the Lands, Queen of Heaven and Earth, Mother of Deities, Creatress of Wisdom, Counsellor of The Gods, Guardian Spirit of Life, Supreme One, River of Life, Judgment Giving, Glorious, Exalted, Lady of Victory, The Heavenly One, Holy One, the Star, the Moon, the Heavenly Virgin, Queen of the Stars, Goddess of all Nourishment.

Now consider some of the nicknames your inner Ishtar has received over the years, both from people you know and in literature, music and the media. Some examples that sprang to my mind included:

Hornbag, floozie, tramp, girl from the gutter, minx, nymphomaniac, whore, femme fatale, slut, bimbo, 'that sort of woman', dollybird, sleeze, loose, ho, hooker, skank, white trash, cocksucker and *tart.*

Words are powerful.

Circle any of the names that jump out at you and question why they carry a charge for you. Who was it that used the word in a derogatory way? Do you still want the approval of this person? How can you reclaim that label in a positive and fun way? Sure, 'Sticks and stones may break your bones but names can psychologically suppress an archetype that's too good to miss!'

Art Therapy: Unveil the Temptress

Find some quiet time and create a temple space in your room in front of a mirror on the floor. You may wish to arrange exotic fruits, flowers, peacock feathers and translucent fabrics, leaving enough space for you to recline amongst them. You may wish to adorn yourself with some jewelry and apply some body oil or kohl pencil to accentuate your eyes. Now light some scented candles, put on some sensual music and using a soft medium such as conti crayons, charcoal, pastels or oil pastels draw yourself naked, paying special attention to the lotus that is the entrance to your temple, your most sacred of flowers, your yoni. Enjoy!

Embracing your Inner High Priestess: Further Suggestions

- So your parents couldn't afford to send you to a Swiss finishing school? Don't despair. Chances are, you'll have more fun serving your own self-appointed apprenticeship in the love arts in an Ishtar Mystery School of your own making.
- Seek out erotic prose, poetry and novels that can stimulate your imagination or can be read aloud to a lover.
- Start collecting pieces of erotic art or books.
- Take up life drawing classes so you can let your lover play the muse.
- Enrol in Latin, Egyptian or Belly dance classes.
- Research sensual and erotic music on the Net and add it to your collection.
- Practise expressing your love in the written and spoken word.
- Read up on the effects different colours have on people and experiment.
- Rent costumes and play fantasy dress-ups with your lover.
- Learn a sensual healing art such as aromatherapy, massage or Reiki.
- House your genitals with love. Discard all the undies that don't do justice to your gateway to the Divine and buy some that do.
- Light a candle at meal times and bless the food. (Try not to watch TV and eat)
- Try to wear rainbow colours and eat a rainbow of colours every meal so you radiate harmoniously
- Take a vow of silence for one day to contain your energy.
- Learn Reiki and give swaps to friends, your partner or yourself regularly.
- Meditate regularly seeing yourself in a prism that refracts white light into the harmonious colours of the rainbow or ask for healing rainbow light from Chiron, the healing planetoid.
- Enjoy your body – this is a definite prerequisite for lovemaking.
- Take time away for Tantric weekends with a lover.
- Striptease for yourself in front of a mirror, unveiling every square millimetre of your sacred temple as you would a priceless one-off piece of art.
- Dance with your eyes closed, imagining yourself as a flame and use this energy to give yourself a healing.
- Pleasure yourself often to release tension and try different fantasy scenarios, e.g. as a temple priestess or 'talk dirty' to yourself in a safe space without the fear of being judged. Take your time and enjoy first relaxing and reconnecting with your body by bathing and pampering

- Love yourself in practical ways that get you out of your head and into the pleasure of your body, heart and soul such as spas, massage and eating delicacies with your fingers.
- Buy yourself some saucy lingerie and wear it often.
- Send erotic emails and text messages to your lover.
- Exercise your pelvic floor muscles by tightening and releasing the muscles inside your vulva.
- Shower when you get home from work to wash away the day and put yourself in a different head space to enjoy your temple.
- Write your partner a love letter and post it (even if you live together).
- Pleasure yourself but avoid climaxing before you see your partner.

Get Wise

Take a leisurely stroll down to your local library or bookstore one Saturday afternoon and enquire about the following titles.

High Priestess Non-Fiction

Sacred Union: Awakening to the Consciousness of Eden by Tanishka

Reclaiming Goddess Sexuality by Linda E. Savage

Aphrodite by Isabelle Allende (Celebrating her sensual side with stories and recipes)

Aphrodite's Daughters by Jalaja Bonheim

The Idiot's Guide to Tantric Sex by Dr. Judy Kuriansky

Aphrodisiacs, An Encyclopedia of Erotic Wisdom

Tantric Sex by Ma Ananda Sarita and Swami Anand Geho

Dear Lover by David Deida

Tantric Massage by Kenneth Ray Stubbs, with Louise-Andree Saulnier

Soul Love by Sanaya Roman

The Naked Bride (Anonymous)

High Priestess Fiction

The Moon Under Her Feet by Clysta Kinstler

Skinny Legs and All by Tom Robbins

The Perfumed Garden translated by Sir Richard Burton

Topics for Discussion

Discuss the following points with your girlfriends and compare experiences:

- Did your parents affirm your blossoming sexuality in the same measure as your intelligence and sporting or cultural talents?
- Did you father react to your burgeoning sexuality with distant aloofness or with overly strict impositions such as dress codes?
- Did your father treat you as a potential 'sex maniac'?
- Did your mother react in a competitive manner to your Ishtar energy?
- Did your parents provide down-to-earth practical guidance and boundaries in regard to dating and safe sex?
- Did your parents or authority figures shame you for having erotic thoughts and urges or for being erotically attractive to others?
- How have you allowed your temple to be desecrated through lack of self-esteem and experiential wisdom?
- How have you judged other women who personify Ishtar?

Questions for Personal Reflection

Sex is an expression of our energy. If our energy is blocked it is because our body is storing unresolved hurt, shame, guilt, anger or resentment. Sexual intimacy reconnects us with our vulnerabilities, making it painful emotionally if we are not with a safe, loving and trustworthy partner. Try asking yourself the following questions:

- Which parts of my body have trouble receiving sensual and sexual attention because of stored shame?
- Do I deny my own sexual needs by performing like a vixen instead of taking the time to really connect with each physical and emotional sensation I receive?
- Do I apologize for needing longer than my partner to feel fully aroused?

- Am I afraid of initiating sexual contact? If so, what parts do I reject or fear are unlovable?
- Am I afraid of losing total control during lovemaking? If so, what makes my head a better lover than the instincts of my soul?
- Is my libido low? If so, who has injured my trust and respect?
- Am I unable to express myself spontaneously, such as when I feel angry? (This tendency inhibits our ability to orgasm.)

Secret Woman's Business: Best Times to Celebrate Ishtar

April 22 (Northern Hemisphere) or **November 22** (Southern Hemisphere) or the nearest full Beltane moon to that date, also full moons in general.

The ancient New Year, **'The Day of The Great Rite'** was held on the Spring Equinox. At Easter (Eostre being the ancient fertility festival where Easter originated from) they would fast to lament the death and resurrection of Ishtar's consort, Dumuzi.

The Sabbath stems from the Sabbatu, the full moon when Ishtar was said to commence her menstrual period and no journeys could be made or food cooked in sympathy, as it was honored as a day of rest. (Patriarchal interpretations of this custom implied that a woman was unclean when menstruating and should not contaminate food by touching it.) Babylonians made the month of Virgo sacred to Ishtar. Virgo being the sign of the priestess. Feel Ishtar's influence at ovulation (14 days before menstruation), when there is the most likelihood of conceiving: our vulva's juice becomes thin and slippery and we are more easily aroused and prone to erotic dreams.

High Priestess Rite of Passage Ceremony

I have included two rites to celebrate Ishtar, one as a solo ritual and one to share with a lover.

Step One: *Prepare a Sacred Space.*

Set up an altar in your room and turn your bed into a sacred union chamber to energetically reconsecrate your priestess connection with the Goddess. Use four clear quartz crystal points and 'charge up' your bedroom with light energy to clarify intentions and consecrate space. Simply place them in the four corners, facing inward and visualize white light linking them. You may also wish to light some incense and prepare some candles to be lit after your bath.

Step Two: *Prepare a special bath.*

Use aphrodisiac oil blends, crystal essence and sprinkle the water with flowers or petals. Light incense and candles around the bath and put on some deeply sensual and erotic music. Recline in the bath and luxuriate. Close your eyes and caress your temple, which feels warm and silky in the perfumed water. Begin to hum and chant (if possible to Middle-Eastern music – try Natasha Atlas or some ambient trance music such as Chicane), then close your eyes and whisper the mantra, 'I

Am Divine' continuously, allowing this knowing to take you into a rapturous trance state, taking you in waves of pleasure so your body writhes like a snake in the warm water.

Step Three: *Evoke Ishtar.*

In your own words, summon the presence of Ishtar. You can either speak this out loud or telepathically. Visualize her consecrating you as a priestess in her order, crowning you with a halo of stars.

Step Four: *Sex Magic.*

Dry yourself with your favourite towel and put on a robe or nightdress that feels silky or sensual on your skin. Enter your bedroom, light the candles and lay on the bed. Visualize a current of rainbow energy streaming down from the heavens and in your crown chakra. Allow the energy to move through your body and into your hands. Ask the Divine to consecrate every part of you with your touch and elevate you into the celestial realms for ecstatic union. Self-pleasure yourself (all over your skin and hair with a loving touch) visualizing energy moving up through your chakras and circling back through you as a current, fuelled by Divine life force that renews every cell in your body. Dedicate your orgasm as a gift of energy to the Divine Feminine, which you now embody.

High Priestess Tantric Union

Step One: *Meditation.*

Set up a ritual space in the bedroom and meditate to call upon the energy of Ishtar.

Step Two: *Purification.*

Run a luxurious bath as in the solo rite and invite your lover to join you. Wash each other using a sea sponge and vegetable blend soap scented with aromatherapy oils.

Step Three: *Creating Intimacy.*

Do the 'In-to-me-see' activity mentioned earlier in this chapter to connect soul to soul.

Step Four: *Anointing the Divine.*

Anoint each other's third eye with oil and honor the God/Goddess within.

Step Five: *Breath Orgasm.*

Sit cross-legged, legs wrapped around each other and synchronize your breathing (energy). Allow the breathing to grow in intensity, clearing your channels with a breath orgasm. Resist the urge to get physical.

Step Six: *Energy Healing.*

Put on some celestial music and ask your lover to lie down on the bed or a fireside faux fur rug with their eyes closed. Place your hands on your heart and visualize energy streaming into you from the creative, Divine Source. Then place your hands on their body intuitively where you're guided and channel healing light/love energy into them. You may like to cleanse their chakras by asking them to breathe in each of the seven charka colours one at a time. Let your imagination run away with you!

Step Seven: *Awaken the Senses.*

Blind fold your partner and heighten the responsiveness of their senses by titillating them one sense at a time. Try using the following:

Smell

Wave the following under their nose: essential oils, incense, fresh herbs, coffee, and flowers.

Touch

Coat your fingers with cornflour and stroke them. Also try fur, feathers, ice and different foods, such as fresh mango.

Sound

Use the following around their ears and body: rainstick, chimes, sing to them, speak erotic suggestions or read erotic poetry.

Taste

Drizzle honey into their mouth, feed them portions of dark chocolate, olives, cucumber, smoked salmon, strips of sweet pineapple, which also sweetens the taste of semen.

Sight

Perform a striptease for them or change into an erotic outfit, which you slowly reveal.

Step Eight: *State the Intention.*

Dedicate the intention of your love ritual. For example, for greater intimacy, to heal, to connect with the Divine, to conceive, or to raise the vibration of human joy. (You may wish to do this as a toast with French champagne.)

Step Nine: *Sensual Appreciation.*

Appreciate and touch every part of each other's body in complete reverence for their Divinity, especially the parts often overlooked, i.e. ankles, underarms, scalp and each vertebrae.

Step Ten: *Rainbow Orgasm.*

Visualize energy as colour both in yourself and your partner as the energy intensifies during love-making. When it escalates into orgasmic ecstasy, see it as a rainbow circle of light that encircles both yourself and your partner, extending the bliss period and uniting the communion even if orgasm is not simultaneous.

Other Suggestions:

Write each other erotic fantasies and share them.

In turn tell each other all the ways you like to be touched, what you love about their body, then about their soul.

Put on some sultry Latin music and cook together naked with a nice bottle of wine, then feed each other.

Leave unexpected notes, erotic suggestions or small trinkets around the house or in their clothes. Alternatively, do them an unexpected favour because true kindness is the greatest aphrodisiac!

Most importantly, make a rule that this time is sacred and commit to make each other the focus of your attention for the specified time (i.e. turn off mobile phones and put on the answering machine).

High Priestess Act of Beauty

Consider now making a violet and crimson mandala to assist the healing of your crown chakra and then adorn a violet altar to your inner Ishtar in your bedroom.

MEET ISIS: THE INNER QUEEN

Isis – The Queen Who Embodies All

Well, hello there Queenly one! Congrats for getting on down your yellow brick road and getting acquainted with the seven superb soul sisters within your psyche.

I have selected Isis as our Queenly role model as she was an ancient Egyptian Queen Goddess, who became so popular as a deity that she was said to have absorbed the qualities of all the other Goddess archetypes. So I thought she'd make a great 'poster gal' for the liberated and integrated woman who knows herself inside out and is therefore as powerful and beguiling to behold as a complex and colourful ever-changing kaleidoscope.

Isis was often portrayed wearing an ornate head dress and huge enfolding wings and her name's hieroglyph became synonymous with the throne of Egypt. Although Egyptian, her influence spread throughout both ancient Greece and Rome and lasted for more than 3000 years. Many of the images and symbols associated with Isis were then incorporated into the figure of the Virgin Mary.

In the myth, Isis restores her dismembered husband back to wholeness after the evil God, Seth murders him and hides his body parts. (Sounds like an episode of 'Law and Order'!) Through her devotion she uncovers both the plot and evidence and uses her feminine gifts to restore him to health, after which they give birth to a child, named Horus. This legend is the symbolic tale of a woman who has integrated her feminine selves and then embarks on a mission to reclaim her inner masculine selves in order to integrate both her masculine and feminine energies. (But that's another inner makeover... stay tuned!)

The colours synonymous with Isis for those planning their next regal outfit are royal blue, gold and turquoise, the same colours that are found in peacock feathers which were said to contain the eye of Isis (and have since been feared superstitiously as an omen of bad luck).

I once attended a fortieth birthday where I had a complete Egyptian Isis outfit made for the guest of honor who we bathed in milk, adorned with perfumes and jewels and sat on a huge cane throne in her backyard. Children sang to her and fanned her with palm fronds and every guest lay a candle and a wish at her feet. (There was not one derogatory hallmark greeting card about old age in sight!)

That said, you also deserve a crown for having served this rite of passage to reclaim your feminine birth rite, so don't be surprised if one comes your way. (I once sang at a wedding and met a lovely man in his seventies who had just bought his wife a crown to wear on a mountain climbing expedition she was undertaking in the Himalayas. Similarly, I was given a beautiful crown spontaneously by a lovely woman at a party after completing my first year of running Goddess archetype seminars.) Alternatively, you may wish to buy some beads, pearls, wire, peacock feathers or anything else that grabs your fancy and make your own ceremonial head dress and have a coming out ball in your honor. (Feel free to let me know how you choose to celebrate your unique Goddess for a subsequent book! Photos most welcome!)

At the very least, treat yourself by committing to doing something you've always dreamed about. After all, it's not important how you mark your homecoming but that you do take the opportunity to honor yourself. So if you are shy of receiving recognition from others who wish to celebrate you, then at least celebrate yourself in a private ritual of sorts.

And last but not least, don't hold back from letting the world see you in all your self-possessed grandeur and newfound empowerment. Try not to shirk at new roles of responsibility and leadership that come your way, for we need more empowered feminine role models in all walks of life, making those necessary feminine touches upon our otherwise man-made world. (Do however, remember to get off your pedestal regularly and dust it yourself for the road to hell is paved with good intentions and often we are the last to see our own mistakes.)

Finally, thanks for having me at your place. Here's some final thoughts for this, my last day of writing: June 8, 2004 the day of the transit of Venus, marking an anchoring of the Divine feminine on to our planet.

The Ten Goddess Commandments

Celebrate your unique beauty, both inner and outer

Honor yourself in every choice you make

Dare to be spontaneous and authentic

Spend equal time being and reflecting

Honor the Divine in all

Speak both your mind's ideas and your heart's wisdom

Support yourself by spending time with those who reflect your inner light

Spend time regularly communing with Mother Nature

Look for the blessing and lesson in every occurrence

Serve the Greater Good with ease and grace

bibliography

Aphrodisiacs, An Encyclopedia of Erotic Wisdom Aphrodite by Isabelle Allende

Aphrodite's Daughters by Jalaja Bonheim

An Introduction to Greek Mythology by David Bellingham

Aspects of The Masculine by Carl J. Jung

A Woman's Worth by Marianne Williamson

Blood, Bread and Roses by Judy Grahn

Buffalo Woman Comes Singing by Brooke Medicine Eagle

Casting the Circle by Diane Stein

Chocolat by Maria Bardoulat

Classic Ancient Mythology by Richard Patrick and Peter Croft

Diet for a Small Planet by Frances Moore Lappe

Dreams and Destinies by Beryl Beare

Dreams. Signs of Things to Come by Quentin Watts and Vicki Canisius

Elderwoman by Marian Van Eyk McCain

Eve's Wisdom – Traditional Secrets of Pregnancy, Birth and Motherhood by Deborah Jackson

Femininity Lost and Regained by Robert A. Johnson

Feminist Fairytales by Barbara G. Walker

Fitonics for Life by Marilyn Diamond and Dr Donald Burton Schnell

Goddesses in Every Woman by Jean Shinoda Bolen

Gods in Every Man by Jean Shinoda Bolen

Gods and Goddesses by Robert Ingpen and Molly Perham

Gods and Myths of Ancient Greece by Mary Barnett

Green Witchcraft by Ann Moura

Harlot, Forbidden Tales of the Bible by Jonathan Hirsch

Healing with the Angels by Doreen Virtue

Intimacy and Solitude by Stephanie Dowrick

Medicine Cards by Jamie Sams and David Carson

Moon Diary by Shekinah Morgan

Moving into Ecstacy by Amoda

Natural Fertility by Francesca Naish

Pocketful of Dreams by Denise Linn

Positive Magic by Marion Weinstein

Reclaiming Goddess Sexuality by Linda Savage PhD

Return to Love by Marianne Williamson

Sacred Contracts, Awakening Your Divine Potential by Caroline Myss

Sacred Path Cards by Jamie Sams and David Carson

Shakti Woman by Vicki Noble

Sister Moon Lodge by Kisma Stepanich

Skinny Legs and All by Tom Robbin

Sophia, Goddess of Wisdom by Caitlin Mathews

Soul Love by Sanaya Roman

Symbols and their Meanings by Jack Tresidder

Take it Personally by Anita Roddick

Tantric Massage by Kenneth Ray Stubbs, with Louise-Andree Saulnier

The Archetypes and the Collective Unconscious second edition by Carl J. Jung

The Body is the Barometer of the Soul by Annette Noontil

The Book of Lilith by Barbara Black Koltuv

The Cauldron of Change by De-Anna Alba

The Different Drum by M. Scott Peck

The Enchanted Broccoli Forest by Mollie Katzen

The Giant Book of Superstitions by Claudia de Lys

The Goddess. A Beginner's Guide by Teresa Moorey

The Goddess Path by Patricia Monaghan

The Goddess Within by Jennifer Barker Woolger and Roger J Woolger

The Good Life in The '90s by Mary Moody

The Hero with a Thousand Faces by Joseph Campbell

The Heroine's Journey by Maureen Murdock

The Homeric Gods by Walter F. Otto

The Idiot's Guide to Tantra by Dr. Judy Kuriansky

The Life You Were Born to Live by Dan Millman

The Magical Name by Ted Andrews

The Manufacture of Madness by Thomas Szasz

The Mask of Motherhood by Susan Maushart

The Moon Under Her Feet by Clysta Kinstler

The Moosewood Cookbook by Mollie Katzen

The Mythic Tarot Book by Juliet Sharman-Burke and Liz Greene

The Naked Bride, Anonymous

The Perfumed Garden translated by Sir Richard Burton

The Red Tent by Anita Diamant

The Seat of the Soul by Gary Zukov

The Secrets of the Rainmaker by Chin-Ning Chu

The Seven Laws of Success by Deepak Chopra

The Three Day Energy Fast by Pamela Serure

The Twelve Trials of Hercules by Alice Bailey

The Whole Woman by Germaine Greer

The Wild Genie by Alexandra Pope

The Wise Wound by Penelope Shuttle and Peter Redgrove

The Woman's Dictionary of Symbols and Sacred Objects by Barbara Walker

The Women's Wheel of Life by Elizabeth Davis and Carol Leonard

The Ultimate Encyclopedia of Mythology by Arthur Cotterell

Unlimited Power by Anthony Robbins

Vein of Gold by Julia Cameron

When God Was a Woman by Merlin Stone

Witch by Fiona Horne

Women in Search of the Sacred by Anne Bancroft

Women's Rituals by Barbara Walker

Women who Run with the Wolves by Clarissa Pinkola Estes

Women Who Love Sex by Gina Ogden

28889339R00125

Printed in Great Britain
by Amazon